READINGS IN EASTERN RELIGIOUS THOUGHT

# HINDUISM

## VOLUME I

Edited by Allie M. Frazier

"This book of readings on Hindu religious thought and practice unites, in one volume, both interpretative essays on the Hindu tradition and selections from the sacred literature of Hinduism. . . . Expert commentaries spaced throughout the readings trace a viable path through the jungle of Indian scriptures and religious history. . . . It includes those original sources and commentaries which highlight the fundamental categories of Hindu thought and experience." Especially interesting to readers who may be approaching Hinduism for the first time.

Primary attention is given those basic themes, doctrines, myths, and practices which are manifest in the germinal (rather than late) stages of Hinduism's development—themes which have been pervasive throughout its history.

*(Continued on back flap)*

0657

*READINGS IN EASTERN RELIGIOUS THOUGHT*

HINDUISM

READINGS IN EASTERN RELIGIOUS THOUGHT

Volume I

# HINDUISM

---

*Edited by*

Allie M. Frazier



THE WESTMINSTER PRESS
PHILADELPHIA

STANDARD BOOK No. 664-20866-5

LIBRARY OF CONGRESS CATALOG CARD No. 69-14197

BOOK DESIGN BY
DOROTHY ALDEN SMITH

PUBLISHED BY THE WESTMINSTER PRESS ®
PHILADELPHIA, PENNSYLVANIA

PRINTED IN THE UNITED STATES OF AMERICA

# Preface

This book of readings on Hindu religious thought and practice unites in one volume both interpretative essays on the Hindu tradition and selections from the sacred literature of Hinduism. The volume is designed to aid college students and readers in general who may be approaching Hinduism for the first time. The Westerner who genuinely desires to comprehend Eastern religions must immerse himself in the original sources of those traditions; he must grapple with the sacred literature without the assistance of detailed commentary and interpretation. The novice in the study of Eastern religion, however, requires a guide that can trace for him a viable path through the jungle of Indian scriptures and religious history. Such guidance is given in this volume by the expert commentaries spaced throughout the selection of readings. These commentaries function as maps, indicating the main thoroughfares through the Hindu tradition, as well as the byways, detours, and uncharted territory. Studying original sources in conjunction with expert commentary brings the reader into direct contact with the persistent values and wisdom of Hinduism.

What is Hinduism? In a broad sense, Hinduism is the whole complex of events, beliefs, practices, and institutions that have appeared in India from the time of the ancient Vedas until the modern age. In a more narrow sense, Hinduism could be defined as that social and religious system which developed in India after the third century B.C. But whether broadly or narrowly conceived, Hinduism represents an extraordinary spectrum of belief and practice ranging from polytheism to monotheism, from pluralism to monism, from ceremonialism to mysticism, and from religious moralism to secular amoralism.

In a volume of first readings, a full representation of the spectrum of the Hindu tradition would be impossible. If, however, we view Hinduism as an upward surge of the human spirit toward a high spirituality which over the centuries has continuously enlarged itself, then we can study those basic themes, doctrines, and practices which have been pervasive throughout its history. Although Hindu thought has undergone major revolutions in the course of its development, its essential ideas have persisted and continue to inform the underlying spirit of all Hindu religion. The principle governing the selection of materials for this volume has always been to include those original sources and commentaries which highlight the fundamental categories of Hindu thought and experience.

I wish to express my thanks to Hollins College, which made available to me the research assistance required to complete this project. I owe a special debt of gratitude to Mrs. Leslie Seyfried Roberts, who greatly assisted me in the final stages of the preparation of the manuscript. To my wife, Ruth, who assisted me at every stage of the project, I express appreciation. She read early drafts, offered valuable critical suggestions, and was a constant source of encouragement. To her I dedicate this volume.

A. M. F.

*Hollins College*
*Hollins College, Virginia*

# Contents

# Introduction

A momentless intensity pure and bare,
I stretch to an eternal everywhere.
I have become what before time I was;
A secret touch has quieted thought and sense.
All things by the Agent mind created pass
Into a void and mute magnificence.
—*Sri Aurobindo*

Human life is caught in the ceaseless movement of time, of perpetual coming-to-be and passing-away. The changing forms of human life and of nature have captured man's reflective attention in the East and West throughout the ages by shaping the main thrust of his philosophical quest and by posing the basic questions of his religious life. Consider for a moment the perpetual change of role, scene, and actor in nature's theater: summer's growth becomes fall's harvest; night follows day; clouds of white alter into ominous thunderheads; children grow into aged men. Is it surprising that the earliest thinkers were amazed at the transience of all forms and contents of the world, including themselves? Yet such coming-to-be and ceasing-to-be essentially define time. In this maelstrom of change, man has sought to understand the meaning of the life given to him and its relationship to the nature of all beings.

At the dawn of Western philosophy, Anaximander expressed the Greeks' wonder at the transience of things in this manner: "And the source of coming-to-be for existing things is that unto which destruction, too, happens according to necessity; for they pay penalty and retribution to each other for their injustice according to the assessment of Time." According to Anaximander, the existence of any particular thing constitutes an encroachment by it upon the rights to existence possessed by other things. To use a simple example, if rainy weather exists at a particular time, it has usurped a portion of the arena of existence to which fair weather has an equal right. Such an "injustice" receives redress by the "assessment of Time." Time sets the basic boundaries for the existence of things—change is inevitable. Anaximander, like all pre-Socratic philosophers, sought the unchanging permanence behind the kaleidoscopic changes in nature. Although the natural scene presented a picture of warring opposites and incessant flux, the pre-Socratic philosophers lived by the faith that a permanence or order of change could be discovered in the cosmic play.

In considering the beginning and development of Western philosophy, Hegel remarked that in the West the "mind's way is roundabout." By this he points to the significant fact that Western thinkers *first* directed their attention to the external world in an effort to understand the nature of the objective world. In pre-Socratic philosophy, for example, no hard-and-fast distinction is made between human subjects and the objective world. The earliest philosophy in the West sought to develop methods for analyzing and comprehending the world of objects. Mathematics was seized upon quite early as an instrument of great usefulness in the effort to understand the structural and permanent characteristics of the world. Only after developing categories of thought appropriate to the exploration of natural objects could Western thinkers come to think of themselves as objects. With this advance, the inner world of the self was opened to objective exploration. Philosophical psychology, ethics, social and political philosophy developed after cosmological speculation had succeeded in perfecting the tools for studying objective things.

Philosophical thought in the pre-Socratic period represented a movement away from the mythicopoetic orientation to life which dominated ancient Greek civilization. The emergence of philosophical speculation on the scene of Greek culture marked the twilight of the gods of the Greek pantheon. This new reflective venture consisted of a progressive rationalization of the mythological content of early Greek religion and epic poetry. The initial problems confronted by the fledgling philosophical movement were the traditional problems implied in the cosmological myths, such as world origination, change, permanence, and the one and the many. Although philosophical speculation originated in the mythical world view, it developed into a rationalized procedure which transcended its mythical foundations. The impulse toward rationalization drove philosophy to disengage (in some measure) cosmogony from its mythical trappings.

Greek thought in the course of its independent development away from the style of mythological thought discovered the power of logos. By the use of their powers of reason and observation, Greek thinkers uncovered the intelligibility (the logos) which lies at the center of the universe. This logos was not understood as being merely a conceptual schema formulated in the mind of the philosopher. That view of logos comprehended it only in its most trivial nature—in its purely subjective mode of being. Logos, rather, was apprehended as the objective constituent of things, and, as such, it was the concrete, existing form of change. Increasingly, however, logos came to mean that *process* by which the arrangement of the world is uncovered to the philosopher's mind in perception and thought. Perception and thought *re*-present the order of the external and internal worlds. Such representations are expressed in judgments which are either true or false—they either truly or falsely represent the order of reality. Eventually, truth was viewed as residing in judgments which accurately correspond to actual states of being in the world.

This is a most significant development in Western philosophy, for the whole tradition builds upon the premise that truth is a *relationship* which exists between judgments and real things. The problem of the relationship between thinking and reality thus emerged as a central concern for Western thinkers. Moreover, the principal categories of interest in Western metaphysics are categories appropriate to the analysis of objective things, e.g., space, quantity, motion, relation.

Yet the consciousness by which things appear to us, which allows the discovery of otherness, cannot be analyzed by these basic categories. Things move; consciousness changes. Things occupy space; consciousness finds itself in situations that are not quite places. Things have sizes and weights; consciousness has desires, emotions, and moods. Because of the basic interest in the problem of the relationship between thinking subjects and real things, an incipient dualism developed in Western philosophy which was consummated in the philosophy of Descartes.

Descartes saw the world as divided absolutely between two kinds of substance: thinking things essentially characterized by awareness, and nonthinking things essentially characterized by space and motion. Such a dualism has extensive practical ramifications for the whole of human life. Nature, the world of physical objects, becomes increasingly alien to man. It becomes the unapproachable, mechanical other to be manipulated and struggled against by man. Human beings, on the other hand, are self-conscious, purposive beings who pursue goals and seek values according to the dictates of their knowledge and their needs. Yet the material world will bend to the wishes of the willing creature only reluctantly, if at all. Thus, man's volitional nature is brought into an inevitable conflict with the powers of the material universe. Man must control indifferent nature by the use of his scientific understanding so as to create out of this recalcitrant world an adequate life for himself. Scientific technology becomes the most prominent way in which Western man makes his will prevail over an alien natural world. By his active labor and knowledge, Western man hopes to become reconciled to the natural world from which his consciousness and thinking have alienated him.

But while man learns to map out the laws of change in the material world and, to some extent, in his own psyche, he progressively is forced into an awareness of the radical limits of his own existence. His life, as well as the lives of all men, is only of a very short duration; his consciousness is a continuous process of changing moods, feelings, desires, thoughts. Our most profound literature, philosophy, and religion continually recall us to the awareness of the radical temporal limits of human life.

Part of our heritage in the West is the recurring attempt to evade the transience of earthly life by means of religious hopes, metaphysical systems, and vigorous activism. Our scientific and philosophical endeavors seek a clarification and expression of those objective factors which condition our existence. Our studies in economics, history, psychology, sociology, and all life-sciences have revealed unmistakably the multiple dimensions of determination which shape our lives. Because we live in time and discover who we are in history, we know that we are subject to the inevitable movement of time. We recognize that each of us is what some other historical moment, as well as our personal history, has determined us to be.

Time exists by virtue of its "perpetual perishing." Any being subject to time is subject to its dominant characteristic, transience. While we may control an indifferent environment by our technological prowess and our scientific genius, we cannot, thereby, alter the essence of time. Even our most magnificent technological achievements (not to mention our artistic ones) cannot finally cancel the essence of time. Although our will rages against human destiny in religious hopes of another, eternal mode of being, such an aversion to time cannot alter the destiny of a temporal being, namely, its perpetually perishing character.

In the West man has set himself and his will against the destructive movement of time. His effort has been to create stabilities in the midst of flux. Such stabilizing factors have taken the form of institutions, traditions, otherworldly religions. The West has restricted its view of history to the span of man's life on earth (often restricting such history to Occidental man). Since history requires the power of perceiving an object in an independent light and understanding it in rational connection with other objects, historical insight has been considered, in the West, as being of crucial importance to a people. By its means, people become aware of the course of their development as it is expressed in their institutions, laws, and actions. Through historical awareness, people attain an image of themselves and of their condition; they become objective to themselves. Historical understanding has been established as a value in the West because it has been presumed that by its light man can *direct* the course of his development in time. Without the knowledge it brings, man is at the mercy of the recurring forces of nature and is blindly involved in temporal change.

Moreover, the West has developed and responded to a linear and evolutionary conception of time (perhaps rooted in and validated by the sciences of geology, history, and paleontology). Each historical moment is presumed to be unique and nonrepeatable. Thus, Western historians focus upon aspects of history which suggest trends and directions. Men in the West look back in order to avoid repeating the mistakes of the past and in the hope that their understanding of the past will enable them to discern how the future can be molded to human advantage. In short, Westerners believe that the destructive ravages of time can be averted only by careful planning and by preservation of existing modes of stability, such as institutions, religions, political orders. Knowledge is to be used as a means of controlling one's temporal destiny and, thereby, shaping one's life in conformity with freely elected values.

While the West focuses principally upon human history, in general, the East focuses upon the history of nature or being. In some Hindu and Buddhist scriptures, the scale of time discussed completely staggers the imagination of the Westerner. Eons follow upon eons in a seemingly endless succession. But even if the scale is somewhat larger and the orientation different, the Easterner also discovers the nature of the human predicament along the horizon of his temporality.

In the East, the great aim of religious men is to find that overall cosmic unity that is hidden behind the veil of temporal succession and cosmic change. Time ought not to be, and man caught up in the endless process of repetitive cycles is ineluctably conditioned by time. Hence, there grows up in Eastern religious thought an aversion to time and a sustained effort to escape the illusory circle of birth, decay, death, and suffering.

According to the Eastern appraisal of the human predicament, the ground of man's bondage to endless suffering, rebirth, and ignorance is his enslavement to the demonic forces of the cosmic illusion. Men, through their ignorance of their real spiritual destinies, are caught in the thralldom of desire and pleasure, and, as a consequence, suffer pain, death, and rebirth. Every attachment to individual selfhood and to the world yields, by an inexorable law, a chain of consequences which bind man ever more firmly to natural existence. Yet, the tighter the chains of illusion become, the more they evoke, in a dialectical fashion, the urge to escape, to be liberated from the ceaseless, meaningless round of pain and illusion.

Desiring absolute emancipation, men seek to realize another dimension of existence which is not subject to the relentless rush of time and universal becoming. The human spirit seeks a realm of freedom that is nontemporal, entirely transcending the human condition. In short, man seeks the death of temporality and rebirth in a mode of being unconditioned by time and change. Such a realm of absolute freedom is symbolized in the concepts of Nirvana, kevola, moksa, tao—the shore completely beyond the chains of illusion. The paths taken to reach such unconditional liberation, whether in Hinduism, Buddhism, Taoism, or Jainism, lead the soul progressively away from involvement in its personal individuality, its world, and their incessant becoming. By the spiritual disciplines of these different faiths, men nurture within themselves a new thirst, a desire for a transtemporal state of being which usually entails a depreciation of and detachment from the world and the narrow confines of individuality.

The aim of most Eastern religious discipline is not simply to comprehend the plight of man's bondage to illusion, but also to overcome that enslavement by the nullification of the factors which cause the bondage, e.g., desire, pleasure, pain, birth, and death. Complete emancipation from the broken character of human life is the great promise and affirmation of most Oriental religions. Enlightenment or release is not equivalent to knowledge of the critical human situation. That knowledge is useful only instrumentally as a means by which men shuck off the chains of ignorance and gain, thereby, the opportunity to achieve absolute liberation.

The contrast between the Christian appraisal of the human predicament and the typical Oriental appraisal of man's situation is quite instructive. The Christian views man's fallen condition as a form of bondage to the destructive consequences of sin—such as anxiety, guilt, pride, self-centeredness. While this is a deplorable condition in which to exist, it is nevertheless a *real* condition. For most Eastern religions, man's enslavement to the world—to individuality, desire, pleasure, pain, rebirth—is not a real condition at all. It is a consequence principally of his spiritual ignorance, his mistaking illusions or appearances for reality. The world of passing forms, so subject to the disintegrating effect of time, does not really participate in eternal being. Hence, most religious persons in the East do not seek a *relationship* with eternal being, but rather they seek a *realization* of an eternal mode of being which is hidden from them by their ignorance.

Western religious thought is produced by the convergence of two traditions—the Greek and the Christian. Its key concepts are revelation, relationship, and community. In the East the key concepts of religious thought are recognition, realization, release, and reunion.

CHAPTER I

# The Meeting of East and West

## Philosophies of Life of East and West

*Heinrich Zimmer*

### The Roar of Awakening

We of the Occident are about to arrive at a crossroads that was reached by the thinkers of India some seven hundred years before Christ. This is the real reason why we become both vexed and stimulated, uneasy yet interested, when confronted with the concepts and images of Oriental wisdom. This crossing is one to which the people of all civilizations come in the typical course of the development of their capacity and requirement for religious experience, and India's teachings force us to realize what its problems are. But we cannot take over the Indian solutions. We must enter the new period our own way and solve its questions for ourselves, because though truth, the radiance of reality, is universally one and the same, it is mirrored variously according to the mediums in which it is reflected. Truth appears differently in different lands and ages according to the living materials out of which its symbols are hewn.

Reprinted from Heinrich Zimmer, *Philosophies of India,* edited by Joseph Campbell (Bollingen Series XXVI, Princeton University Press, 1967), pages 1-7, 12-14, 23-27, 30-36, 38-50, 56-58, 63, 65-66. Copyright 1951 by the Bollingen Foundation, New York. Used by permission of Princeton University Press.

Concepts and words are symbols, just as visions, rituals, and images are; so too are the manners and customs of daily life. Through all of these a transcendent reality is mirrored. They are so many metaphors reflecting and implying something which, though thus variously expressed, is ineffable, though thus rendered multiform, remains inscrutable. Symbols hold the mind to truth but are not themselves the truth, hence it is delusory to borrow them. Each civilization, every age, must bring forth its own.

We shall therefore have to follow the difficult way of our own experiences, produce our own reactions, and assimilate our sufferings and realizations. Only then will the truth that we bring to manifestation be as much our own flesh and blood as is the child its mother's; and the mother, in love with the Father, will then justly delight in her offspring as His duplication. The ineffable seed must be conceived, gestated, and brought forth from our own substance, fed by our blood, if it is to be true child through which its mother is reborn: and the Father, the divine Transcendent Principle, will then also be reborn—delivered, that is to say, from the state of non-manifestation, non-action, apparent non-existence. We cannot borrow God. We must effect His new incarnation from within ourselves. Divinity must descend, somehow, into the matter of our own existence and participate in this peculiar life-process.

According to the mythologies of India, this is a miracle that will undoubtedly come to pass. For in the ancient Hindu tales one reads that whenever the creator and sustainer of the world, Viṣṇu, is implored to appear in a new incarnation, the beseeching forces leave him no peace until he condescends. Nevertheless, the moment he comes down, taking flesh in a blessed womb, to be again made manifest in the world which itself is a reflex of his own ineffable being, self-willed demonic forces set themselves against him; for there are those who hate and despise the god and have no room for him in their systems of expansive egoism and domineering rule. These do everything within their power to hamper his career. Their violence, however, is not as destructive as it seems; it is no more than a necessary force in the historic process. Resistance is a standard part in the recurrent cosmic comedy that is enacted whenever a spark of supernal truth, drawn down by the misery of creatures and the imminence of chaos, is made manifest on the phenomenal plane.

"It is the same with our spirit," states Paul Valéry, "as with our flesh: both hide in mystery what they feel to be most important. They conceal it from themselves. They single it out and protect it by this profundity in which they ensconce it. Everything that really counts is well veiled; testimony and documents only render it the more obscure; deeds and works are designed expressly to misrepresent it."

The chief aim of Indian thought is to unveil and integrate into consciousness what has been thus resisted and hidden by the forces of life—not to explore and describe the visible world. The supreme and characteristic achievement of the Brāhman mind (and this has been decisive, not only for the course of Indian philosophy, but also for the history of Indian civilization) was its discovery of the Self (*ātman*) as an independent, imperishable entity, underlying the conscious personality and bodily frame. Everything that we normally know and express about ourselves belongs to the sphere of change, the sphere of time and space, but this Self (*ātman*) is forever changeless, beyond time, beyond space and the veiling net of causality, beyond measure, beyond the dominion of the eye. The effort of Indian philosophy has been, for millenniums, to know this adamantine Self and make the knowledge effective in human life. And this enduring concern is what has been responsible for the supreme morning calm that pervades the terrible histories of the Oriental world—histories no less tremendous, no less horrifying, than our own. Through the vicissitudes of physical change a spiritual footing is maintained in the peaceful-blissful ground of Ātman; eternal, timeless, and imperishable Being.

Indian, like Occidental, philosophy imparts information concerning the measurable structure and powers of the psyche, analyzes man's intellectual faculties and the operations of his mind, evaluates various theories of human understanding, establishes the methods and laws of logic, classifies the senses, and studies the processes by which experiences are apprehended and assimilated, interpreted, and comprehended. Hindu philosophers, like those of the West, pronounce on ethical values and moral standards. They study also the visible traits of phenomenal existence, criticizing the data of external experience and drawing deductions with respect to the supporting principles. India, that is to say, has had, and still has, its own disciplines of psychology, ethics, physics, and metaphysical theory. But the primary concern—in striking contrast to the interests of the modern philosophers of the West—has always been, not information, but transformation: a radical changing of man's nature and, therewith, a renovation of his understanding both of the outer world and of his own existence; a transformation as complete as possible, such as will amount when successful to a total conversion or rebirth.

In this respect Indian philosophy sides with religion to a far greater extent than does the critical, secularized thinking of the modern West. It is on the side of such ancient philosophers as Pythagoras, Empedocles, Plato, the Stoics, Epicurus and his followers, Plotinus, and the Neoplatonic thinkers. We recognize the point of view again in St. Augustine, the medieval mystics such as Meister Eckhart, and such later mystics as Jakob Böhme of Silesia. Among the Romantic philosophers it reappears in Schopenhauer.

The attitudes toward each other of the Hindu teacher and the pupil bowing at his feet are determined by the exigencies of this supreme task of transformation. Their problem is to effect a kind of alchemical transmutation of the soul. Through the means, not of a merely intellectual understanding, but of a change of heart (a transformation that shall touch the core of his existence), the pupil is to pass out of bondage, beyond the limits of human imperfection and ignorance, and transcend the earthly plane of being.

There is an amusing popular fable which illustrates this pedagogical idea. It is recorded among the teachings of the celebrated

Hindu saint of the nineteenth century, Śrī Rāmakrishna. Anecdotes of this childlike kind occur continually in the discourses of the Oriental sages; they circulate in the common lore of the folk and are known to everyone from infancy. They carry the lessons of India's timeless wisdom to the homes and hearts of the people, coming down through the millenniums as everybody's property. Indeed India is one of the great homelands of the popular fable; during the Middle Ages many of her tales were carried into Europe. The vividness and simple aptness of the images drive home the points of the teaching; they are like pegs to which can be attached no end of abstract reasoning. The beast fable is but one of the many Oriental devices to make lessons catch hold and remain in the mind.

The present example is of a tiger cub that had been brought up among goats, but through the enlightening guidance of a spiritual teacher was made to realize its own unsuspected nature. Its mother had died in giving it birth. Big with young, she had been prowling for many days without discovering prey, when she came upon this herd of ranging wild goats. The tigress was ravenous at the time, and this fact may account for the violence of her spring; but in any case, the strain of the leap brought on the birth throes, and from sheer exhaustion she expired. Then the goats, who had scattered, returned to the grazing ground and found the little tiger whimpering at its mother's side. They adopted the feeble creature out of maternal compassion, suckled it together with their own offspring, and watched over it fondly. The cub grew and their care was rewarded; for the little fellow learned the language of the goats, adapted his voice to their gentle way of bleating, and displayed as much devotion as any kid of the flock. At first he experienced some difficulty when he tried to nibble thin blades of grass with his pointed teeth, but somehow he managed. The vegetarian diet kept him very slim and imparted to his temperament a remarkable meekness.

One night, when this young tiger among the goats had reached the age of reason, the herd was attacked again, this time by a fierce old male tiger, and again they scattered; but the cub remained where he stood, devoid of fear. He was of course surprised. Discovering himself face to face with the terrible jungle being, he gazed at the apparition in amazement. The first moment passed; then he began to feel self-conscious. Uttering a forlorn bleat, he plucked a thin leaf of grass and chewed it, while the other stared.

Suddenly the mighty intruder demanded: "What are you doing here among these goats? What are you chewing there?" The funny little creature bleated. The old one became really terrifying. He roared, "Why do you make this silly sound?" and before the other could respond, seized him roughly by the scruff and shook him, as though to knock him back to his senses. The jungle tiger then carried the frightened cub to a nearby pond, where he set him down, compelling him to look into the mirror surface, which was illuminated by the moon. "Now look at those two faces. Are they not alike? You have the pot-face of a tiger; it is like mine. Why do you fancy yourself to be a goat? Why do you bleat? Why do you nibble grass?"

The little one was unable to reply, but continued to stare, comparing the two reflections. Then it became uneasy, shifted its weight from paw to paw, and emitted another troubled, quavering cry. The fierce old beast seized it again and carried it off to his den, where he presented it with a bleeding piece of raw meat remaining from an earlier meal. The cub shuddered with disgust. The jungle tiger, ignoring the weak bleat of protest, gruffly ordered: "Take it! Eat it! Swallow it!" The cub resisted, but the frightening meat was forced between his teeth, and the tiger sternly supervised while he tried to chew and prepared to swallow. The toughness of the morsel was unfamiliar and was causing some difficulty, and he was just about to make his little noise again, when he began to get the taste of the blood. He was amazed; he reached with eagerness for the rest. He began to feel an unfamiliar gratification as the new food went down his gullet, and the meaty substance came into his stomach. A strange, glowing strength, starting from there, went out through his whole organism, and he commenced to feel elated, intoxicated. His lips smacked; he licked his jowls. He arose and opened his mouth with a mighty yawn, just as though he were waking from a night of sleep—a night that had held him long under its spell, for years and years. Stretching his form, he arched his back, extending and spreading his paws. The tail lashed the ground, and suddenly from his throat there burst the terrifying, triumphant roar of a tiger.

The grim teacher, meanwhile, had been watching closely and with increasing satisfaction. The transformation had actually taken place. When the roar was finished he demanded gruffly: "Now do you know what you really are?" . . .

According to the thinking and experience of India, the knowledge of changing things does not conduce to a realistic attitude; for such things lack substantiality, they perish. Neither does it conduce to an idealistic outlook; for the inconsistencies of things in flux continually contradict and refute each other. Phenomenal forms are by nature delusory and fallacious. The one who rests on them will be disturbed. They are merely the particles of a vast universal illusion which is wrought by the magic of Self-forgetfulness, supported by ignorance, and carried forward by the deceived passions. Naïve unawareness of the hidden truth of the Self is the primary cause of all the misplaced emphases, inappropriate attitudes, and consequent self-torments of this auto-intoxicated world.

There is obviously implicit in such an insight the basis for a transfer of all interest not only from the normal ends and means of people of the world, but also from the rites and dogmas of the religion of such deluded beings. The mythological creator, the Lord of the Universe, is no longer of interest. Only introverted awareness bent and driven to the depth of the subject's own nature reaches that borderline where the transitory superimpositions meet their unchanging source. And such awareness can finally succeed even in bringing consciousness across the border, to merge—perish and become therewith imperishable—in the omnipresent substratum of all substance. That is the Self (*ātman*), the ultimate, enduring, supporting source of being. That is the giver of all these specialized manifestations, changes of form, and deviations from the true state, these so-called *vikāras:* transformations and evolutions of the cosmic display. Nor is it through praise of and submission to the gods, but through knowledge, knowledge of the Self, that the sage passes from involvement in what is here displayed to a discovery of its cause.

And such knowledge is achieved through either of two techniques: 1. a systematic disparagement of the whole world as illusion, or 2. an equally thoroughgoing realization of the sheer materiality of it all.

This we recognize as precisely the non-theistic, anthropocentric position that we ourselves are on the point of reaching today in the West, if indeed we are not already there. For where dwell the gods to whom we can uplift our hands, send forth our prayers, and make oblation? Beyond the Milky Way are only island universes, galaxy beyond galaxy in the infinitudes of space —no realm of angels, no heavenly mansions, no choirs of the blessed surrounding a divine throne of the Father, revolving in beatific consciousness about the axial mystery of the Trinity. Is there any region left in all these great reaches where the soul on its quest might expect to arrive at the feet of God, having become divested of its own material coil? Or must we not now turn rather inward, seek the divine internally, in the deepest vault, beneath the floor; hearken within for the secret voice that is both commanding and consoling; draw from inside the grace which passeth all understanding?

We of the modern Occident are at last prepared to seek and hear the voice that India has heard. But like the tiger cub we must hear it not from the teacher but from within ourselves. Just as in the period of the deflation of the revealed gods of the Vedic pantheon, so today revealed Christianity has been devaluated. The Christian, as Nietzsche says, is a man who behaves like everybody else. Our professions of faith have no longer any discernible bearing either on our public conduct or on our private state of hope. The sacraments do not work on many of us their spiritual transformation; we are bereft and at a loss where to turn. Meanwhile, our academic secular philosophies are concerned rather with information than with that redemptive transformation which our souls require. And this is the reason why a glance at the face of India may assist us to discover and recover something of ourselves.

The basic aim of any serious study of Oriental thought should be, not merely the gathering and ordering of as much detailed inside information as possible, but the reception of some significant influence. And in order that this may come to pass—in line with the parable of the goat-fosterling who discovered he was a tiger—we should swallow the meat of the teaching as red and rare as we can stand it, not too much cooked in the heat of our ingrained Occidental intellect (and, by no means, from any philological pickle jar), but not raw either, because then it would prove unpalatable and perhaps indigestible. We must take it rare, with lots of the red juices gushing, so that we may really taste it, with a certain sense of surprise. Then we will join, from our transoceanic distance, in the world-reverberating jungle roar of India's wisdom. . . .

## The Meeting of East and West

Occidental philosophy, as developed through the long and stately series of its distinguished masters, from Pythagoras to Empedocles and Plato, from Plotinus and the Neoplatonic thinkers to the mystics of the Middle Ages, and again in Spinoza and Hegel, deals with problems beyond the sphere of common sense, such as can be expressed only in cryptic difficult formulae, and by paradox. Indian philosophy does the same. The Oriental thinkers are as fully aware as the Western of the fact that the means offered by the mind and the powers of reason are not adequate to the problem of grasping and expressing truth. Thinking is limited by language. Thinking is a kind of soundless interior talk. What cannot be formulated in the current words or symbols of the given tradition does not exist in current thinking. And it requires, therefore, a specific creative effort on the part of a bold, fervent mind to break through to what is not being said—to view it at all; and then another effort to bring it back into the field of language by coining a term. Unknown, unnamed, non-existing as it were, and yet existing verily, the truth must be won to, found, and carried back through the brain into speech —where, inevitably, it will again be immediately mislaid.

The possibilities for thought, practical or otherwise, at any period, are thus rigidly limited by the range and wealth of the available linguistic coinage: the number and scope of the nouns, verbs, adjectives, and connectives. The totality of this currency is called, in Indian philosophy, *nāman* (Latin *nomen,* our word "name"). The very substance on and by which the mind operates when thinking consists of this name-treasury of notions. *Nāman* is the internal realm of concepts, which corresponds to the external realm of perceived "forms," the Sanskrit term for the latter being *rūpa,* "form," "shape," "color" (for there are no shapes or forms without color). *Rūpa* is the outer counterpart of *nāman; nāman* the interior of *rūpa. Nāma-rūpa* therefore denotes, on the one hand, man, the experiencing, thinking individual, man as endowed with mind and senses, and on the other, all the means and objects of thought and perception. *Nāma-rūpa* is the whole world, subjective and objective, as observed and known.

Now, all of the schools of Indian philosophy, though greatly diverging in their formulations of the essence of ultimate truth or basic reality, are unanimous in asserting that the ultimate object of thought and final goal of knowledge lies beyond the range of nāma-rūpa. Both Vedāntic Hinduism and Mahāyāna Buddhism constantly insist on the inadequacy of language and logical thought for the expression and comprehension of their systems. According to the classical Vedāntic formula, the fundamental factor responsible for the character and problems of our normal day-world consciousness, the force that builds the ego and leads it to mistake itself and its experiences for reality, is "ignorance, nescience" (*avidyā*). This ignorance is to be described neither as "being or existent" (*sat*), nor as "non-being, non-existent" (*a-sat*), but as "ineffable, inexplicable, indescribable" (*a-nirvacanīya*). For if it were "unreal, non-existent"—so the argument runs—it would not be of force sufficient to bind consciousness to the limitations of the individual and shroud from man's inner eye the realization of the immediate reality of the Self, which is the only Being. But on the other hand, if it were "real," of absolute indestructibility, then it could not be so readily dispelled by knowledge (*vidyā*); the Self (*ātman*) would never have been discovered as the ultimate substratum of all existences, and there would be no doctrine of Vedānta capable of guiding the intellect to enlightenment. "Ignorance" cannot be said to *be,* because it changes. Transiency is its very character—and this the seeker recognizes the moment he transcends its deluding spell. Its form is "the form of becoming" (*bhāva-rūpa*)—ephemeral, perishable, conquerable. And yet this "ignorance" itself differs from the specific transient phenomena within its pale, because it has existed—though ever changing—from time immemorial. Indeed, it is the root, the very cause and substance, of time. And the paradox is that though without beginning it can have an end. For the individual, bound by it to the everlasting round-of-rebirth, and subject to what is popularly called the law of the transmigration of the life-monad or soul, can become aware of the whole sphere of "ignorance" as an existence of no final reality—simply by an act of interior awareness (*anubhava*), or a moment of the uncomplicated realization, "I am nescient" (*aham ajña*).

Indian philosophy insists that the sphere of logical thought is far exceeded by that of the mind's possible experiences of reality. To express and communicate knowledge gained in moments of grammar-transcending insight metaphors must be used, similes and allegories. These are then not mere embellishments, dispensable accessories, but the very vehicles of the meaning, which could not be rendered, and could never have been attained, through the logical formulae of normal verbal thought. Significant images can comprehend and make manifest with clarity and pictorial consistency the paradoxical character of the reality known to the sage: a translogical reality, which, expressed in the abstract language of normal thought, would seem inconsistent, self-contradictory, or even absolutely meaningless. Indian philosophy, therefore, frankly avails itself of the symbols and images of myth, and is not finally at variance with the patterns and sense of mythological belief.

The Greek critical philosophers before Socrates, the pre-Socratic thinkers and the Sophists, practically destroyed their native mythological tradition. Their new approach to the solution of the enigmas of the universe and of man's nature and destiny conformed to the logic of the rising natural sciences—mathematics, physics, and astronomy. Under their powerful influence the older mythological symbols degenerated into mere elegant and amusing themes for novels, little better than society gossip about the complicated love-affairs and quarrels of the celestial upper class. Contrariwise in India, however: there mythology never ceased to support and facilitate the expression of philosophic thought. The rich pictorial script of the epic tradition, the features of the divinities whose incarnations and exploits constituted the myth, the symbols of religion, popular as well as esoteric, loaned themselves, again and again, to the purpose of the teachers, becoming the receptacles of their truth-renewing experience and the vehicles of their communication. In this way a co-operation of the latest and the oldest, the highest and the lowest, a wonderful friendship of mythology and philosophy, was effected; and this has been sustained with such result that the whole edifice of Indian civilization is imbued with spiritual meaning. The close interdependence and perfect harmonization of the two serve to counteract the natural tendency of Indian philosophy to become recondite and esoteric, removed from life and the task of the education of society. In the Hindu world, the folklore and popular mythology carry the truths and teachings of the philosophers to the masses. In this symbolic form, the ideas do not have to be watered down to be popularized. The vivid, perfectly appropriate pictorial script preserves the doctrines without the slightest damage to their sense.

Indian philosophy is basically skeptical of words, skeptical of their adequacy to render the main topic of philosophical thought, and therefore very cautious about trying to bring into a purely intellectual formula the answer to the riddle of the universe and man's existence. "What is all this around me, this world in which I find myself? What is this process carrying me on, together with the earth? Whence has it all proceeded? Whither is it tending? And what is to be my role, my duty, my goal, amidst this bewildering breath-taking drama in which I find myself involved?" That is the basic problem in the mind of men when they start philosophizing and before they reduce their aspirations to questions of methodology and the criticism of their own mental and sensual faculties. "All this around me, and my own being": that is the net of entanglement called māyā, the world creative power. Māyā manifests its force through the rolling universe and evolving forms of individuals. To understand that secret, to know how it works, and to transcend, if possible, its cosmic spell—breaking outward through the layers of tangible and visible appearance, and simultaneously inward through all the intellectual and emotional stratifications of the psyche—this is the pursuit conceived by Indian philosophy to be the primary, and finally undeniable, human task. . . .

A close and continuous interrelationship with rational science has been a distinguishing trait of Western philosophy; consider, for instance, the role of applied mathematics in Greek astronomy, mechanics, and physics, or the approach to zoology and botany of such thinkers as Aristotle and Theophrastus—methodical, and unclouded by any theological or mythical conceptions. It has been argued that Indian thought, at its best, may be compared not with the great line of Western philosophy, but only with the Christian thinking of the Middle Ages, from the Fathers to St. Thomas Aquinas, when philosophical speculation was kept subservient to the claims of the "revealed" faith and compelled to enact the part of helpmate or handmaid of theology (*ancilla theologiae*), and was never permitted to challenge or analyze the dogmatic foundations laid down and interpreted by the decrees of the popes and maintained by the persecution of all heretics and freethinkers. Greek philosophy, and then likewise modern philosophy—as represented by Giordano Bruno (who perished at the stake) and Descartes—has invariably brought intellectual revolution in its wake, effecting a radical and ever increasing disentanglement of thought from the meshes of religious traditionalism. Already in the middle of the fifth century B.C. Anaxagoras was banished from Athens for declaring that the sun was not the sun-god Helios but an incandescent celestial sphere. Among the crimes of which Socrates was accused, and for which he had to drain the deadly cup, was a lack of faith in the established religion, that of the local tutelary deities of Athens. While from the days of Bruno and Galileo on, our modern sciences and philosophy have arrived at their present maturity only by battling at every step the doctrines of man and nature that were the tradition and established treasure of the Church. Nothing comparable, or at least nothing of such a revolutionizing and explosive magnitude, has ever shown itself in the traditional East.

Western philosophy has become the guardian angel of right (i.e., unprejudiced, critical) thinking. It has earned this position through its repeated contacts with, and unwavering loyalty to, the progressive methods of thought in the sciences. And it will support its champion even though the end may be the destruction of all traditional values whatsoever, in society, religion, and philosophy. The nineteenth-century thinkers who declined to accept Indian philosophy on the par level did so because they felt responsible to the truth of the modern sciences. This had been established by experiment and criticism. And philosophy, as they conceived it, was to expound the methods of such rational progress, while safeguarding them against dilettantism, wishful thinking, and the ingrained prepossessions of any undisciplined speculation conducted along the discredited lines of archaic man.

There is, on the other hand, an attitude of hallowed traditionalism conspicuous in most of the great documents of Eastern thought, a readiness to submit to the authoritative utterances of inspired teachers claiming direct contact with transcendental truth. This would seem to indicate an incorrigible preference for vision, intuition, and metaphysical experience rather than experiment, laboratory work, and the reduction of the exact data of the senses to mathematical formulae. There was never in India any such close affinity between natural science and philosophy as to bring about a significant cross-fertilization. Nothing in Hindu physics, botany, or zoology can compare with the mature achievements of Aristotle, Theophrastus, Eratosthenes, and the scientists in Hellenistic Alexandria. Indian reasoning has remained uninfluenced by such criticism, new raw material, and inspiration as the Occidental thinkers have continually received from sources of this kind. And if the Indian natural sciences cannot be said ever to have equaled those known to Europe even in the time of the Greeks, how much greater is the inequality today!

Under the impact of the sweeping achievements of our laboratories, modern philosophy has completely refashioned its conception of its problems. Without the development of a modern mathematics, physics, and astronomy, through the work of Galileo, Torricelli, and their contemporaries, the new way of thought represented by Descartes and Spinoza would never have been found. Spinoza earned his livelihood as an optician, making lenses—a modern, advanced tool of the newest sciences. The versatile lifework of Leibnitz exhibited most conspicuously the close interrelationship, nay fusion, of mathematics and physics, with seventeenth-century philosophy. And one cannot study Kant without becoming aware of Newton. During the nineteenth century, science found its counterpart in the positivistic, empiristic philosophies of Comte, Mill, and Spencer. Indeed, the whole course of modern Western thought has been established by the pacemaking, relentless progress of our secularized, rational sciences, from the day of Francis Bacon and the rise of the New Learning, even to the present moment, when the staggering theories of Einstein, Heisenberg, Planck, Eddington, and Dirac on the structure of the atom and the universe, have projected the new task for the philosophers not only of today but of generations to come.

Absolutely nothing of this kind will be found in the history of India, though in classical antiquity a corresponding situation is marked by the grand sequence from Thales to Democritus, and through Plato and Aristotle to Lucretius. Not a few of the pre-Socratics were distinguished in mathematics, physics, and astronomy, as well as in philosophical speculation. Thales won more fame when he predicted an eclipse of the sun by means of mathematics applied to problems of cosmology than he ever gained among his contemporaries by declaring water to be the primary element of the universe—an idea that had been common to various earlier mythologies. Pythagoras, similarly, is celebrated as the discoverer of certain basic principles of acoustics. Aristotle writes of the followers of Pythagoras that they "applied themselves to the study of mathematics and were the first to advance that science." Regarding the principles of number as the first principles of all existing things, Pythagoras, by experiment, discovered the dependence of the musical intervals on certain arithmetical ratios of lengths of string at the same tension; and the laws of harmony thus discovered he applied to the interpretation of the whole structure of the cosmos. Thus in ancient Greece, as in Europe today, philosophical speculation concerning the structure and forces of the universe, the nature of all things, and the essential character of man was already largely actuated by a spirit of scientific inquiry; and the result was a dissolution of the archaic, established, mythological and theological ideas about man and the world. Traditionalism based on revelation and time-honored visions became discredited. A series of intellectual revolutions followed, which were in part the cause and spiritual prototype of the collapse, centuries later, of our established social systems—from the French Revolution in 1789 to the Russian and Central European revolutions of the present century, and, last but not least, the recent upheavals in Mexico, South America, and China.

Indian philosophy, on the contrary, has remained traditional. Supported and refreshed not by outward-directed experiment, but by the inward-turned experiences of yoga-practice, it has interpreted rather than destroyed inherited belief, and in turn been both interpreted and corrected by the forces of religion. Philosophy and religion differ in India on certain points; but there has never been a dissolving, over-all attack from the representatives of pure criticism against the immemorial stronghold of popular belief. In the end, the two establishments have reinforced each other, so that in each may be found characteristics which in Europe we should attribute only to its opposite. This is why the professors in our universities who for so long were reluctant to dignify Indian thinking about our everlasting human problems with the Greek and Western title "philosophy" were far from being unjustified. Nevertheless—and this is what I hope to be able to show—there exists and has existed in India what is indeed a real philosophy, as bold and breath-taking an adventure as anything ever hazarded in the Western world. Only, it emerges from an Eastern situation and pattern of culture, aims at ends that are comparatively unfamiliar to the modern academic schools, and avails itself of alien methods—the ends or goals being precisely those that inspired Plotinus, Scotus Erigena, and Meister Eckhart, as well as the philosophic flights of such thinkers of the period before Socrates as Parmenides, Empedocles, Pythagoras, and Heraclitus.

## The Four Aims of Life

The fact remains: there is no one word in Sanskrit to cover and include everything in the Indian literary tradition that we should be disposed to term philosophical. The Hindus have several ways of classifying the thoughts which they regard as worth learning and handing down, but no single heading under which to comprehend all of their basic generalizations about reality, human nature, and conduct. The first and most important of their systems of classification is that of the four aims, or ends, or areas, of human life.

1. *Artha,* the first aim, is material possessions. The arts that serve this aim are those of economics and politics, the techniques of surviving in the struggle for existence against jealousy and

competition, calumny and blackmail, the bullying tyranny of despots, and the violence of reckless neighbors. Literally, the word *artha* means "thing, object, substance," and comprises the whole range of the tangible objects that can be possessed, enjoyed, and lost, and which we require in daily life for the upkeep of a household, raising of a family, and discharge of religious duties, i.e., for the virtuous fulfillment of life's obligations. Objects contribute also to sensuous enjoyment, gratification of the feelings, and satisfaction of the legitimate requirement of human nature: love, beautiful works of art, flowers, jewels, fine clothing, comfortable housing, and the pleasures of the table. The word *artha* thus connotes "the attainment of riches and wordly prosperity, advantage, profit, wealth," also, "result"; in commercial life: "business-matter, business-affair, work, price"; and in law: "plaint, action, petition." With reference to the external world, *artha,* in its widest connotation, signifies "that which can be perceived, an object of the senses"; with reference to the interior world of the psyche: "end and aim, purpose, object, wish, desire, motive, cause, reason, interest, use, want, and concern"; and as the last member of a compound, *-artha*: "for the sake of, on behalf of, for, intended for." The term thus bundles together all the meanings of 1. the object of human pursuit, 2. the means of this pursuit, and 3. the needs and the desire suggesting this pursuit.

There exists in India a special literature on the subject wherein the field of the inquiry is narrowed to the specific area of politics: the politics of the individual in everyday life, and the politics of the gaining, exercise, and maintenance of power and wealth as a king. This art is illustrated by the beast fable—a most remarkable vehicle for the presentation of a realistic philosophy of life. Case histories from the animal realm develop and illuminate a ruthless science of survival, a completely unsentimental craft of prospering in the face of the constant danger that must ever lurk in the clandestine and open struggle of beings for life and supremacy. Like all Indian doctrines, this one is highly specialized and designed to impart a skill. It is not confused or basically modified by moral inhibitions; the techniques are presented chemically pure. The textbooks are dry, witty, merciless, and cynical, reflecting on the human plane the pitiless laws of the animal conflict. Beings devouring each other, thriving on each other, maintaining themselves against each other, inspire the patterns of the thought. The basic principles are those of the deep sea; hence the doctrine is named *Matsya-nyāya,* "The Principle or Law (*nyāya*) of the Fishes (*matsya*)"—which is to say, "the big ones eat the little ones." The teaching is also called *Arthaśāstra,* "The Authoritative Handbook (*śāstra*) of the Science of Wealth (*artha*)," wherein are to be found all the timeless laws of politics, economy, diplomacy, and war. . . .

2. *Kāma,* the second of the four ends of life, is pleasure and love. In Indian mythology, Kāma is the counterpart of Cupid. He is the Hindu god of love, who, with flower-bow and five flower-arrows, sends desire quivering to the heart. Kāma is desire incarnate, and, as such, lord and master of the earth, as well as of the lower celestial spheres.

The principal surviving classic of India's Kāma teaching is Vātsyāyana's celebrated *Kāmasūtra.* This work has earned India an ambiguous reputation for sensuality that is rather misleading; for the subject is presented on an entirely secularized and technical level, more or less as a textbook for lovers and courtesans. The dominant attitude of the Hindu, in actuality, is austere, chaste, and extremely restrained, marked by an emphasis on purely spiritual pursuits and an absorption in religious and mystical experiences. Kāma teaching came into existence to correct and ward off the frustration in married life that must have been all too frequent where marriages of convenience prevailed and marriages of love were the rare exception. Through the centuries, marriage became increasingly a family affair. Bargains struck by the heads of families, based on the horoscopes cast by astrologers and on economic and social considerations, determined the fate of the young bride and groom. No doubt there were many dull and painful households where a little study of the courtesan's science could have been of immense service. It was for a society of frozen emotions, not libertine, that this compendium of the techniques of adjustment and stimulation was compiled.

Though the Kāma literature that has come down to us is thus excessively technical, nevertheless some basic insights concerning the attitude of the sexes toward each other can still be extracted from it—some notion of the Hindu psychology of love, analysis of the feelings, and manners of emotional expression, as well as a view of the recognized task and sphere of love. Better, however, than the *Kāmasūtra* for this purpose is another class of textbooks devoted to the various arts of pleasure, namely the handbooks of poetics and acting, the so-called *Nāṭyaśāstras,* which are summaries, for professionals, of the techniques of dancing, pantomime, singing, and the drama. The standard Hindu types of hero and heroine are here presented and discussed. The traits of their psychology are delineated, and the sequences of feeling described which they normally experience in different standard situations. We find reflected in these texts an exquisitely developed psychology of the heart, comparable to the typology and tapestry of human emotions and reactions that developed in the West with the Italian opera and the French tragedy of the seventeenth and eighteenth centuries. The works continually remind one of the essays and aphorisms of such French littérateur-psychologists as La Bruyère, La Rochefoucauld, Chamfort, and Vauvenargues—revivers of the Greek tradition of Theophrastus, who in his turn had been inspired by the Greek art of the stage.

3. *Dharma,* the third of the four aims, comprises the whole context of religious and moral duties. This too is personified as a deity, but he is one of comparatively abstract character.

The texts are the *Dharmaśāstras* and *Dharmasūtras,* or Books of the Law. Some are attributed to mythical personages such as Manu, forefather of man, others to certain eminent Brāhman saints and teachers of antiquity. The style of the most ancient—for example, that of Gautama, of Āpastamba, and of Baudhāyana, who belong to the fifth and following centuries B.C.—resembles that of the later Vedic prose tradition. These earlier works are filled with social, ritual, and religious prescriptions intended for one or another of the Vedic schools. But the later law books—and most notably the great compendium assigned to Manu—reach out to cover the whole context of orthodox Hindu life. The rituals and numerous social regulations of the three upper castes, Brāhman (priest), Kṣatriya (noble), Vaiśya (merchant and agriculturalist), are meticulously formulated on the basis of immemorial practices ascribed to the teaching of the Creator himself. Not the king or the millionaire, but the sage, the saint, the Mahātma (literally "magnanimous": "great (*mahat*) Self or Spirit (*ātman*)"), receives the highest place and honor in this system. As the seer, the tongue or mouthpiece of the timeless truth, he is the one from whom all society derives its order. The king is, properly, but the administrator of that order; agriculturalists and merchants supply the materials that give embodiment to the form; and the workers (*śūdras*) are those who contribute the necessary physical labor. Thus all are co-ordinated to the revelation, preservation, and experience of the one great divinely-intended image. Dharma is the doctrine of the duties and rights of each in the ideal society, and as such the law or mirror of all moral action.

4. *Mokṣa, apavarga, nirvṛtti,* or *nivṛtti,* the fourth of the four aims, is redemption, or spiritual release. This is regarded as the ultimate aim, the final human good, and as such is set over and against the former three.

Artha, Kāma, and Dharma, known as the *trivarga,* the "group of three," are the pursuits of the world; each implies its own orientation or "life philosophy," and to each a special literature is dedicated. But by far the greatest measure of Indian thought, research, teaching, and writing has been concerned with the supreme spiritual theme of liberation from ignorance and from the passions of the world's general illusion. *Mokṣa,* from the root *muc,* "to loose, set free, let go, release, liberate, deliver; to leave, abandon, quit," means "liberation, escape, freedom, release; rescue, deliverance; final emancipation of the soul." *Apavarga,* from the verb *apavṛj,* "to avert, destroy, dissipate; tear off, pull out, take out," means "throwing, discharging (a missile), abandonment; completion, end; and the fulfillment, or accomplishment of an action." *Nirvṛtti* is "disappearance, destruction, rest, tranquility, completion, accomplishment, liberation from worldly existence, satisfaction, happiness, bliss"; and *nivṛtti*: "cessation, termination, disappearance; abstinence from activity or work; leaving off, desisting from, resignation; discontinuance of worldly acts or emotions; quietism, separation from the world; rest, repose, felicity." All of which dictionary terms taken together suggest something of the highest end of man as conceived by the Indian sage.

India's *paramārtha*—"paramount (*parama*) object (*artha*)"—is nothing less than the basic reality which underlies the phenomenal realm. This is apprehended when the mere impressions conveyed by the physical senses to a nervous brain in the service of the passions and emotions of an ego no longer delude. One is then "dis-illusioned." *Paramārtha-vid,* "he who knows (*vid*) the paramount object (*paramārtha*)," is consequently the Sanskrit word that the dictionary roughly translates "philosopher."

## Release and Progress

The gist of any system of philosophy can best be grasped in the condensed form of its principal terms. An elementary exposition must be concerned, therefore, with presenting and interpreting the words through which the main ideas have to be conceived. Indian thought is excellently adapted to such an approach; for all of its terms belong to Sanskrit and have long served in the everyday language of poetry and romance as well as in such technical literatures as that of medicine. They are not terms confined to the strange and unfamiliar atmosphere of the specialized schools and doctrines. The nouns, for example, which constitute the bulk of the philosophic terminology, stand side by side with verbs that have been derived from the same roots and denote activities or processes expressive of the same content. One can always come to the basic meaning through a study of the common uses of the word in daily life and by this means ascertain not only its implied shades and values, but also its suggested metaphors and connotations. All of which is in striking contrast with the situation in the contemporary West, where by far the greater number of our philosophical terms have been borrowed from Greek and Latin, stand detached from actual life, and thus suffer from an inevitable lack of vividness and clarity. The word "idea" means very different things, for example, according to whether it is Plato, Locke, the modern history of ideas, psychology, or everyday talk that one is trying to understand. Each case, each authority for the term, every author, period, and school, must be taken by itself. But the Indian vocabulary is so closely connected with the general usage of the civilization that it can always be interpreted through the way of the general understanding.

By reviewing the whole range of values covered by any Sanskrit term one can watch Indian thought at work, as it were from within. This technique corrects the unavoidable misinterpretations that arise, even in the best intended translations, as a result of the vastly differing range of associations of our European terms. Actually, we have no precise verbal equivalents for translations from Sanskrit, but only misleading approximations resounding with Occidental associations that are necessarily very different from those of the Indian world. This fact has led the West to all sorts of false deductions as to the nature, ends, and means of Oriental thought. Even the most faithful interpreter finds himself spreading misinformation simply because his words slip into a European context the moment they leave his lips. It is only by referring continually to the Sanskrit dictionary that one can begin to perceive something of the broader backgrounds of the phrases that for centuries have served to carry the living burden of Indian thought.

For example, the emphasis placed by the ascetic philosophies on the paramount ideal and end of mokṣa, and the consequent mass of literature on the subject, leads the Western student to an extremely one-sided view of Indian civilization. The true force of the ideal cannot be understood out of context—and that context is the traditional Indian, not the modern industrial, world. Mokṣa is a force that has impressed itself on every feature, every trait and discipline, of Indian life and has shaped the entire scale of values. It is to be understood, not as a refutation, but as the final flowering, of the success of the successful man. Briefly: the greater part of Indian philosophy proper is concerned with guiding the individual during the second, not the first, portion of his life. Not before but after one has accomplished the normal worldly aims of the individual career, after one's duties have been served as a moral member and supporter of the family and community, one turns to the tasks of the final human adventure. According to the Hindu dharma, a man's lifetime is to be divided into four strictly differentiated stages (*āśrama*). The first is that of the student, "he who is to be taught" (*śiṣya*), "he who attends, waits upon, and serves his guru" (*antevāsin*). The second is that of the householder (*gṛhastha*), which is the great period of a man's maturity and enactment of his due role in the world. The third is that of retirement to the forest for meditation (*vanaprastha*). And the fourth is that of the mendicant wandering sage (*bhikṣu*). Mokṣa is for the latter two; not for the first or second.

*Grāma,* "the village," and *vana,* "the forest": these stand as opposites. For grāma, men have been given the "group of three" (*trivarga*), and the handbooks of the normal aims and ends of worldly life; but for vana—the forest, the hermitage, the work of getting rid of this earthly burden of objects, desires, duties, and all the rest—a man will require the other disciplines, the other way, the other, quite opposite, ideals, techniques, and experiences of "release." Business, family, secular life, like the beauties and hopes of youth and the successes of maturity, have now been left behind; eternity alone remains. And so it is to that—not to the tasks and worries of this life, already gone, which came and passed like a dream—that the mind is turned. Mokṣa looks beyond the stars, not to the village street. Mokṣa is the practical discipline of metaphysics. Its aim is not to establish the foundations of the sciences, evolve a valid theory of knowledge, or control and refine methods of scientific approach to either the spectacle of nature or the documents of human history, but to rend the tangible veil. Mokṣa is a technique of transcending the senses in order to discover, know, and dwell at one with the timeless reality which underlies the dream of life in the world. Nature and man, in so far as they are visible, tangible, open to experience, the sage cognizes and interprets, but only to step through them to his ultimate metaphysical good.

On the other hand, in the Occident, we have had no metaphysics—practical or otherwise—since the middle of the eighteenth century. In diametric contrast to the dominant Oriental view of the insubstantiality of the world of change and decay, our materialistic minds have developed and favored an optimistic view of evolution and, together with this, a fervent faith in the perfectibility of human affairs through better planning, technology, a wider spread of education, and the opening of opportunities for all. Whereas the Hindu feels himself to be utterly at the mercy of the destructive forces of death (diseases, plagues, warfare, human tyranny and injustice), and the inevitable victim of the relentless flow of time (which swallows individuals, wipes out the bloom of realms and towns, and crumbles even the ruins to dust), we feel the power of human genius to invent and organize, the sovereign strength of man to achieve collective discipline, and both the urge and the capacity to control the moving forces of nature. *We* are the ones who work changes; nature remains ever the same. And this nature, conquered by scientific analysis, can be compelled to submit to the harness of the triumphant chariot of our human advance. Europe's eighteenth-century thinkers believed in progressive collective enlightenment: wisdom as a dispeller of darkness, making society perfect, noble, and pure. The nineteenth century believed in collective material and social progress: the conquest of nature's forces, the abolition of violence, slavery, and injustice, and the victory over not only suffering but even premature death. And now the twentieth century feels that only by intense and extensive planning and organization can our human civilization hope to be saved.

The frailty of human life does not really obsess us, as it did our ancestors in the fifteenth and sixteenth centuries. We feel more sheltered than did they against vicissitudes, better insured against setbacks; decay and decline do not fill us with such despair and resignation. We believe that it is we ourselves who constitute our providence—as we all press onward in the historic human battle to dominate the earth and its elements, to control its mineral, vegetable, animal, and even sub-atomic kingdoms. The secret forces of existence, the complex chemistry and organic alchemy of the life process, whether in our own psyches and physiques or in the world around, we are now gradually unveiling. No longer do we feel caught in the meshes of an unconquerable cosmic web. And so, accordingly, we have our logic of science, experimental methods, and psychology, but no metaphysics.

The airy flights do not really interest us any more. We do not found our lives on fascinating or consoling total interpretations of life and the universe, along lines such as those of traditional theology or meditative speculation; rather, we have all these questions of detail in our numerous systematic sciences. Instead of an attitude of acceptance, resignation, and contemplation, we cultivate a life of relentless movement, causing changes at every turn, bettering things, planning things, subduing to schedule the spontaneous wild growths of the world. In place of the archaic aim of understanding life and the cosmos as a whole, by means of general speculation, we have for our thought the ideal of a multifarious, ever more refined activity of highly specialized understandings, and the mastery of concrete details. Religion and philosophy have become transformed into science, technology, and political economics. Since this is so, and since the main object of Indian philosophy, on the other hand, is mokṣa, we may well ask whether we have any qualifications at all for the understanding of that remote doctrine—fixed as we are to our pursuit of artha, kāma, and dharma, and feeling fully satisfied to be this way.

And so here we hit upon another of the fundamental differences between the philosophies of the modern West and the traditional East. Viewed from the standpoints of the Hindu and Buddhist disciplines, our purely intellectual approach to all theoretical matters that are not directly concerned with the trivarga would seem dilettante and superficial. Through the course of its evolution during comparatively modern times, Western thought has become completely exoteric. It is supposed to be open to the approach and accredited investigation of every intellectual who can meet the general requirements of a) a basic education, and b) some specialized intellectual training to enable him to keep up with the argument. But this was not the way in Plato's ancient time. Μηδεὶς ἀγεωμέτρητος εἰσίτω ἐμὴν στέγην: "Nobody untrained in mathematics may cross this my threshold." Plato is said to have inscribed this warning above his door in homage to Pythagoras and the contemporary revolutionary mathematicians of Sicily—such men as Archytas of Tarentum; whereas in modern times, a high-school education and four years of college are supposed to open an access to the sanctum sanctorum of ultimate Truth. India, in this respect, is where Plato was; and that is another of the reasons why the professors of the European and American universities were justified in refusing to admit Indian thought to *their* temple of "philosophy."

## Philosophy as a Way of Life

In ancient India each department of learning was associated with a highly specialized skill and corresponding way of life. The knowledge was not to be culled from books primarily, or from lectures, discussions, and conversation, but to be mastered through apprenticeship to a competent teacher. It required the wholehearted surrender of a malleable pupil to the authority of the guru, its elementary prerequisites being obedience (*śuśrūṣā*) and implicit faith (*śraddhā*). *Suśrūṣā* is the fervent desire to hear, to obey, and to retain what is being heard; it implies dutifulness, reverence, and service. *Śraddhā* is trust and composure of mind; it demands the total absence of every kind of independent thought and criticism on the part of the pupil; and here again there is reverence, as well as strong and vehement desire. The Sanskrit word means also "the longing of a pregnant woman."

The pupil in whom the sought truth dwells as the jungle tiger dwelt within the cub submits without reserve to his guru, paying him reverence as an embodiment of the divine learning to be imparted. For the teacher is a mouthpiece of the higher knowledge and a master of the special skill. The pupil in his religious worship must become devoted to the presiding divinity of the department of skill and wisdom that is to be the informing principle, henceforward, of his career. He must share the household of the teacher for years, serve him in the home and assist him in his work—whether the craft be that of priest, magician, ascetic, physician, or potter. The techniques must be learned by constant practice, while the theory is being taught through oral instruction supplemented by a thoroughgoing study of the basic textbooks. And most important of all, a psychological "transference" between the master and pupil has to be effected; for a kind of transformation is to be brought to pass. The malleable metal of the pupil is to be worked into the pattern of the model teacher, and this with respect not only to matters of knowledge and skill but also, much more deeply, to the whole personal attitude. As for the life and morals of the guru himself: it is required that there should be an identity—an absolute, point-for-point correspondence—between his teachings and his way of life; the sort of identity that we should expect to find in the West only in a monk or priest.

No criticism, but a gradual growing into the mold of the discipline, is what is demanded. The training is accepted and followed, as it were, blindfold; but in the course of time, when the pupil's grasp of his subject increases, understanding comes of its own accord. Such blind acceptance and subsequent intuitive comprehension of a truth through the enactment of its corresponding attitude is known to Europe primarily in the practice of the Roman Catholic church. In one of the novels, for example, of Flaubert, *Bouvard et Pécuchet,* the case is described of two freethinkers, disappointed with their way of life, who, following an attempt at suicide, become reconverted to the faith of their childhood and early peasant environment. They turn to the priest and assail him with unsettled doubts and skepticism, but he replies merely, *"Pratiquez d'abord."* That is to say: "Take up and practice first the orthodox, established way of the ritualistic duties—attending mass regularly, praying, going to confession and communion. Then gradually you will understand, and your doubts will vanish like mist in sunshine. You need not fathom the great depths of the dogma of the Trinity, nor the other mysteries, but you must indeed profess and feel an implicit faith that ultimately, somehow, these must be true. Then abide with the hope that their meaning may dawn upon you with the increasing operation within you of supernatural grace."

Precisely in this way, Oriental philosophy is accompanied and supported by the practice of a way of life—monastic seclusion, asceticism, meditation, prayer, yoga-exercises, and daily devotional hours of worship. The function of the worship is to imbue the devotee with the divine essence of the truth; this being made manifest under the symbolic thought-directing forms of divinities or other superhuman holy figures, as well as through the teacher himself, who, standing for truth incarnate, reveals truth continually, both through his teaching and in his way of daily life. In this respect Indian philosophy is as closely linked with religion, sacraments, initiations, and the forms of devotional practice as is our modern Western philosophy with the natural sciences and their methods of research.

This Indian view of the identity of personality and conduct with teaching is well rendered in the apt comment of a Hindu friend of mine in criticism of a certain popular book on Oriental philosophy. "After all," said he, "real attainment is only what finds confirmation in one's own life. The worth of a man's writing depends on the degree to which his life is itself an example of his teaching." . . .

## Philosophy as Power

In the Orient, philosophic wisdom does not come under the head of general information. It is a specialized learning directed to the attainment of a higher state of being. The philosopher is one whose nature has been transformed, re-formed to a pattern of really superhuman stature, as a result of being pervaded by the magic power of truth. That is why the prospective pupil must be carefully tested. The word *adhikārin* means, literally, as adjective, "entitled to, having a right to, possessed of authority, possessed of power, qualified, authorized, fit for"; also, "belonging to, owned by"; and as noun, "an officer, a functionary, head, director, rightful claimant, master, owner, a personage qualified to perform some sacrifice or holy work."

Philosophy is but one of many kinds of wisdom or knowledge (*vidyā*), each leading to some practical end. As the other vidyās lead to such attainments as belong to the special masterships of the craftsman, priest, magician, poet, or dancer, so philosophy ends in the attainment of a divine state both here and hereafter. Every kind of wisdom brings to its possessor its specific power, and this comes inevitably in consequence of the mastery of the respective materials. The doctor is the master of diseases and drugs, the carpenter the master of wood and other building materials, the priest of demons and even of gods by virtue of his charms, incantations, and rituals of offering and propitiation. Correspondingly, the yogī-philosopher is the master of his own mind and body, his passions, his reactions, and his meditations. He is one who has transcended the illusions of wishful thinking and of all other kinds of normal human thought. He feels no challenge or defeat in misfortune. He is absolutely beyond the touch of destiny.

Wisdom, in the Orient, no matter what its kind, is to be guarded jealously and communicated sparingly, and then only to one capable of becoming its perfect receptacle; for besides representing a certain skill, every department of learning carries with it a power that can amount almost to magic, a power to bring to pass what without it would seem a miracle. Teaching not intended to communicate such a power is simply of no consequence, and the communication to one unfit to wield the power properly would be disastrous. Furthermore, the possession of the wisdom and its special potencies was in ancient times regarded as one of the most valuable portions of the family heritage. Like a treasure, it was handed down with all care, according to the patrilineal order of descent. Charms, spells, the techniques of the various crafts and professions, and, finally, philosophy itself originally were communicated only in this way. Son followed father. For the growing generation there was little leniency of choice. This is how the instruments of family prestige were kept from slipping away.

And so it is that the Vedic hymns originally belonged exclusively to certain great family lines. Of the ten books of the *Ṛg-veda* (which is the oldest of the Vedas and indeed the oldest extant document of any of the Indo-European traditions) the second and those following it are the so-called "Family Books." They contain groups of potent verses which formerly were the guarded property of the ancient families of priests, seers, and holy singers. The ancestors of the various clans composed the stanzas in order to conjure gods to the sacrifice, propitiate them, and win their favor—the hymns having been revealed to those ancestral singers during their intercourse (in vision) with the gods themselves. The owners then occasionally marked their property, either by letting their names appear somewhere in the verses or, as was more frequently the case, by a characteristic closing stanza, which would be generally recognized as an earmark. Just as the ranging herds of the cattle-breeding Āryan families in Vedic times were distinguished by some brand or cut on the ear, flank, or elsewhere, so likewise the hymns—and with the same aristocratic sense of the force, and consequent preciousness, of property.

For if the wisdom that produces a special art and mastery is to be guarded jealously, then the higher the powers involved the more careful the guardianship must be—and this particularly when the powers are the gods themselves, the moving forces of nature and the cosmos. Cautious, complex rituals designed to conjure them and link them to human purposes occupied in Vedic (as also in Homeric) antiquity precisely the place held today by such sciences as physics, chemistry, medicine, and bacteriology. A potent hymn was as precious for those people as the secret of a new super-bomber is for us, or the blueprint of the latest device for a submarine. Such things were valuable not only for the art of war but also for the commercial competition of the times of peace....

In the West, on the other hand, the pride of philosophy is that it is open to the understanding and criticism of all. Our thought is exoteric, and that is regarded as one of the signs and proofs of its universal validity. Western philosophy has no secret doctrine, but challenges all to scrutinize her arguments, demanding no more than intelligence and an open-minded fairness in discussion. By this general appeal she has won her ascendency over the wisdom and teaching of the Church—which required that certain things should be taken for granted as once and for all established by divine revelation, and unquestionably settled by the interpretations of the inspired fathers, popes, and councils. Our popular modern philosophy, sailing in the broad wake of the natural sciences, recognizes no other authority than proof by experiment and pretends to rest upon no other assumptions than those rationally drawn as the logical theoretical result of critically and methodically digested data derived through sense-experience, registered and controlled by the mind and the faultless apparatus of the laboratories. . . .

India, dreamy India, philosophical, unpractical, and hopelessly unsuccessful in the maintenance of her political freedom, has always stood for the idea that wisdom can be power if (and this is an "if" that must be kept in mind) the wisdom permeates, transforms, controls, and molds the whole of the personality. The sage is not to be a library of philosophy stalking about on two legs, an encyclopedia with a human voice. Thought itself is to be converted in him into life, into flesh, into being, into a skill in act. And then the higher his realization, the greater will be his power. The magic of Mahātma Gandhi is to be understood, for example, in this way. The force of his model presence on the Hindu masses derives from the fact that in him is expressed an identity of ascetic wisdom (as a style of existence) with politics (as an effective attitude toward worldly issues, whether of daily life or of national policy). His spiritual stature is expressed and honored in the title bestowed upon him: Mahātma: "whose essence of being is great," "he in whom the supra-personal, supra-individual, divine essence, which pervades the whole universe and dwells within the microcosm of the human heart as the animating grace of God (*ātman*), has grown to such magnitude as to have become utterly predominant (*mahat*)." The Spiritual Person has swallowed and dissolved in him all traces of ego, all the limitations proper to personal individuation, all those limiting, fettering qualities and propensities that belong to the normal human state, and even every trace remaining from ego-motivated deeds (*karma*), whether good or evil, whether derived from this life or from deeds in former births. Such traces of personality bias and distort a man's outlook on worldly affairs and prevent his approach to divine truth. But the Mahātma is the man who has become transformed in his being through wisdom; and the power of such a presence to work magic we may yet live to see.

## CHAPTER II

# The Formative Stages of Hindu Religion

### Historical Background

*The Indus Civilization: ca. 2500–1500* B.C. The Indus Valley is the home of one of the world's oldest civilizations. Archaeological evidence indicates that a Bronze Age civilization appeared in the Indus Valley about 2500 B.C. Two major sites have yielded a massive amount of archaeological treasure: Harappa on the river Ravi (in Punjab) and Mohenjo-Daro on the Indus River (in Sind). The artifacts uncovered at these twin cities suggest that both sites manifest a common Indus civilization, a notion further supported by the discovery of characteristic artifacts from this ancient world in over sixty other sites covering wide areas of India.

While this civilization made an abrupt appearance and lasted almost a thousand years, the remains clearly suggest that during the course of its life it exhibited very little development or innovation. Moreover, as it moved toward the conclusion of its first millennium of existence, it dramatically deteriorated and fell into utter ruin. Its life history resembles very closely a shooting star which abruptly appears on the horizon, blazes brilliantly for a brief period, and then is utterly extinguished.

Skeletons unearthed at the sites at Harappa and Mohenjo-Daro disclose the presence in the Indian civilization of two broad categories of peoples: (1) an aboriginal population; and (2) a population with Mediterranean affinities. The aboriginal stock were the indigenous tribes of India. They were a dark-skinned people (almost black), small of stature, having broad, flat noses and protruding lips. Descendants of these people, even today, are found in the lower castes of Indian society. The people of Mediterranean stock have close affinities with people found in predynastic Egypt, Arabia, and North Africa. Evidently, their skin complexion was lighter (olive-brown) and their physique more slender. They had prominent, patrician noses and large, wide-set eyes. It is generally conceded that this stock of people migrated into the Indus Valley, since such peoples have always been associated with agricultural settlements throughout the Near East and Western Asia.

The artifacts of the Indus civilization point to the presence of phallic cults, usually associated in the primitive world with the worship of a mother-goddess. A small collection of steatite sealstones with representations of human figures have been recovered, and they suggest the possibility of human sacrifice (frequently found in worship of a mother-goddess) as an important part of the religious ritual. As Joseph Campbell suggests:

> The underlying myth is of a divine being, slain, cut up, and the parts buried, which thereupon turn into the food plants on which the community lives; and the leading theme . . . is the coming of death into the world. . . . The second point being that the food plants on which man lives derive from that death. And finally, the sexual organs . . . appeared at the time of that coming of death; for reproduction without death would have been a calamity, as would death without reproduction.[1]

Two other features of this ancient Indus civilization deserve mention. First, several seals uncovered portray a figure seated in the yoga position. Some scholars find in this remarkable figure a prototype of the Hindu god, Shiva. However, such a posture is also characteristic of the Buddha in meditation. Second, the ground plans for the cities of Harappa and Mohenjo-Daro clearly show that they were carefully laid out in districts reflecting the social and economic status of the inhabitants. The

---

[1] Joseph Campbell, *The Masks of God: Oriental Mythology* (The Viking Press, 1962), p. 164.

Indus cities had their slums and their higher-class dwellings. The division of classes in these cities presages the later development of the caste system when the Aryans arrived to subjugate the native inhabitants.

*The Aryan Migration: The Vedic Age ca. 1500–500* B.C. Sometime between 1700 B.C. and 1400 B.C. the first wave of the Aryan migration pushed through the passes of the Hindu Kush Mountains in northern India and began to spread out over the fertile Indian plain along the branches of the Indus River. The geographical origin of the Aryan invaders remains shrouded in mystery but is usually fixed somewhere in the great Eurasian land mass between the Rhine and Don Rivers. A coherent picture of the character of the Aryans can be pieced together from their oral tradition (later to be collected in the Vedas) which celebrates their adventures of conquest and appropriation of their new home in India. They were a lusty, warlike people, who brought the horse and chariot with them in their migration. The Vedic hymns reflect their wandering spirit and zest for life. Whether or not they were an agricultural or nomadic people is a disputed question, but we know that they raised cattle and pastured flocks of sheep and goats. For some period of time, they had been pressing eastward toward the sun, so that theirs was principally a mobile society in contrast to the land-rooted agricultural settlements of the Indus civilization.

During the Vedic age, we witness a gradual change in the Aryans' style of existence from that of nomadic wanderers to that of agricultural settlers. The spearhead of the Aryan migration was in constant struggle with the indigenous tribes and later with the Dravidian civilization to the south. Meanwhile, successive waves of Aryan migrants poured through the passes of the mountains in the north creating an irresistible pressure to move farther into the subcontinent. This pressure from successive waves of Aryan migrations led to inevitable intertribal conflicts. Such clashes are graphically described in the epic literature of the Vedic period, e.g., in the *Mahabharata* and the *Ramayana*.

This period of Indian prehistory is frequently referred to as the Dark Millennium because of the chaos that ensued from the Aryans' simultaneous efforts to subdue the indigenous tribes, to settle into their new territory, and to maintain their "squatter's rights" in the face of late migrations of their own stock. From the Vedic hymns, we gather that they brought with them an extensive religious tradition and mythology.

The invading Aryans were a warrior aristocracy interested in conquering, drinking, eating, and generally oriented to heroic enterprises. They were not unlike the adventuresome peoples of other heroic ages, such as the Homeric Greeks. Their mastery of the horse and their use of the chariot gave them a revolutionary weaponry enabling them to create a "mechanized blitzkrieg" against which the older, land-rooted civilization was helpless.

As the Aryan invaders gradually settled in the new land, a natural division of labor occurred which produced the first vestiges of a class system. Chieftains (rajahs) assumed the responsibility of continuing the struggle against the stubbornly resisting Dravidians. As more territory and people came under their sway, they became responsible for administering a crudely organized system of labor and exchange of goods. The Vedic literature indicates that a priestly class developed quickly in the early Aryan settlements. The priests were usually under the protection of the warrior class. At the bottom of the social scale was a vast multitude of subjects who performed diverse, but simple, social and economic functions.

Since it was during this period that the extensive oral tradition developed which was later to be collected in the Vedas, we must now turn to a consideration of the Vedic literature and religion.

## Vedic Literature and Religion

Vedic literature constitutes an indispensable source for the study of Hinduism. Most Hindus accept the total corpus of the Vedas (which is enormous indeed!) as divinely inspired knowledge. The orthodox schools of Hindu religious thought view the Vedas as divine revelation (sruti). "Vedic verses are not made, they are eternal." In this literature of the most remote antiquity one finds the germs of the whole future development of Hindu religion.

The Vedas are four in number: (1) Rg-Veda; (2) Sama-Veda; (3) Yajur-Veda; (4) Atharva-Veda. The Rg-Veda is composed mainly of hymns, brought into India by the Aryan conquerors during their migrations. Because the Aryans came into constant contact with the aboriginal inhabitants and their religious myths and practices, they cultivated an extensive oral tradition to preserve their most precious religious possession. No doubt much of this oral tradition is lost, but what is preserved is found in the Rg-Veda. The Sama-Veda and Yajur-Veda are essentially liturgical collections, which often repeat hymns found in the Rg-Veda and add nothing distinctive to the tradition. The organization of the Yajur-Veda and the Sama-Veda suggests that they were collected to serve the purposes of a complex, ceremonial religion. This probably indicates that they were collected after the Rg-Veda at a time when a highly systematized ritualism was emerging. The Atharva-Veda stands next in importance to the Rg-Veda. Although it was collected at a later date, when the Vedic Aryans were subduing and assimilating the primitive religious figures of pre-Aryan India, some of its contents clearly predate the hymns of the Rg-Veda.

The essence of the Vedas are the collections of metrical hymns, prayers, charms, and infrequent prose passages called "samhitas." Other supplementary writings are also considered to be part of the Vedas: (1) the Brahmanas, catalogs of moral precepts and religious duties; (2) the Upanishads, highly meditative poetry and prose dealing with the most basic religious and philosophical issues. The Brahmanas contain also a collection of writings, largely mystical in character, called the "Forest Books," or Aranyakas. These meditative and speculative tracts represent a late stage in the development of Hindu religious thought and are often considered transitional to the intensely spiritual and philosophical Upanishads. These latter, exceeding two hundred in number (of which about twelve are very ancient), come from a very late period in Indian history. The Upanishads constitute the foundation of the Hindu systems of religious and philosophical thought.

Composed of roughhewn allegories, half-formed myths, opaque symbols and allusions, the Vedic hymns nevertheless are an essential starting point for the study of Hindu religion and its subsequent development. The problem of dating the genesis of the Vedic hymns has been rigorously debated among scholars, with some placing their origin as early as 6000 B.C. and others as late as 1500 B.C.

As previously suggested, the Rg-Veda, composed of approximately 1,017 hymns, is unquestionably the oldest and the most important of the Vedas. The most common form given of the collection is to divide the hymns into ten mandalas, or circles. There is evidently a principle at work in this arrangement. Hymns addressed to the god Agni come first, those addressed to Indra second, and the remainder follow. Each of the next six books or mandalas is thought to have originated from a single family. Mandala Eight has no particular order and is usually ascribed to various authors, whereas Mandala Nine is addressed to the god Soma. Mandala Ten, where one finds the most interesting speculative material, is probably a later appendage.

What precisely do the Vedic hymns teach? This is an enormously difficult question, and to illustrate this point, here is a rough catalog of some of the possible interpretations that this literature has evoked from modern scholars:

1. The gods of the Vedic pantheon are symbols for highly complex psychological functions. When viewed in this manner, the Vedic literature is thought to teach a cleverly disguised form of mystical religion.

2. The teachings of the Vedic hymns concerning the pantheon of gods should be viewed as fundamentally allegorical. The action, character, and powers of the different Vedic gods are allegorical representations of the charter of one supreme deity.

3. The Vedic hymns celebrate a world-affirming mode of nature worship, extremely primitive in character, but carefully worked out in ritual and prayer.

4. The Vedic hymns reveal a primitive groping for a form of monotheism.

This small sample of the variety of interpretation that has been advanced points to the great heterogeneity of the hymns. It suggests to us that they should be treated as an archaeologist treats the site of an ancient ruin, namely, as containing different strata of material. Some of this material originates in a very primitive unsophisticated age, whereas other material is a later accretion formed during a more reflective, syncretistic age.

What strikes our attention most in studying the hymns of the Rg-Veda is how close an affinity the Vedic gods have with nature. The Aryans lived in close touch with nature and experienced both the harshness of its demands and the bounty of its productivity. These people knew what it was to encounter the mystery, wonder, and danger of natural events. For them, nature constituted a living presence with which they communed daily in both their struggle to survive and their efforts to conquer this new land. It should not surprise us that they came to worship those vital forces of the natural world which played such a large part in their lives.

Nor should it surprise us that these powers were at least partially personified. The tendency of primitive man to project human qualities such as will, intention, knowledge, and anger upon natural forces is a basic characteristic of primitive religions. By means of such projections, the seemingly erratic forces of nature may be brought into a kind of kinship with man. Chaos can be brought into a semblance of order by subduing the unknown (nature) to the known (self).

The unique characteristic of the Vedic pantheon was that it was primarily polytheistic rather than animistic. An animistic religion views nature as totally populated by spirits. The Vedic pantheon, however, was more systematically arranged and more selective in terms of the powers which were deified. Evidently there were three groupings of gods, with each grouped according to the actual range of the god's abode. There were gods of the sky, such as Mitra and Varuna, gods of the "midair," such as the storm gods, the Maruts and Indra, and there were gods of the earth, such as Soma and Agni. In the Vedas, no single god is elevated to supremacy—certainly not in any uniform or lasting sense. Different hymns, however, do cultivate reverence for one god as supreme, but many gods are elevated to this rank in different hymns.

Another striking characteristic of the Vedic gods is what might be termed the "overlapping of divinities." This may have been a consequence of the arrested anthropomorphism or incomplete personification of the powers of nature. To illustrate: the Vedic god Agni is clearly associated with fire, but is also associated with the sun (frequently addressed as a separate deity, Surya), with light, with water, indeed with a whole range of natural powers. Such overlapping might be accounted for by the fact that many natural events exhibit a close affinity to each other, e.g., wind, rain, storms, clouds, and so on. Gods in the Vedic pantheon, then, have individual characters but not idiosyncratic characters. Moreover, hymns praising Agni, Varuna, Indra, or Soma frequently read as though addressed to a supreme deity, incorporating and manifesting all natural powers. This tendency to overlap or merge the multiple deities into one supreme deity has frequently been described as an incipient (if unconscious) urge to monotheism, or perhaps monism, in Vedic religion.

Our natural expectation is that out of this seeming mergence of the many deities into one godhead, a monotheism would certainly develop. The natural avenue for such a progression would appear to be the elevation of one of the more prominent gods, such as Varuna or Indra, to the rank of supremacy. Such a movement never occurred during the Vedic age, probably because the gods of the Vedic pantheon were never sufficiently individualized. Rather, the development seems to have been toward the discovery of a common divine ground manifesting itself in the powers and relative individualities of all the separate gods. Hence, we find references to Visve-devas (all-gods), Prajapati (father-god), Visva-Karman (lord of all beings), Prana (deified breath), and Kala (time).

The human spirit as a theogenic zone is nowhere more evident than in Vedic literature. Striking features of the new land were elevated to the level of gods, such as river deities like Sarasvati. The dominant style of their everyday existence as conquerors of the indigenous tribes brought the war god, Indra, into prominence. The Maruts, gods of the wind and storm, received considerable attention because the Aryans were overawed by the crashing, thunderous storms which raged out of the mountains to the north. In the later speculative period of Vedic religion, we find qualities that are shared by several well-known deities becoming themselves deified.

Special attention should be given to the three most prominent gods of the Vedic pantheon: Varuna, Indra, and Agni. Varuna was the god of the sky and of heavenly light. Just as the sky is all-encompassing, so was Varuna. He was believed to be the custodian of law, Rta. The concept of Rta recurs throughout the Vedic hymns in reference to many deities, but Varuna stands in a special relationship to Rta. Literally, the principle of Rta means the "course of things," that order governing both the physical and moral worlds. Originally, this notion must have referred to the orderly course of the stars, moon, sun, and other natural events, but eventually, by extrapolation, was thought to govern man-god and man-man relationships. Behind the flux of events stands Rta (Greek counterpart: Moira). When Vedic religion developed into a highly organized ceremonialism, Rta became associated with the ceremony of sacrifice. Varuna was believed to be the guarantor of the continuous functioning of Rta and, hence, was the guardian of moral order. No evildoing or plotting escaped his all-searching vision.

Varuna, however, as a god of peace could offer little support to a people engaged in a violent struggle to subdue the indigenous tribes of India. Hence, the god Indra became the center of attention in the Vedic hymns. Indra is the prototype of the

Aryan warrior-hero—a god of thunder and lightning who strikes terror and awe into the hearts of the Aryans. Indra, like Zeus, wields the thunderbolt and releases or holds back the rain at his pleasure. Not only is Indra capable of banishing the demons of drought (literally, he slays the dragon holding back the water in the mountains), but Indra also leads the Aryans in battle and guarantees their victory. Many gods are closely associated with the powerful Indra, including the Maruts, the destructive but sometimes beneficent storm gods, and Rudra, a militant god addressed with awe and fear, but also considered to be a healer.

Agni is second only in importance to Indra and was thought to have his origin either in scorching sun, water, flintstone, or lightning from the clouds. The dispeller of darkness and the consumer of wood in sacrifice, Agni is the helpmate of humans and the mediator between man and the gods. The fire in the hearth (identified with Agni) provided the Aryans with light and warmth and banished the demons who approached and threatened in the darkness.

The world we enter with the subject matter of the Atharva-Veda constitutes both a degrading of Vedic religion and, to some extent, a sophisticated step beyond the confused nature worship of the Rg-Veda. On the one hand, the Atharva-Veda is filled with magical incantations, charms, and prayers that are oriented to a world peopled with goblins, ghosts, and demons. The superstitions of primitive man are rampant in the Atharva-Veda, which provides spells and incantations for deliverance from almost every imaginable catastrophe or human dilemma. A spirit of fear and terror suffuses the pages of the Atharva-Veda, bringing a vision of the world as populated by demonic agencies whose favor must be courted by ritual and whose displeasure must be avoided by charms. While the hymns of the Rg-Veda overflow with praise and devotion, the prayers and charms of the Atharva-Veda unleash the superstitions and terrors of the primitive imagination. In these incantations, man achieves direct participation in divine power by the instrumentality of magic. This weird orientation provides a striking contrast to the reverence, awe, and confidence manifested in the expansive hymns of the Rg-Veda.

Clearly the magical formulas of the Atharva-Veda breathe the atmosphere of a more prehistoric age. Probably it is an amalgamation of the popular, religious superstitions of the Aryan invaders and the more primitive religious world view of the indigenous tribes.

The Atharva-Veda, however, contains some beautiful prose passages. Its hymns in praise of Kala (time) and Prana (breath) are highly speculative and mystical, having much in common with the Upanishads.

*Brahminism*

The simplicity of the nature worship of early Vedic religion gradually gave way to a priestly oriented ritualism which was artificial and excessively symbolic. The reasons for this line of development in the focus of religious concern are diverse. The hymns of the Rg-Veda introduce us to a vigorous people confidently facing the challenges of life and, through their nature worship, existing in direct communion with the forces of nature which they had deified. As previously noted, the motives for the earliest Vedic rituals had been such things as the desire to express gratitude to the gods for their bounty, the effort to persuade the gods to grant favors to man and to withhold their displeasure, and, at times, the desire to enter into direct communion with the gods in a sacramental fashion.

But during the second stage in the development of Vedic religion, prayer and ritual outgrew their proper functions and became the central concerns of religious life. Some very curious features mark this transition; for example, in the literature of this period (Sama-Veda, Yajur-Veda, Brahmanas) we frequently find the accouterments of ceremony (e.g., a sacrificial post or clay bowl for oblations) elevated to the level of deity simply because they occupied such a significant place in the sacrificial rites. An even more remarkable change transformed the spirit in which the rituals and prayers were performed. Conciliation was replaced by conjuring. Persuasion gave way to compulsion. Communion dropped into the background and the divine agencies were activated by the Brahmins (priests) repeating the sacred formulas and performing the proper rites.

During the period of the Rg-Veda, the gods' bounty had been implored to yield a large crop of grain or a healthy stock of cattle. The later Vedas and the Brahmins give the impression that the conjuring rites themselves forced these blessings from the gods. The Aryans were led to the simple conclusion, as a result of this development, that the rituals, formulas, and incantations must therefore be greater than the gods themselves. So that in the second stage in the development of Vedic religion, the Aryans came to believe that ceremonial acts were the principal instrumentalities by means of which the gods were to be contacted and controlled in the interest of human needs. Indeed, we find the suggestion made during this period that the responsibility of the gods to maintain Rta (world order) depends entirely upon the maintenance of a more significant Rta (orderly sacrifice).

Speech in the form of formulas or charms accompanying sacrificial ceremonies took on occult powers. In the Rg-Veda the divine energies of the universe had been addressed through hymns inspired by the gods. During the ritualistic stage, divine energy was thought to reside *in* the formulas and rites, awaiting their activation by Brahminic action. Hence, there developed a sense of the mystery, even secretiveness, of the language of the conjuring rites. Words hid the truth rather than revealed it, but in the hands of priests, the words of prayer could be made to unleash their divine powers. The priests, then, came to be viewed as the custodians of Vedic truth. Rta, which previously had been thought to control the total physical and moral world, was seen to reside in the hands of humans (Brahmins).

What factors account for the emergence into priority of the forms of ritualism at the expense of the spirit of religion? The most plausible explanation seems to be the dramatic achievement of power by the Brahmins, or priestly class, and this shift in the base of authority in the Aryan societies may be seen as a consequence of several factors. Most important was the fact that the religious treasures of the Vedas, which were thought to be divinely revealed, had to be preserved in the face of challenges from other religious practices and beliefs held by the indigenous Dravidians. The Vedas as repositories of revealed truth were placed in the care of the priests, who then devoted their lives to preserving and interpreting them. The warrior class was so occupied with winning and protecting the new land that many administrative powers fell to the Brahmins by default. The priestly claim to final authority in all aspects of life was reinforced by the realities of the situation. They were thought to be able to control the whole range of human and divine life by their prayers and sacred formulas. They could, it was believed, guarantee victory over enemies, a bountiful harvest, and even such things as relief from the bite of a poisonous snake. Therefore, a professional priesthood developed to conduct those ceremonies so essential for energizing divine power in behalf of human desire. A rigid orthodoxy, not of creed but of ceremony, was the result of this shift of power in the Aryan settlements.

Brahministic religion apparently had three basic focuses: (1) observance of ritual, (2) maintenance of caste, and (3) the supremacy of the Brahmins in all phases of societal life. In the Brahmanas, a set of ritual texts containing complicated details of rites and the sacred formulas associated with them, we discover the first writings concerned with the rules of the caste system. The flexible class structure of the Aryans hardened into a rigid caste system during the phase of ritualism. Obviously, the Aryan conquerors occupied the upper strata of the social order, with the conquered, indigenous population being relegated to slavery. The peoples of the Aryan settlements were roughly divided into two large segments or classes, the victors and the vanquished, and these categories were further broken into four subclassifications. These were the warrior-aristocrats (noblemen-Kshatriyas), the priests (Brahmins), the Aryan masses (Vaisyas), and finally, the non-Aryan blacks (Shudras). Increasingly the three upper strata held themselves aloof from the lowest class. The Brahmins, because of their special responsibility to preserve the Vedas, probably set the example for the other classes in the society by forming strict rules to guard themselves against contamination of their ceremonial purity. Such defilement was thought to come from undesirable marriages or contact with unholy food. Hence, the priests enforced the most stringent regulations upon themselves in order to ensure their separateness from society. Quite possibly, the more worldly classes of the Aryan society were drawn by the priests' efforts to guarantee their purity, and eventually came to emulate the self-restraint of their spiritual leaders. What had originated as a stratification of the social order resulting from a division of labor, during this period took on the rigidity of a caste system containing both social and religious sanctions and taboos.

The caste system is a mode of social organization in which a person's place and duties in society are determined by his birth and then by the particular set of rules regarding social behavior which define his caste. In the Hindu world, each caste is unified internally by a rigid set of ceremonial rules relating especially to diet and marriage. Caste membership has been thought to entail descent from a common ancestor and may involve rigid strictures regarding occupation, religious creed, moral and religious duties. Violation of the duties and regulations (dharma) of one's caste may result in severe penalties and possibly expulsion. One is born into one's "station and its duties" in the Hindu society and is under a categorical obligation to confine himself to his given place in society. Each person in Hindu society stands under the practical morality of his caste (varna-dharma) and a more general ethic applying to all mankind (dharma).

Quite obviously the institution of caste has had, and continues to have, some pernicious effects upon the development of India. It has inhibited fruitful contact of India with the outside world, for under the caste system, anyone who disregards Hindu dharma is a barbarian. Moreover, the rigidity and complexity of the caste system prohibit social mobility within India itself, creating at times insuperable barriers to cooperation for any practical purposes, political, social, religious, or economic. Because of the myriad castes and subcastes that have been produced over the centuries, Indian society is fragmented into thousands of separate units. Hostility and jealousy frequently exhibited between diverse castes have rendered cooperative activities exceedingly difficult. No doubt the practical regulations of caste conflict incessantly with the conditions of modern life. A mode of social organization that perhaps worked well in ancient times cannot easily adapt itself to the requirements of a quite different modern age. Moreover, the caste system creates differences between human beings which have no basis in fact. In fostering a kind of caste pride, it builds unnecessary walls between man and man.

But some mention should be made of those qualities of the caste system which recommend it to both its ancient and modern proponents. The caste system does provide an established basis for the cohesion and harmony of a society. Through its moral and religious undergirding of social action, it provides an unshakable foundation for ensuring that individual conduct will be oriented to the welfare of the social whole. It generates the sense that all of human life is sacrificial in a sacramental universe, in effect reducing the unstabilizing factors of individual competitiveness and selfish aspiration.

Any account of the caste system would be incomplete without viewing it in relation to the Hindu doctrines of karma and rebirth. To treat the caste system as an institution unrelated to the totality of Hindu religion, its beliefs, practices, and mythology, is to miss its integral connection with all of Hinduism. The concepts of karma and rebirth are organically connected with the world view elaborated and developed in the Upanishads. Hence, we must turn to a consideration of this literature as the next stage in the development of Hindu religion.

### *The Upanishads*

In the lofty speculations and spiritual insights of the Upanishads we encounter a movement away from the anthropomorphic nature deities toward a new source of concern—the inner life of man, the mystery of the self. The creative thinkers of the Upanishads alter the center of Indian religious concern, somehow managing to avoid a clash with the priests and their ritualistic theology. And yet, because of the profundity of Upanishadic speculation, ritualistic theology is totally reevaluated. The new generation of religious thinkers who produced the earliest Upanishads turn toward an exploration of that all-transcending, divine principle which is only partially manifested in the deified agencies of nature in the early Vedic thought. Moreover, this pervading, spiritual unity is to be found within oneself.

"That Thou Art." These words of the Hindu father to his son become the great formula which dominates the Upanishads. It is the great source of Vedantic truth. In it, the entire spectacle of nature with its diversity of powers and beings is reduced to a single, all-pervasive, spiritual unity. The spiritual essence of the universe must be viewed as invisible, hidden, and yet, paradoxically, all-suffusing and omnipresent (like salt in water). Although nature unfolds itself in a multiplicity of forms and beings, these are to be viewed as manifestations of the Divine Essence—as transformations of one divine substance. The whole movement of religious aspiration is toward the realization that each one of us, in our innermost essence, is identical with the spiritual substance suffusing all things.

The Upanishads appear at the end of the Vedas, and hence, are called Veda-anta (Vedanta), literally, "end of the Vedas." Almost every subsequent philosophy and religion in India rests upon the wealth of speculation contained in these works. While there are over two hundred Upanishads, most of them derive from a relatively late period in Indian religious history. The traditional number usually given is one hundred eight, of which about twelve are extremely ancient (from the ninth to the fourth century B.C.). The most ancient Upanishads are sometimes called the "canonical" Upanishads. Even among the canonical Upanishads there appears to be a wide chronological discontinuity, but they do seem to exhibit a kinship both in language and thought. This family likeness in the canonical Upanishads is all the more remarkable in view of the fact that they are the products of a variety of authors writing in ages widely separate in time.

Most of the earliest Upanishads are written in prose style in the form of dialogues. They contain a rich diversity of symbol, metaphor, and allegory and in form seem to alternate between poetry and a more mystical, philosophical style of expression.

The meaning of the word "upanishad" has been vigorously debated, but apparently it is closely associated with the word *rahasya,* or "secret." Perhaps the kernel of Upanishadic thought, prior to its being committed to writing, was in the form of short pithy sayings or formulas, such as "That Thou Art." Possibly in this form, the secrets of spiritual truth could be safely preserved and easily communicated to aspiring Brahmins. Such formulas would constitute a kind of shorthand of the basic truths of Hindu religion which the teacher would later elaborate upon and develop. Such a view is supported by the etymology of the word "upanishad," which literally means "sitting (*sad*) close by (*upa*) devotedly (*ni*)." Probably, then, the Upanishads were the secret instructions given to aspiring religious novitiates who sat at the feet of the great religious sages and speculators.

Because the Upanishads issued from many authors and widely divergent times, they contain a heterogeneity of thought and theme. Not only is this true from Upanishad to Upanishad, but it also holds within a single Upanishad. On the surface, this would appear to offer an immense barrier with respect to the question of the effectiveness of the teachings of the Upanishads. However, when one considers this heterogeneity more closely, it becomes evident that because of it the Upanishads can serve a valuable function in stimulating profound thought on a great diversity of themes and concepts. The obscurity and mystical character of Upanishadic writings provide a continuous source of provocative and suggestive subject matter for religious thought. All the major systems of Hindu philosophy derive from the Upanishads, and all claim the Upanishads as authoritative for their particular interpretations of religious truth. An interesting feature of the Upanishads is that almost all commentators and interpreters claim that there is an essential unity to Upanishadic thought, but they widely disagree as to the precise nature of that unity. If one measure of greatness for a religious corpus is its provocativeness and suggestiveness, the Upanishads have manifested this quality for over two thousand years.

The canonical Upanishads constitute an indispensable resource for the understanding of Hindu thought. This is particularly true in the light of the fact that most of them are pre-Buddhistic and were the inspiration for almost all later Upanishads. It would be utter folly to undertake a systematic analysis of Upanishadic literature, for that enterprise is the story of Hindu philosophy as a whole. Despite the heterogeneous nature of Upanishadic thought there do seem to be pervasive themes in the canonical works which have received attention in many later Upanishads and in almost every system of Hindu religious thought. Some limited attention should be given here to these pervasive themes.

In contrast to the hymns of Vedic religion, which centered upon the deified powers of nature, the canonical Upanishads concentrate on the inner realm of the spirit. Moreover, the monistic suggestions found in some Vedic hymns receive, in the ancient Upanishads, extensive exploration and development. The tendency in the Vedic hymns to merge all the gods of the Vedic pantheon into a single spiritual unity becomes, in the early Upanishads, a speculative exploration of the meaning of spiritual unity. The polytheistic elements, so deeply rooted in the Indian consciousness, are subordinated to the principle of unity. No "twilight of the gods" occurs, however, for in the Upanishads the gods of the Vedic pantheon are cast as manifestations of the Divine Unity which pervades all of nature and is identical with the self.

The name given to the supernatural principle which is manifested in all being is Brahman-Atman. The term "Brahman" probably derives from the root (*brh*) meaning "to grow," or "to burst forth." Since in the period of the Rg-Veda what grew, or burst forth, of primary religious significance were the hymns and prayers, "Brahman" first meant the hymns and prayers manifested in the spoken word. In the language of the Vedic hymns and prayers the Divine Energy of the universe burst forth and expressed itself. We are reminded here of Nietzsche's sentence in Book III of *Thus Spake Zarathustra:*

> Here the words and word-shrines of all being open up before you; here all being wishes to become word, all becoming wishes to learn from you how to speak.

In the ritualistic stage of Vedic religion, Brahman was the crystallization of divine energy in the form of charms and ceremonial formulas. As previously suggested, as so conceived the divine energy was then placed at the disposal of the priesthood to use for the benefit of man. In the Upanishads, Brahman's manifestations are not restricted to verses or formulas, but encompass the totality of the universe. Brahman is the fundamental ground from which the whole universe of beings bursts forth.

The term "Atman" probably originally referred to "breath." Since breath is essential to life, "Atman" may in time have come to mean the principle of the essence of life, i.e., selfhood. In the Atharva-Veda, there is a speculative hymn to Prana (breath), in which breath, personified as a god, is addressed as the creator and substance of all being.

In Upanishadic literature the terms "Brahman" and "Atman" are used in their more restricted designations, but increasingly they come to mean the same thing—the ground of all being, including nature and man. Already in the Rg-Veda we find a hymn to Purusa (man) in which the universe is praised as a gigantic man. Thus, Atman, which is clearly a psychological principle and has a psychological referent, is transformed in the Upanishads into a cosmic principle. What is discovered most immediately through introspection, the self, becomes the principle which opens to us the whole cosmic reality. Inner and outer reality are realized to be identical. Brahman, who is the primal source of all objective reality, *is* Atman, that reality discovered subjectively and immediately from within.

The religious perspective of the Upanishads represents a reawakening of the Indian mind to the spiritual ground of the religious life that is in sharp contrast to the arid formalism of ceremonial religion. The earlier Upanishads take a dim view of the notion that man achieves salvation by performing sacrificial rites. Religious enlightenment is realized by achieving a vision of the true spirituality of all reality, through consciousness of one's identity with Brahman-Atman. In underplaying the role of ritual and sacrifice, the Upanishads were able to bring about a devaluation of artificial ritualism and to effect a change in the whole spiritual life of the Hindu. The concept of sacrifice undergoes a subtle, but far-reaching, change. Earlier sacrifice was the means by which the holy powers were manipulated to serve man's ends. In the Upanishads, the notion of sacrifice is elevated to a cosmic principle, implying that Brahman-Atman brings all beings into existence by a sacrificial act. Sacrifice is related to human conduct by considering that all human actions should be devotional offerings to the Supreme Being.

The Upanishads support the doctrine that all of the Veda is revealed truth, but at the same time they introduce the notion that knowledge articulated in the earlier hymns has been superseded by a higher form of truth, i.e., the knowledge of Brahman. In a similar fashion, the ceremonies of the Vedic tradition are a "lower" path to salvation and divine vision, ancillary to that path of knowledge achieved through self-renunciation, observance of moral duty, and full devotion in all one's acts to Brahman-realization.

The man who lives a self-centered life lives in ignorance (avidya). He lives in forgetfulness of his essential identity with Brahman. To be ensnared by one's own individuality and uniquenesss is to be caught in samsara. Samsara is the veil of illusion that man weaves around himself because of his ignorance. It represents the fruitless efforts of the finite to rest upon itself and to affirm itself as a final reality. Samsara is unreal in that it inhibits a man from perceiving the fundamental truth about himself and his relation to Brahman-Atman. At the same time, samsara provides continual opportunities for a man to realize the error upon which his life is predicated. The suffering, transience, and disharmony of samsara generate in man the aspiration to achieve complete liberation through perfected knowledge.

Samsara brings to light the Hindu conception of the fundamental conditions of human existence. Humans are chained to the relentless round of birth, suffering, death, and rebirth so long as they live in ignorance of their true spiritual destiny and nature. Associated with the doctrine of samsara is the conception of the law of karma. Karma guarantees, in the moral world, that all of our actions will have their consequences. It supports the principle that character-building is an orderly process in which good actions produce good results, bad actions bad results. Life, however, is something more than a succession of mechanically controlled states, for man, through initiative, discipline, and meditation, can transcend karmic determination. Whatever we sow, that must we reap, but the more we center our life in Brahman, the more freedom we can achieve. The deeds we perform have consequences both for the world and for ourselves. In other words, karma has both a cosmic and a psychological application. By our conduct, we unleash an inevitable chain of consequences in the natural world and initiate a disposition within ourselves to act in a similar fashion in the future. By spiritual discipline and knowledge we can master tendencies to act in habitual ways or at least modify such behavior. Discipline (yoga) may take the form of intensive self-renunciation, self-control, devotional and sacrificial action, or self-knowledge. Through such discipline we can bring our narrower self under rigorous restraint and hopefully transcend it to realize our higher selfhood, i.e., Brahman-Atman.

Failure to realize our higher spirituality entails rebirth. So long as we do not transcend the bounds of samsara, we are subject to the transience of time, and hence, subject to birth, death, and rebirth. Absolute liberation brings us into an eternal mode of being, but short of that, our destiny is to continue from life to life until final liberation is achieved. The particular form of our future rebirths is determined by the law of karma which works inexorably to tie us to that future existence of which we are most deserving. Life and death are inextricably intertwined in samsara. Typically, the doctrine of rebirth assumed or discussed in the Upanishads entails the view that from one life to the next there is a persisting identity of the self. Such an identity, however, is not a conscious one. It is the "karma-laden" character which persists from one birth to the next and not the self-consciousness of the individual. Rebirth is but the consequence of the diverse karmic conditionings of the human life that has not realized Brahman. The great paradox of Hinduism is that this union which is to be *realized,* has always been *achieved*. Only our ignorance hides this from us and blinds us with the unreality of samsara.

### *The* Bhagavad-Gita

The *Bhagavad-Gita* is a part of the *Mahabharata*. This latter work belongs to the Epic period of Indian history which is usually designated as beginning around 500 B.C. The *Mahabharata* records the struggles between two royal families, the Pandavas and the Kauravas. More importantly, this epic composition reveals the ferment within Indian civilization during this period, drawing in bold outline the history, mythology, practical religion, law, and politics of both the Epic age and the preceding ages. It was at approximately this time that Hinduism was confronted by the radical challenge of heretical movements and ideas, including the heterodox systems of Jainism and Buddhism, while from the philosophical side, Carvaka, or the materialist school, challenged the idealism of the Upanishads. The

*Mahabharata* purports to record the events of an earlier age, and, in so doing, it manifests a spirit of accommodation, compromise, and synthesis, particularly with respect to movements of thought and religious mythologies quite diverse from the Vedic tradition. In its pages we find outlined and developed such moral and social codes as the four aims of life, the four stages of life, the four castes, and a systematic elaboration of the social customs then in vogue.

The *Bhagavad-Gita* shares the spirit of accommodation, tolerance, and synthesis of the larger work in which it is contained. It is probably the most popular religious work in the corpus of Indian literature. While the *Gita* derives its main inspiration from the Upanishads, it does reflect the ferment of Indian thought during the time of its composition. The date ascribed to its writing is usually somewhere between 500 B.C. and 200 B.C.

The *Gita* owes its great popularity to its spirit of practicality, its exceptional tolerance, its style, and its subject matter. In contrast to the highly speculative concerns of the Upanishads, the *Gita* concerns itself principally with the problems of religious devotion and moral living. Metaphysical themes are subordinated to a practical concern for the fate of dharma (righteousness-moral order), and how it can be achieved and preserved. Written in dialogue form, the *Gita* presents the great issues of religious and moral duty in a dramatic, easily accessible fashion, and with a charming clarity. Through the use of a dramatic dialogue between Krishna, an incarnation of Vishnu, and Arjuna, a warrior-prince confronting a moral dilemma, the *Gita* explores the great questions of self-purification and service to God. It achieves, thereby, a concreteness of style and approach that makes it have a natural appeal.

The situation with which the *Gita* opens is one episode in the conflict between the Pandavas and their relatives, the Kauravas (symbolically, between good and evil). Arjuna, a warrior-hero of the Pandavas, has entered the battlefield with his relatives and supporters, to reclaim his ancestral kingdom which has been usurped by the Kauravas. Being confronted by friends and relations among the ranks of the enemy, Arjuna's resolve to fight is weakened and doubts assail him. Krishna, his charioteer (later revealed as Vishnu incarnate), at the command of his master, drives the chariot some distance from the battlefield, where Arjuna ponders his doubts and explores his conscience. There ensues the dialogue in which Krishna urges Arjuna to follow his dharma as a warrior and explains why this is necessary.

During the course of this explanation, Krishna does not restrict himself to the immediate situation, but elaborates a general theory of action, discusses the paths toward union with the divine, reveals to Arjuna the nature of the divine ground of all existence, and elaborates the goal of religious devotion and of all human life. As the dialogue unfolds, the synthetic and eclectic spirit of the *Gita* becomes increasingly evident. Krishna reveals to Arjuna the diverse paths (yogas) which lead to union of the soul with the divine: (1) the way of knowledge (jnana-yoga); (2) the way of devotion (bhakti-yoga); and (3) the way of action (karma-yoga). These different avenues lead to the same goal, liberation or unity with divine reality (moksa).

The doctrine of action taught in the *Gita* weaves a middle path between the two extremes of renunciation of action (*nivrtti*), sometimes advocated in the Upanishads, and positive involvement in society (*pravrtti*), which was often motivated by utilitarian goals and involved some measure of selfishness. Arjuna's tendency at the beginning of the *Gita* is to renounce all action, to withdraw from the everyday world, in order to avoid the evil consequences (karma) of acting in the world—such as having to kill his friends, relatives, and old teachers in battle. The central teaching of the *Gita* regarding action is that men should harness (yoga) themselves to the duties of their station in society (karma). In the *Gita,* the term "karma" is often used to mean those deeds or obligations which are customarily associated with one's particular place in society. According to the principle of karma-yoga, we should apply ourselves to "our station and its duties," not from motives of personal ambition or for private gain, but rather from a spirit of sacrificial devotion to God. Thus, the *Gita* teaches not renunciation *of* action, but renunciation *in* action. Karma-yoga, then, lifts our attention to a higher self than the narrow confines of our individuality and bids us renounce the fruits of action in activity of devotional self-sacrifice. In so doing, we emulate that higher self who is the primary cause of all nature and society, and who is immanent in each of us. Thus, Krishna's explanation of the yoga of action preserves both the spirit of activism and the spirit of self-renunciation. It enables these two ideals to exist by eliminating the play of selfish impulses and providing one overarching motive for action: self-purification through devotion to God.

While the *Gita* is a practical handbook for redeeming man and the world, it also contains elements from a diversity of sources. It considers the rituals of sacrifice advocated by the Vedas as important, but secondary to those paths of sacrificial discipline leading to the realization of unity with God. Certain passages in the *Gita* explore the Upanishadic notion of Brahman-Atman. Others suggest a kind of dualism, very much like that found in the Samkhya system. Altogether, it is a rich treasury of concepts and attitudes which were produced by the ferment which existed during the time when it was composed.

# A. Selections from the Rg-Veda

*Translated by Ralph T. H. Griffith, F. Max Müller, and Hermann Oldenberg*

## To Indra

1. I will declare the manly deeds of Indra, the first that he achieved, the thunder-wielder.
   He slew the dragon, then disclosed the waters, and cleft the channels of the mountain torrents.
2. He slew the dragon lying on the mountain: his heavenly bolt of thunder Tvashtar fashioned.
   Like lowing kine in rapid flow descending the waters glided downward to the ocean.
3. Impetuous as a bull, he chose the Soma, and in three sacred beakers drank the juices.
   The Bounteous One grasped the thunder for his weapon, and smote to death this firstborn of the dragons.
4. When, Indra, thou hadst slain the dragons' firstborn, and overcome the charms of the enchanters,
   Then, giving life to sun and dawn and heaven, thou foundest not one foe to stand against thee.
5. Indra with his own great and deadly thunder smote into pieces Vritra, worst of Vritras.
   As trunks of trees, what time the axe hath felled them, low on the earth so lies the prostrate dragon.
6. He, like a mad weak warrior, challenged Indra, the great impetuous many-slaying hero.

---

Reprinted from:
F. Max Müller, tr., *Vedic Hymns* (Part I), in *The Sacred Books of the East,* Vol. XXXII (1889). Modified.
Hermann Oldenberg, tr., *Vedic Hymns* (Part II), in *The Sacred Books of the East,* Vol. XLVI (1897). Modified.
Ralph T. H. Griffith, tr., *The Hymns of the Rigveda* (2 vols., Benares: E. J. Lazarus and Company, 1896). Modified.

He, brooking not the clashing of the weapons, crushed—Indra's foe—the shattered forts in falling.

7. Footless and handless still he challenged Indra, who smote him with his bolt between the shoulders.
Emasculate yet claiming manly vigour, thus Vritra lay with scattered limbs dissevered.

8. There as he lies like a bank-bursting river, the waters taking courage flow above him.
The dragon lies beneath the feet of torrents which Vritra with his greatness had encompassed.

9. Then humbled was the strength of Vritra's mother: Indra hath cast his deadly bolt against her.
The mother was above, the son was under, and like a cow beside her calf lay Danu.

10. Rolled in the midst of never-ceasing currents flowing without a rest for ever onward,
The waters bear off Vritra's nameless body: the foe of Indra sank to during darkness.

11. Guarded by Ahi stood the thralls of Dasas, the waters stayed like kine held by the robber.
But he, when he had smitten Vritra, opened the cave wherein the floods had been imprisoned.

12. A horse's tail wast thou when he, O Indra, smote on thy bolt; thou, god without an equal,
Thou hast won back the kine, hast won the Soma; thou hast let loose to flow the seven rivers.

13. Nothing availed him lightning, nothing thunder, hailstorm or mist which he had spread around him:
When Indra and the dragon strove in battle, the Bounteous One gained the victory for ever.

14. Whom sawest thou to avenge the dragon, Indra, that fear possessed thy heart when thou hadst slain him;
That, like a hawk affrighted through the regions, thou crossedst nine-and-ninety flowing rivers?

15. Indra is king of all that moves and moves not, of creatures tame and horned, the thunder-wielder.

Over all living men he rules as sovran, containing all as spokes within the felly.

[Rg-Veda I. 32 *Griffith*]

## To the Maruts and Indra

### THE PROLOGUE

The sacrificer speaks:

1. To what splendour do the Maruts all equally cling, they who are of the same age, and dwell in the same nest? With what thoughts?—from whence are they come? Do these heroes sing forth their own strength, wishing for wealth?

2. Whose prayers have the youths accepted? Who has turned the Maruts to his own sacrifice? By what strong desire may we arrest them, they who float through the air like hawks?

### THE DIALOGUE

The Maruts speak:

3. From whence, O Indra, dost thou come alone, thou who art mighty? O lord of men, what has thus happened to thee? Thou greetest us when thou comest together with us, the bright Maruts. Tell us then, thou with thy bay horses, what thou hast against us!

Indra speaks:

4. The sacred songs are mine, mine are the prayers; sweet are the libations! My strength rises, my thunderbolt is hurled forth. They call for me, the hymns yearn for me. Here are my horses, they carry me hither.

The Maruts speak:

5. From thence, in company with our strong friends, having adorned our bodies, we now harness our fallow deer with all

our might;—for, Indra, according to custom, thou hast come to be with us.

Indra speaks:

6. Where, O Maruts, was that custom with you, when you left me alone in the killing of Ahi? I indeed am terrible, powerful, strong,—I escaped from the blows of every enemy.

The Maruts speak:

7. Thou hast achieved much with us as companions. With equal valour, O hero! let us achieve then many things, O thou most powerful, O Indra! whatever we, O Maruts, wish with our mind.

Indra speaks:

8. I slew Vritra, O Maruts, with Indra's might, having grown powerful through my own vigour; I, who hold the thunderbolt in my arms, have made these all-brilliant waters to flow freely for man.

The Maruts speak:

9. Nothing, O mighty lord, is strong before thee: no one is known among the gods like unto thee. No one who is now born comes near, no one who has been born. Do what thou wilt do, thou who art grown so strong.

Indra speaks:

10. Almighty strength be mine alone, whatever I may do, daring in my heart; for I indeed, O Maruts, am known as terrible: of all that I threw down, I, Indra, am the lord.

11. O Maruts, now your praise has pleased me, the glorious hymn which you have made for me, ye men!—for me, for Indra, for the joyful hero, as friends for a friend, for your own sake, and by your own efforts.

12. Truly, there they are, shining towards me, bringing blameless glory, bringing food. O Maruts, wherever I have looked for you, you have appeared to me in bright splendour: appear to me also now!

### THE EPILOGUE

The sacrificer speaks:

13. Who has magnified you here, O Maruts? Come hither, O friends, toward your friends. Ye brilliant Maruts, welcoming these prayers, be mindful of these my rites.

14. The wisdom of Manya has brought us hither, that he should help as the poet helps the performer of a sacrifice: turn hither quickly! Maruts, on to the sage! the singer has recited these prayers for you.

15. May this your praise, O Maruts, this song of Mandarya, the son of Mana, the poet, bring offspring for ourselves with food. May we have an invigorating autumn, with quickening rain.

[Rg-Veda I. 165 *Müller*]

## To Indra-Agni

1. Indra-Agni, in consequence of our prayers come hither to the pressed Soma, to the precious cloud. Drink of it incited by our thoughts.
2. Indra-Agni, the brilliant sacrifice of him who praises you goes forward together with the Soma libations, the praises, etc. Thus drink this pressed Soma!
3. By this stirring sacrifice I choose Indra and Agni who show themselves as sages; may they here satiate themselves with Soma.
4. I call the bounteous, the killers of foes, the united conquerors, unconquered, Indra-Agni, the greatest winners of booty.
5. The praisers rich in hymns, knowing all the ways of the sacrifice, laud you. Indra-Agni, I choose the food which you give.
6. Indra-Agni, you have hurled down by one deed the ninety strongholds together of which the Dasas were the lords.
7. Indra-Agni, the thoughts of the worshippers go forward towards you from the work of sacrifice along the paths of Rta.
8. Indra and Agni, yours are powerful abodes and delights. You cross the waters: this is the deed which belongs to you.

9. Indra and Agni, you display the lights of heaven in your deeds of strength; that mighty deed of yours has been known far and wide.

[Rg-Veda III. 12 *Oldenberg*]

## To Varuna

1. This laud of the self-radiant wise Aditya shall be supreme o'er all that is in greatness.
   I beg renown of Varuna the mighty, the god exceeding kind to him who worships.
2. Having extolled thee, Varuna, with thoughtful care may we have high fortune in thy service,
   Singing thy praises like the fires at coming, day after day, of mornings rich in cattle.
3. May we be in thy keeping, O thou leader, wide-ruling Varuna, lord of many heroes.
   O sons of Aditi, for ever faithful, pardon us, gods, admit us to your friendship.
4. He made them flow, the Aditya, the sustainer: the rivers run by Varuna's commandment.
   These feel no weariness, nor cease from flowing: swift have they flown like birds in air around us.
5. Loose me from sin as from a bond that binds me: may we swell, Varuna, thy spring of order.
   Let not my thread, while I weave song, be severed, nor my work's sum, before the time, be shattered.
6. Far from me, Varuna, remove all danger: accept me graciously, thou holy sovran.
   Cast off, like cords that hold a calf, my troubles: I am not even mine eyelid's lord without thee.
7. Strike us not, Varuna, with those dread weapons which, Asura, at thy bidding wound the sinner.
   Let us not pass away from light to exile. Scatter, that we may live, the men who hate us.
8. O mighty Varuna, now and hereafter, even as of old, will we speak forth our worship.

For in thyself, invincible god, thy statutes ne'er to be moved are fixed as on a mountain.

9. Move far from me what sins I have committed: let me not suffer, king, for guilt of others.

Full many a morn remains to dawn upon us: in these, O Varuna, while we live direct us.

10. O king, whoever, be he friend or kinsman, hath threatened me affrighted in my slumber—

If any wolf or robber fain would harm us, therefrom, O Varuna, give thou us protection.

11. May I not live, O Varuna, to witness my wealthy, liberal, dear friend's destitution.

King, may I never lack well-ordered riches. Loud may we speak, with heroes, in assembly.

[Rg-Veda II. 28 *Griffith*]

## To Rudra

1. What could we say to Rudra, the wise, the most liberal, the most powerful, that is most welcome to his heart,—

2. So that Aditi may bring Rudra's healing to the cattle, to men, to cow, and kith,

3. So that Mitra, that Varuna, that Rudra hear us, and all the united Maruts.

4. We implore Rudra, the lord of songs, the lord of animal sacrifices, the possessor of healing medicines, for health, wealth, and his favour.

5. He who shines like the bright sun, and like gold, who is the best Vasu among the gods,

6. May he bring health to our horse, welfare to ram and ewe, to men, to women, and to the cow!

7. Bestow on us, O Soma, the happiness of a hundred men, great glory of strong manhood;

8. O Soma, let not those who harass and injure overthrow us; O Indu, help us to booty!

9. Whatever beings are thine, the immortal, in the highest

place of the law, on its summit, in its centre, O Soma, cherish them, remember them who honour thee.

[Rg-Veda I. 43 *Müller*]

## To Rudra

1. Offer ye these songs to Rudra whose bow is strong, whose arrows are swift, the self-dependent god, the unconquered conqueror, the intelligent, whose weapons are sharp—may he hear us!

2. For, being the lord, he looks after what is born on earth; being the universal ruler, he looks after what is born in heaven. Protecting us, come to our protecting doors, be without illness among our people, O Rudra!

3. May that thunderbolt of thine, which, sent from heaven, traverses the earth, pass us by! A thousand medicines are thine, O thou who art freely accessible; do not hurt us in our kith and kin!

4. Do not strike us, O Rudra, do not forsake us! May we not be in thy way when thou rushest forth furiously. Let us have our altar and a good report among men—protect us always with your favours!

[Rg-Veda VII. 46 *Müller*]

## To Soma and Rudra

1. Soma and Rudra, may you maintain your divine dominion, and may the oblations reach you properly. Bringing the seven treasures to every house, be kind to our children and our cattle.

2. Soma and Rudra, draw far away in every direction the disease which has entered our house. Drive far away Nirriti, and may auspicious glories belong to us!

3. Soma and Rudra, bestow all these remedies on our bodies. Tear away and remove from us whatever evil we have committed, which clings to our bodies.

4. Soma and Rudra, wielding sharp weapons and sharp bolts, kind friends, be gracious unto us here! Deliver us from the snare of Varuna, and guard us, as kind-hearted gods!

[Rg-Veda VI. 74 *Müller*]

### To Agni

1. Driving away evil with thy light, Agni, shine upon us with wealth—driving away evil with thy light.

2. Longing for rich fields, for a free path, and for wealth, we sacrifice—driving away evil with thy light.

3. When he stands forth as the most glorious one among them, and when our liberal lords excel—driving away evil with thy light—

4. When through thee, Agni, the liberal lords, and when through thee we may multiply with offspring—driving away evil with thy light—

5. When the rays of the mighty Agni go forth on all sides—driving away evil with thy light—

6. For thou indeed, O god whose face is turned everywhere, encompassest the world everywhere—driving away evil with thy light.

7. Do thou carry us, as with a boat, across hostile powers, O god whose face is turned everywhere—driving away evil with thy light.

8. Do thou carry us across evil to welfare, as across a stream with a boat—driving away evil with thy light.

[Rg-Veda I. 97 *Oldenberg*]

### To Agni

1. Produce thy stream of flames like a broad onslaught. Go forth impetuous like a king with his elephant; . . . after thy greedy onslaught, thou art an archer; shoot the sorcerers with thy hottest arrows.

2. Thy whirls fly quickly. Fiercely flaming touch them. O Agni, send forth with the ladle thy heat, thy winged flames; send forth unfettered thy firebrands all around.

3. Being the quickest, send forth thy spies against all evil-doers. Be an undeceivable guardian of this clan. He who attacks us with evil spells, far or near, may no such foe defy thy track.

4. Rise up, O Agni! Spread out against all foes! Burn down the foes, O god with the sharp weapon! When kindled, O Agni, burn down like dry brushwood, the man who exercises malice against us.

5. Stand upright, strike the foes away from us! Make manifest thy divine powers, O Agni! Unbend the strong bows of those who incite demons against us. Crush all enemies, be they relations or strangers.

6. He knows thy favour, O youngest one, who makes a way for a sacred speech like this. Mayst thou beam forth to his doors all auspicious days and the wealth and the splendour of the niggard.

7. May he be fortunate and blessed with good rain, who longs to gladden thee with constant offerings and hymns through his life in his house. May such longing ever bring aupicious days to him, O Agni.

8. I praise thy favour; it resounded here. May this song which is like a favourite wife, awaken for thee. Let us brighten thee, being rich in horses and chariots. Mayst thou maintain our knightly power day by day.

9. May the worshipper here frequently of his own accord approach thee, O god who shinest in darkness, resplendent day by day. Let us worship thee sporting and joyous, surpassing the splendour of other people.

10. Whoever, rich in horses and rich in gold, approaches thee, O Agni, with his chariot full of wealth—thou art the protector and the friend of him who always delights in showing thee hospitality.

11. Through my kinship with thee I break down the great foes by my words. That kinship has come down to me from my

father Gotama. Be thou attentive to this our word, O youngest, highly wise Hotri, as the friend of our house.

12. May those guardians of thine, infallible Agni, sitting down together protect us, the never sleeping, onward-pressing, kind, unwearied ones, who keep off the wolf, who never tire.

13. Thy guardians, O Agni, who seeing have saved the blind son of Mamata from distress—He the possessor of all wealth has saved them who have done good deeds. The impostors, though trying to deceive, could not deceive.

14. In thy companionship we dwell, protected by thee. Under thy guidance let us acquire gain. Accomplish both praises, O thou who art the truth! Do so by thy present power, O fearless one!

15. May we worship thee, O Agni, with this log of wood. Accept the hymn of praise which we recite. Burn down those who curse us, the sorcerers. Protect us, O god who art great like Mitra, from guile, from revilement, and from disgrace.

[Rg-Veda IV. 4 *Oldenberg*]

## Creation

1. Then was not non-existent nor existent: there was no realm of air, no sky beyond it.
   What covered in, and where? and what gave shelter? Was water there, unfathomed depth of water?
2. Death was not then, nor was there aught immortal: no sign was there, the day's and night's divider.
   That One Thing, breathless, breathed by its own nature: apart from it was nothing whatsoever.
3. Darkness there was: at first concealed in darkness this All was indiscriminated chaos.
   All that existed then was void and formless: by the great power of warmth was born that unit.
4. Thereafter rose desire in the beginning, desire, the primal seed and germ of spirit.
   Sages who searched with their heart's thought discovered the existent's kinship in the non-existent.

5. Transversely was their severing line extended: what was above it then, and what below it?
   There were begetters, there were mighty forces, free action here and energy up yonder.
6. Who verily knows and who can here declare it, whence it was born and whence comes this creation?
   The gods are later than this world's production. Who knows then whence it first came into being?
7. He, the first origin of this creation, whether he formed it all or did not form it,
   Whose eye controls this world in highest heaven, he verily knows it, or perhaps he knows not.

[Rg-Veda X. 129 *Griffith*]

### To Purusha

1. A thousand heads hath Purusha, a thousand eyes, a thousand feet.
   On every side pervading earth he fills a space ten fingers wide.
2. This Purusha is all that yet hath been and all that is to be;
   The lord of immortality which waxes greater still by food.
3. So mighty is his greatness; yea, greater than this is Purusha.
   All creatures are one-fourth of him, three-fourths eternal life in heaven.
4. With three-fourths Purusha went up: one-fourth of him again was here.
   Thence he strode out to every side over what eats not and what eats.
5. From him Viraj was born; again Purusha from Viraj was born.
   As soon as he was born he spread eastward and westward o'er the earth.
6. When gods prepared the sacrifice with Purusha as their offering,
   Its oil was spring, the holy gift was autumn; summer was the wood.

7. They balmed as victim on the grass Purusha born in earliest time.
With him the deities and all Sadhyas and Rishis sacrificed.
8. From that great general sacrifice the dripping fat was gathered up.
He formed the creatures of the air, and animals both wild and tame.
9. From that great general sacrifice Rig-Veda and Sama-Veda were born:
Therefrom were spells and charms produced; the Yajur-Veda had its birth from it.
10. From it were horses born, from it all cattle with two rows of teeth:
From it were generated kine, from it the goats and sheep were born.
11. When they divided Purusha how many portions did they make?
What do they call his mouth, his arms? What do they call his thighs and feet?
12. The Brahman was his mouth, of both his arms was the Rajanya made.
His thighs became the Vaisya, from his feet the Sudra was produced.
13. The moon was gendered from his mind, and from his eye the sun had birth;
Indra and Agni from his mouth were born, and Vayu from his breath.
14. Forth from his navel came mid-air; the sky was fashioned from his head;
Earth from his feet, and from his ear the regions. Thus they formed the worlds.
15. Seven fencing-sticks had he, thrice seven layers of fuel were prepared,
When the gods, offering sacrifice, bound, as their victim, Purusha.
16. Gods, sacrificing, sacrificed the victim: these were the earliest holy ordinances.

The mighty ones attained the height of heaven, there where the Sadhyas, gods of old, are dwelling.

[Rg-Veda X. 90 *Griffith*]

### To the Unknown God

1. In the beginning there arose the Golden Child; as soon as born, he alone was the lord of all that is. He stablished the earth and this heaven:—Who is the God to whom we shall offer sacrifice?

2. He who gives breath, he who gives strength, whose command all the bright gods revere, whose shadow is immortality, whose shadow is death:—Who is the God to whom we shall offer sacrifice?

3. He who through his might became the sole king of the breathing and twinkling world, who governs all this, man and beast:—Who is the God to whom we shall offer sacrifice?

4. He through whose might these snowy mountains are, and the sea, they say, with the distant river, he of whom these regions are indeed the two arms:—Who is the God to whom we shall offer sacrifice?

5. He through whom the awful heaven and the earth were made fast, he through whom the ether was stablished, and the firmament; he who measured the air in the sky:—Who is the God to whom we shall offer sacrifice?

6. He to whom heaven and earth, standing firm by his will, look up, trembling in their mind; he over whom the risen sun shines forth:—Who is the God to whom we shall offer sacrifice?

7. When the great waters went everywhere, holding the germ, and generating light, then there arose from them the sole breath of the gods:—Who is the God to whom we shall offer sacrifice?

8. He who by his might looked even over the waters which held power and generated the sacrifice, he who alone is God above all gods:—Who is the God to whom we shall offer sacrifice?

9. May he not hurt us, he who is the begetter of the earth,

or he, the righteous, who begat the heaven; he who also begat the bright and mighty waters:—Who is the God to whom we shall offer sacrifice?

10. Pragapati, no other than thou embraces all these created things. May that be ours which we desire when sacrificing to thee: may we be lords of wealth!

[Rg-Veda X. 121 *Müller*]

## B. Selections from the Atharva-Veda

*Translated by Maurice Broomfield*

### CHARM AGAINST TAKMAN (FEVER)

1. As if from this Agni (fire), that burns and flashes, the takman comes. Let him then, too, as a babbling drunkard, pass away! Let him, the impious one, search out some other person, not ourselves! Reverence be to the takman with the burning weapon!

2. Reverence be to Rudra, reverence to the takman, reverence to the luminous king Varuna! Reverence to heaven, reverence to earth, reverence to plants!

3. To thee here, that burns through, and turns all bodies yellow, to the red, to the brown, to the takman produced by the forest, do I render obeisance.

[Atharva-Veda VI. 20]

### THE SOMA-OBLATION DIRECTED AGAINST DEMONS (RAKSHAS)

1. Press the soma, ye priests, and rinse it for renewed pressing, in behalf of Indra who shall listen to the song of the worshipper, and to my call!

---

Reprinted from Maurice Broomfield, tr., *Hymns of the Atharva-Veda,* in *The Sacred Books of the East,* Vol. XLII (1897). Modified.

2. Do thou, O Indra, whom the drops of soma enter as birds a tree, beat off the hostile brood of the Rakshas!

3. Press ye the soma for Indra, the soma-drinker, who wields the thunderbolt! A youthful victor and ruler is he, praised by many men.

[Atharva-Veda VI. 2]

### Prayer to Varuna for Protection Against Treachery

1. The great guardian among these gods sees as if from anear. He that thinks he is moving stealthily—all this the gods know.

2. If a man stands, walks, or sneaks about, if he goes slinking away, if he goes into his hiding-place; if two persons sit together and scheme, king Varuna is there as a third, and knows it.

3. Both this earth here belongs to king Varuna, and also yonder broad sky whose boundaries are far away. Moreover, these two oceans are the loins of Varuna; yea he is hidden in this small drop of water.

4. He that should flee beyond the heaven far away would not be free from king Varuna. His spies come hither to the earth from heaven, with a thousand eyes do they watch over the earth.

5. King Varuna sees through all that is between heaven and earth, and all that is beyond. He has counted the winkings of men's eyes. As a winning gamester puts down his dice, thus does he establish these laws. . . .

[Atharva-Veda IV. 16]

### Frustration of the Sacrifice of an Enemy

1. Whenever yonder person in his thought, and with his speech, offers sacrifice accompanied by oblations and benedictions, may Nirriti (the goddess of destruction), allying herself with death, smite his offering before it takes effect!

2. May sorcerers, Nirriti, as well as Rakshas (demons), mar

his true work with error! May the gods, despatched by Indra, scatter his sacrificial butter; may that which yonder person offers not succeed!

3. The two agile supreme rulers, like two eagles pouncing down, shall strike the sacrificial butter of the enemy, whosoever plans evil against us!

4. Back do I tie both thy two arms, thy mouth I shut. With the fury of god Agni have I destroyed thy oblation.

5. I tie thy two arms, I shut thy mouth. With the fury of terrible Agni have I destroyed thy oblation.

[Atharva-Veda VII. 70]

## Charm to Deprive Enemies of Their Strength

1. As the rising sun takes away the lustre of the stars, thus do I take away the strength of both the women and the men that hate me.

2. As many enemies as ye are, looking out against me, as I come on—of those that hate me do I take away the strength, as the sun takes away the strength of persons asleep while it rises.

[Atharva-Veda VII. 13]

## Charm to Secure the Love of a Woman

1. As the creeper embraces the tree on all sides, thus do thou embrace me, so that thou, woman, shalt love me, so that thou shalt not be averse to me!

2. As the eagle when he flies forth presses his wings against the earth, thus do I fasten down thy mind, so that thou, woman, shalt love me, so that thou shalt not be averse to me.

3. As the sun day by day goes about this heaven and earth, thus do I go about thy mind, so that thou, woman, shalt love me, so that thou shalt not be averse to me.

[Atharva-Veda VI. 8]

### Charm to Appease Anger

1. As the bowstring from the bow, thus do I take off thy anger from thy heart, so that, having become of the same mind, we shall associate like friends!

2. Like friends we shall associate—I take off thy anger. Under a stone that is heavy do we cast thy anger.

3. I step upon thy anger with my heel and my fore-foot, so that, bereft of will, thou shalt not speak, shalt come up to my wish!

[Atharva-Veda VI. 42]

### Blessing During the Sowing of Seed

1. Raise thyself up, grow thick by thy own might, O grain! Burst every vessel! The lightning in the heavens shall not destroy thee!

2. When we invoke thee, god grain, and thou dost listen, then do thou raise thyself up like the sky, be inexhaustible as the sea!

3. Inexhaustible shall be those that attend to thee, inexhaustible thy heaps! They who give thee as a present shall be inexhaustible, they who eat thee shall be inexhaustible!

[Atharva-Veda VI. 142]

### Prayer to Kala (Time)

1. Time, the steed, runs with seven reins (rays), thousand-eyed, ageless, rich in seed. The seers, thinking holy thoughts, mount him, all the beings are his wheels.

2. With seven wheels does this Time ride, seven naves has he, immortality is his axle. He carries hither all these beings. Time, the first god, now hastens onward.

3. A full jar has been placed upon Time; him, verily, we see existing in many forms. He carries away all these beings; they call him Time in the highest heaven.

4. He surely did bring hither all the beings, he surely did en-

compass all the beings. Being their father, he became their son; there is, verily, no other force, higher than he.

5. Time begot yonder heaven, Time also begot these earths. That which was, and that which shall be, urged forth by Time, spreads out.

6. Time created the earth, in Time the sun burns. In Time are all beings, in Time the eye looks abroad.

7. In Time mind is fixed, in Time breath is fixed, in Time names are fixed; when Time has arrived all these creatures rejoice.

8. In Time tapas (creative fervour) is fixed; in Time the highest being is fixed; in Time brahma (spiritual exaltation) is fixed; Time is the lord of everything, he was the father of Pragapati.

9. By him this universe was urged forth, by him it was begotten, and upon him this universe was founded. Time, truly, having become the brahma, supports Parameshthin (the highest lord).

10. Time created the creatures, and Time in the beginning created the lord of creatures (Pragapati); the self-existing Kasyapa and the tapas (creative fervour) from Time were born.

[Atharva-Veda XIX. 53]

## C. Selections from the *Bhagavad-Gita*

*Translated by Kashinath Trimbak Telang*

### The Way of Ultimate Reality

#### Chapter II

ARJUNA: Seeing these kinsmen, O Krishna! standing here wanting to engage in battle, my limbs droop; my mouth is dry; a tremor comes over my body; and my hair stands on end; the bow slips from my hand; my skin burns intensely. I am unable to stand up; my head spins; I see adverse omens; and I do not perceive any good to follow upon killing my kinsmen in the battle. I do not wish for victory, nor sovereignty, nor pleasures: What is sovereignty to us, what are enjoyments, and even life? Even those, for whose sake we desire sovereignty, enjoyments, and pleasures, are standing here for battle, abandoning life and wealth—preceptors, fathers, sons as well as grandfathers, maternal uncles, fathers-in-law, grandsons, brothers-in-law, and other relatives. These I do not wish to kill, though they kill me, even for the sake of sovereignty over the three worlds, how much less then for this earth alone? What joy shall be ours after killing Dhritarashtra's sons? Killing these felons we shall only incur sin. It is not proper for us to kill our own kinsmen, the sons of Dhritarashtra. For how shall we be happy after killing our own relatives? Although their consciences are corrupted by avarice, they do not see the evils flowing from the extinction of a family, and the sin in treachery to friends. Still, should not we, who do see the evils, learn to refrain from that sin? On the extinction of a family, the eternal rites of families are destroyed. Those rites destroyed, impiety predominates over the whole family. In consequence of impiety, the women of the family become corrupt;

---

Reprinted from *The Bhagavadgita,* translated by Kashinath Trimbak Telang, in *The Sacred Books of the East,* Vol. VIII (1882). Chapters II to XII, XVIII. Modified.

and with the women corrupt, intermingling of castes results; that intermingling necessarily leads the family and the destroyers of the family to hell; for when the ceremonies of offering the balls of food and water to them fail, their ancestors fall down to hell. By these transgressions against the family, occasioning the intermінglings of castes, the eternal rites of caste and families are subverted. We have heard that men whose family-rites are subverted must necessarily live in hell. Alas! we are engaged in committing a heinous sin, seeing that we are preparing to kill our own kinsmen out of greed for the pleasures of sovereignty. If the sons of Dhritarashtra, weapon in hand, should kill me in battle, me weaponless and not defending myself, that would be better for me.

KRISHNA: How comes it that this delusion has overtaken you in this place of peril? Such lowness of spirit is dishonorable and an obstacle to the attaining of heaven. Be not unmanly: it is not worthy of you. Cast off this base weakness of heart and arise.

ARJUNA: But how can I fight with arrows on the battlefield against Bhishma and Drona, both entitled to my reverence? It would be better to live on alms in this world than to slay such men of great glory. But if I kill them, even though they are avaricious of worldly goods, I should enjoy wealth and desires stained with their blood. Nor do we know which of the two is better for us—whether we should vanquish them or they should vanquish us. With a heart contaminated by the taint of helplessness; with a mind confounded about my duty, I ask you. Tell me what is good for me. I am your disciple; instruct me, who have thrown myself on your indulgence. For I do not see what is to destroy the grief that is drying up my very senses—even the attainment of unrivalled and flourishing dominion on earth and lordship over the gods in heaven.

KRISHNA: You have grieved for those who deserve no grief; yet you speak words of wisdom. Neither for the living nor for the dead do the wise grieve. Never did I not exist, nor you, nor these rulers of men; nor will any one of us ever hereafter cease to be.

Even as the embodied self passes, in this body, through the stages of infancy and youth and old age, so does it pass into another body. A sensible man is not deceived about that. The contacts of the senses with external objects, which produce cold and heat, pleasure and pain, are not permanent; they are ever coming and going. Bear them. For that sensible man who remains unchanged in pain and pleasure, whom these cannot disturb, he alone merits immortality. There is no existence for that which is unreal; there is no non-existence for that which is real. And the correct conclusion about both is perceived by those who perceive the truth. Know that to be indestructible which pervades all this; the destruction of that inexhaustible principle none can bring about. Only the bodies, of which this eternal, imperishable, incomprehensible self is the indweller, are said to have an end. Therefore, do engage in battle, descendant of Bharata! He who thinks the self to be the killer and he who thinks it to be killed, both know nothing. It kills not, is not killed. It is not born, nor does it ever die, nor, having existed, does it exist no more. Unborn, everlasting, unchangeable, and primeval, it is not killed when the body is killed.

How can that man who knows it thus to be indestructible, everlasting, unborn, and inexhaustible, how and whom can he kill, whom can he cause to be killed? As a man, casting off old clothes, puts on others and new ones, so the embodied self, casting off old bodies, goes to others and new ones. Weapons do not divide it into pieces; fire does not burn it; waters do not moisten it; the wind does not dry it up. It is not divisible; it is not combustible; it is not to be moistened; it is not to be dried up. It is everlasting, all-pervading, stable, firm, and eternal. It is said to be unperceived, to be unthinkable, to be unchangeable. Therefore knowing it to be such, you should not grieve. But even if you think that it is constantly born, and constantly dies, still you should not grieve thus. For to one that is born, death is certain; and to one that dies, birth is certain. Therefore you should not grieve over the unavoidable. The source of things is unperceived; their middle state is perceived; and their end again is unperceived.

What occasion is there for any lamentation regarding them? One looks upon the self as a wonder; another speaks of it as a wonder; another too hears of it as a wonder; and even after having heard of it, no one does really know it. This embodied self within every one's body is ever indestructible. Therefore you ought not to grieve for any being. Having regard to your own duty also, you ought not to falter, for there is nothing better for a Kshatriya than a righteous battle. Happy those Kshatriyas who can find such a battle to fight—come of itself—an open door to heaven! But if you will not fight this righteous battle, then you will have abandoned your own duty and your fame, and you will incur sin. All beings, too, will tell of your everlasting infamy; and to one who has been honoured, dishonour is a greater evil than death.

Great warriors will think that you abstained from the battle through fear, and having been highly thought of by them, you will fall down in their esteem. Your enemies, too, decrying your power, will speak much about you that should not be spoken. And what, indeed, is more lamentable than that? Killed, you will obtain heaven; victorious, you will enjoy the earth. Therefore arise resolved to fight. Looking alike on pleasure and pain, on gain and loss, on victory and defeat, then prepare for battle, and thus you will not incur sin. The knowledge here declared to you is that relating to the Sankhya. Now hear that relating to the Yoga. Possessed of this knowledge you will cast off the bonds of action. In this path to final emancipation nothing that is begun is aborted; no obstacles exist; and even a little of this form of piety protects one from great danger. There is here but one state of mind consisting in firm understanding. But the states of mind of those who have no firm understanding are many-branched and endless. The state of mind consisting in firm understanding regarding steady contemplation does not belong to those who are strongly attached to worldly pleasures and power, and whose minds are drawn away by that flowery talk which is full of ordinances of specific acts for the attainment of those pleasures and that power, and which promises birth as the fruit of acts—that flowery talk which the unwise ones utter, who are enamoured of Vedic words, who say there is nothing else, who are full of desires, and whose goal is heaven.

The Vedas merely relate to the effects of the three qualities. You, Arjuna, rise above those effects of the three qualities, and be free from the pairs of opposites. Always preserve courage, be free from anxiety for new acquisitions or protection of old acquisitions, and be self-controlled. To the instructed Brahmana, there is in all the Vedas as much usefulness as in a reservoir of water into which waters flow from all sides. Your business is with action alone; not by any means with fruit. Let not the fruit of action be your motive to action. Let not your attachment be fixed on inaction. Having recourse to devotion, perform actions, casting off all attachment, and being equable in success or ill-success; such equability is called devotion. Action is far inferior to the devotion of the mind. In that devotion seek refuge. Wretched are those whose motive to action is the fruit of action. He who has obtained devotion in this world casts off both merit and sin. Therefore apply yourself to devotion; devotion in all actions is wisdom. The wise who have obtained devotion cast off the fruit of action; and released from the fetters of repeated births, repair to that seat where there is no unhappiness. When your mind shall have crossed beyond the taint of delusion, then will you become indifferent to all that you have heard or will hear. When your mind, now confounded by what you have heard, will stand firm and steady in contemplation, then will you have attained devotion.

Arjuna: What are the characteristics of one whose mind is steady, and who is intent on contemplation? How should one of steady mind speak, how sit, how move?

Krishna: When a man abandons all the desires of his heart, his self finding satisfaction in itself alone, he is then called one of steady mind. He whose heart is not agitated in the midst of calamities, who has no longing for pleasures, and from whom the feelings of affection, fear, and wrath have departed, is called a sage of steady mind. He who is not attached to anything, who feels no exultation and no aversion on encountering the various agreeable and disagreeable things of this world, is one of steady mind. When he withdraws his senses from all objects of sense, as the tortoise draws in its limbs from all sides, then is one of steady mind. Objects of sense draw back from a person who is abstinent; not so the taste for those objects. But even the taste departs from him, when he has seen the Supreme. The boisterous senses forcefully carry away the mind even of a wise man striving for perfection. Restraining them all, a man should remain engaged in devotion, making me his only resort. For his mind is steady whose senses are under his control. The man who ponders over objects of sense forms an attachment to them; from that attachment is produced desire; and from desire anger is produced; from anger results want of discrimination; from want of discrimination, confusion of the memory; from confusion of the memory, loss of reason; and in consequence of loss of reason he is utterly ruined. But the self-restrained man who moves among objects with his senses under the control of his own self, and free from affection and aversion, obtains serenity of mind. When there is such tranquillity, all miseries are destroyed, for the mind of him whose heart is tranquil soon becomes steady.

He who is not self-restrained has no steadiness of mind, nor has he perseverance in the pursuit of self-knowledge; there is no tranquillity for him who does not persevere in the pursuit of self-knowledge; and whence can there be happiness for one who is not tranquil? For the heart which follows the rambling senses leads away his judgment, as the wind leads a boat astray upon the waters. Therefore his mind is steady whose senses are restrained on all sides from objects of sense. The self-restrained man is awake when it is night for all beings; and when all beings are awake that is the night of the right-seeing sage. He into whom all objects of desire enter, as waters enter the ocean, which, though full to the brim is grounded in stillness—he only obtains tranquillity; not he who desires those objects of desire. The man who, casting off all desires, lives free from attachments, who is free from egoism, and from the feeling that this or that is mine, obtains tranquillity. This is the Brahmic state; attaining it, one is never deluded; and remaining in it in one's last moments, one attains (brahma-nirvana) the Brahmic bliss.

## The Way of Action

### Chapter III

Arjuna: If devotion is superior to action, then why do you prompt me to this fearful action? You seem, indeed, to confuse my mind by equivocal words. Therefore, tell me one thing definitely, by which I may attain the highest good.

Krishna: I have already declared, that in this world there is a twofold path—that of the Sankhyas by devotion in the shape of true knowledge; and that of the Yogins by devotion in the shape of action. A man does not attain freedom from action merely by not engaging in action; nor does he attain perfection merely by renunciation. For nobody ever remains even for an instant without performing some action; since the qualities of nature constrain everybody, not having free-will in the matter, to some action. The deluded man who, restraining the organs of action, continues to think about objects of sense, is called a hypocrite. But he who restrains his senses, and being free from attachments, engages in devotion in the form of action, with the organs of action, is far superior. Do your prescribed action, for action is better than inaction, and the maintenance of your body, too, cannot be accomplished with inaction. The world is fettered by all action unless it is done for the purpose of the sacrifice. Therefore cast off attachment and perform action for that purpose.

The Creator, having in olden times created men together with the sacrifice, said: 'Propagate with this. May it be the giver to you of the things you desire. Please the gods with this, and may the gods please you. Pleasing each other, you will attain the highest good. For pleased with the sacrifices, the gods will give you the enjoyments you desire. And he who enjoys himself without giving them anything in return is, indeed, a thief.' The good, who eat the leavings of a sacrifice, are released from all sins. But the unrighteous ones, who prepare food for themselves only, incur sin. From food all creatures are born; from rain food is produced; from sacrifice comes rain; sacrifices are the result of action; know that action has its source in the Vedas, and the Vedas come from the Indestructible. Therefore the all-comprehending Vedas are always concerned with sacrifices. He who in this world does not turn round the wheel as it revolves, is of sinful life, indulging his senses, and he lives in vain. But the man who is attached to his self only, who is contented in his self, and is pleased with his self, has nothing to do. He has no interest at all in what is done, and none whatever in what is not done, in this world; nor is any interest of his dependent on any being. Therefore always perform action, which must be performed, without attachment. For a man, performing action without attachment, attains the Supreme. By action alone, did Ganaka and the rest work for perfection.

Further, you should perform work with a view to guiding people along the right path. Whatever a great man does, that other men do also. And people follow whatever he sets up as a standard. There is nothing for me to do in all the three worlds, nothing to acquire which has not been acquired. Still I do engage in action. For should I at any time not engage without sloth in action, men would follow in my path from all sides. If I did not perform actions, these worlds would be destroyed: I should be the cause of caste-interminglings; and I should be ruining these people. As the ignorant act with attachment to action, so should a wise man act without attachment, wishing to keep the people to their duties. A wise man should not shake the convictions of the ignorant who are attached to action, but acting with devotion himself should make them apply themselves to all action. He whose mind is deluded by egoism thinks himself the doer of the actions, which, in every way, are done by the qualities of nature. But he who knows the truth about the difference from qualities and the difference from actions, forms no attachments, believing that qualities deal with qualities. But those who are deluded by the qualities of nature form attachments to the actions of the qualities.

A man of perfect knowledge should not shake these men of imperfect knowledge in their convictions. Dedicating all actions to me with a mind knowing the relation of the supreme and individual self, engage in battle without desire, without any feeling that this or that is mine, and without any grief. Those men who always act on this opinion of mine, full of faith, and without carping, are released from all actions. But those who carp at my opinion and do not act upon it, know them to be devoid of discrimination, deluded as regards all knowledge, and ruined. Even a man of knowledge acts in accordance with his own nature. All beings follow nature. What will restraint effect? Every sense has fixed affections and aversions towards its objects, but one should not become subject to them, for they are one's opponents. One's own duty, though defective, is better than another's duty well performed. Death in performing one's own duty is preferable; the performance of the duty of others is perilous.

ARJUNA: But by whom is man impelled, even though unwilling, and, as it were, constrained by force, to commit sin?

KRISHNA: It is desire, it is wrath, born of passion; it is very ravenous, very sinful. Know that this is the foe in the world. As fire is concealed by smoke, a mirror by dust, the foetus by the womb, so is knowledge concealed by desire. Knowledge is enveloped by this constant foe of the man of knowledge, in the shape of desire, which is like a fire and insatiable. The senses, the mind, and the understanding are said to be its seat; with these it deludes the embodied self after deluding knowledge. Therefore, first restrain your senses, then cast off this sinful thing which destroys knowledge and experience. It has been said, great are the senses, greater than the senses is the mind, greater than the mind is the understanding. What is greater than the understanding is that. Thus knowing that which is higher than the understanding, and restraining yourself by yourself destroy this unmanageable enemy in the shape of desire.

## The Way of Knowledge

### Chapter IV

Krishna: This everlasting system of devotion I declared to the sun, the sun declared it to Manu, and Manu communicated it to Ikshvaku. Coming thus by steps, it became known to royal sages. But that devotion was lost to the world by a long lapse of time. That same primeval devotion I have declared to you to-day, seeing that you are my devotee and friend, for it is the highest mystery.

Arjuna: Later was your birth, and earlier the birth of the sun. How then shall I understand that you taught him in the beginning?

Krishna: I have passed through many births, Arjuna, and so have you. I know them all, but you do not know them. Even though I am unborn and inexhaustible in my essence, even though I am lord of all beings, still I take up the control of my own nature, and am born by means of my delusive power. Whensoever piety languishes, and impiety is in the ascendant, I create myself. I am born age after age, for the protection of the good, for the destruction of evildoers, and the establishment of piety. Whoever truly knows thus my divine birth and work, casts off this body and is not born again. He comes to me. Many from whom affection, fear, and wrath have departed, who are full of me, who depend on me, and who are purified by the penance of knowledge, have come into my essence. I serve men in the way in which they approach me. In every way men follow in my path. Desiring the success of actions, men in this world worship the divinities, for in this world of mortals, success produced by action is soon obtained.

The fourfold division of castes was created by me according to the apportionment of qualities and duties. But though I am its author, know me to be inexhaustible, and not the author. Actions defile me not. I have no attachment to the fruit of actions. He who knows me thus is not tied down by actions. Knowing this, the men of old who wished for final emancipation, performed action. Therefore do you, too, perform action as was done by men of old in olden times. Even sages are confused as to what is action, what inaction. Therefore I will speak to you about action, and learning that, you will be freed from evil. One must possess knowledge about action; one must also possess knowledge about prohibited action; and again one must possess knowledge about inaction. The truth regarding action is abstruse. He is wise among men, he is possessed of devotion, and performs all actions, who sees inaction in action, and action in inaction. The wise call him learned, whose acts are all free from desires and fancies, and whose actions are consumed by the fire of knowledge. Forsaking all attachment to the fruit of action, always contented, dependent on none, he does nothing at all, though he engages in action. Devoid of expectations, restraining the mind and the self, and casting off all belongings, he incurs no sin, performing actions merely for the sake of the body. Satisfied with what comes to him spontaneously, rising above the pairs of opposites, free from all animosity, and equable whether successful or unsuccessful, he is not fettered, even though he performs actions.

The acts of one who is devoid of attachment, who is free, whose mind is fixed on knowledge, and who performs action for the purpose of the sacrifice are all destroyed. Brahman is the oblation; with Brahman as a sacrificial instrument it is offered up; Brahman is in the fire; and by Brahman it is thrown; and Brahman, too, is the goal to which he proceeds who meditates on Brahman in the action. Some perform the sacrifice to the gods, some offer up the sacrifice by the sacrifice itself in the fire of Brahman. Others offer up the senses, such as the sense of hearing and others, in the fires of restraint; others offer up the objects of sense, such as sound and so forth, into the fires of the senses. Some again offer up all the operations of the senses and the operations of the life-breaths into the fire of devotion by self-restraint, kindled by knowledge. Others perform the sacrifice of wealth, the sacrifice of penance, the sacrifice of concentration of mind, the sacrifice of Vedic study, and of knowledge, and others are ascetics of rigid vows. Some offer up the upward life-breath into the downward life-breath, and the downward life-breath into the upper life-breath, and stopping up the motions of the upward and downward life-breaths, devote themselves to the restraint of the life-breaths. Others, who take limited food, offer up the life-breaths into the life-breaths. All of these, conversant with the sacrifice, have their sins destroyed by the sacrifice. Those who eat the nectar-like leavings of the sacrifice repair to the eternal Brahman.

This world is not for those who perform no sacrifice, much less the other. Thus sacrifices of various sorts are laid down in the Vedas. Know them all to be produced from action, and knowing this you will be released from the fetters of this world. The sacrifice of knowledge is superior to the sacrifice of wealth, for all action is wholly and entirely comprehended in knowledge. That you should learn by salutation, question, and service. The men of knowledge who perceive the truth will teach knowledge to you. Having learnt that you will not again fall thus into delusion; and by means of it, you will see all beings, without exception, first in yourself, and then in me. Even if you are the most sinful of all sinful men, you will cross over all trespasses by means of the boat of knowledge alone. As a fire well kindled reduces fuel to ashes, so the fire of knowledge reduces all actions to ashes. For there is in this world no means of sanctification like knowledge, and one who is perfected by devotion finds it within one's self in time. He who has faith, whose senses are restrained, and who is assiduous, obtains knowledge. Obtaining knowledge, he acquires, without delay, the highest tranquillity. He who is ignorant and devoid of faith, and whose self is full of misgivings, is ruined. Not this world, not the next, nor happiness, is for him whose self is full of misgivings. Actions do not fetter one who is self-possessed, who has renounced action by devotion, and who has destroyed misgivings by knowledge. Therefore destroy with the sword of knowledge, these misgivings of yours which fill your mind, and which are born of ignorance. Engage in devotion. Arise!

## The Way of Renunciation

### Chapter V

Arjuna: O Krishna! you praise renunciation of actions and also the pursuit of them. Tell me definitely which one of these two is superior.

Krishna: Renunciation and pursuit of action are both instruments of happiness. But of the two, pursuit of action is superior to renunciation of action. He should be understood to be always an ascetic, who has no aversion and no desire. For he who is free from the pairs of opposites is easily released from all bonds. Children—not wise men—talk of sankhya and yoga as distinct. One who pursues either well obtains the fruit of both. The seat which the sankhyas obtain is reached by the yogas also. He sees truly who sees the sankhya and yoga as one. Renunciation is difficult to reach without devotion; the sage possessed of devotion attains Brahman without delay. He who is possessed of devotion, whose self is pure, who has restrained his self, and who has controlled his senses, and who identifies his self with every being, is not tainted though he performs actions. The man of devotion, who knows the truth, thinks he does nothing at all, when he sees, hears, touches, smells, eats, moves, sleeps, breathes, talks, throws out, takes, opens or closes the eyelids; he holds that the senses deal with the objects of the senses. He who, casting off all attachment, performs actions dedicating them to Brahman, is not tainted by sin, as the lotus-leaf is not tainted by water. Devotees, casting off attachment, perform actions for attaining purity of self, with the body, the mind, the understanding, or even the senses. He who is possessed of devotion, abandoning the fruit of actions, attains the highest tranquillity. He who is without devotion, and attached to the fruit of action, is tied down by reason of his acting in consequence of some desire. The self-restrained, embodied self lies at ease within the city of nine portals, renouncing all actions by the mind, not doing nor causing any thing to be done.

The Lord is not the cause of actions, or of the capacity to perform actions amongst men, or of the connexion of action and fruit. But nature only works. The Lord receives no one's sin, nor merit either. Knowledge is veiled by ignorance, hence all creatures are deluded. But to those who have destroyed that ignorance by knowledge of the self, such knowledge, like the sun, shows forth that supreme principle. And those whose mind is centred on it, whose very self it is, who are thoroughly devoted to it, and whose final goal it is, go never to return, having their sins destroyed by knowledge. The wise look upon a Brahmana possessed of learning and humility, on a cow, an elephant, a dog, and a Svapaka, as alike. Even here, those who have conquered the material world, whose mind rests on sameness, they rest in Brahman. He who knows Brahman, whose mind is steady, who is not deluded, and who rests in Brahman, does not exult on finding anything agreeable, nor does he grieve on finding anything disagreeable. One whose self is not attached to external objects, obtains the happiness that is in one's self; and by means of concentration of mind, joining one's self with the Brahman, one obtains indestructible happiness. For the enjoyments born of contact between senses and their objects are, indeed, sources of misery; they have a beginning as well as an end. A wise man feels no pleasure in them. He who even in this world, before his release from the body, is able to bear the agitations produced from desire and wrath, is a devoted man, he is a happy man. The devotee whose happiness is within himself, whose recreation is within himself, and whose light of knowledge also is within himself, becoming one with the Brahman, obtains the Brahmic bliss.

The sages whose sins have perished, whose misgivings have been destroyed, who have achieved self-restraint, and who are intent on the welfare of all beings, obtain the Brahmic bliss. To the ascetics, who are free from desire and wrath, and whose minds are restrained, and who have knowledge of the self, the Brahmic bliss is on both sides of death. The sage who excludes from his mind external objects, concentrates his visual power between his brows, and makes even the upward and downward life-breaths, confining their movements within the nose, who restrains senses, mind, and understanding, whose highest goal is final emancipation, from whom desire, fear, and wrath have departed, is, indeed, forever released from birth and death. He, knowing me to be the enjoyer of all sacrifices and penances, the great Lord of all worlds, and the friend of all beings, attains tranquillity.

## The Way of Meditation

### Chapter VI

Krishna: He who, regardless of the fruit of actions, performs the actions which ought to be performed, is the devotee and renouncer; not he who discards the sacred fires, nor he who performs no acts. Know that what is called renunciation is devotion; for nobody becomes a devotee who has not renounced all desires. To the sage who wishes to rise to devotion, action is said to be a means, and to him, when he has risen to devotion, tranquillity is said to be a means. When one does not attach oneself to objects of sense, or to action, renouncing all desires, then is one said to have risen to devotion. A man should elevate his self by his self; he should not debase his self, for a man's own self is his friend, but a man's own self is also his enemy. To him who has subjugated his self by his self, his self is a friend; but to him who has not restrained his self, his own self behaves inimically, like an enemy.

The self of one who has subjugated his self and is tranquil, is absolutely concentrated on itself the same in the midst of cold and heat, pleasure and pain, as well as in honour and dishonour. The devotee whose self is contented with knowledge and experience, who is unmoved, who has restrained his senses, and to whom a sod, a stone, and gold are alike, is said to be devoted. And he is esteemed highest who thinks alike about well-wishers, friends, and enemies, and those who are indifferent, and those who take part with both sides, and those who are objects of hatred, and relatives, as well as about the good and the sinful. A devotee should constantly devote his self to abstraction, remaining in a secret place, alone, with his mind and self restrained, without expectations, and without belongings. Fixing his seat firmly in a clean place, not too high nor too low, and covered over with a sheet of cloth, a deerskin, and blades of Kusa grass,—and there seated on that seat, fixing his mind exclusively on one point, with the workings of the mind and senses restrained, he should practice devotion for purity of self. Holding his body, head, and neck even and unmoved, remaining steady, looking at the tip of his own nose, and not looking about in all directions, with tranquillity, devoid of fear, and adhering to the rules of Brahmakarins, he should restrain his mind, and concentrate it on me, and sit down engaged in devotion, regarding me as his final goal.

Thus constantly devoting his self to abstraction, a devotee whose mind is restrained, attains that tranquillity which culminates in final emancipation, and assimilation with me. Devotion is not his who eats too much, nor his who eats not at all; not his who is addicted to too much sleep, nor his who is ever awake. That devotion which destroys all misery is his, who takes due food and exercise, who toils duly in all works, and who sleeps and awakes in due time. When a man's mind, well restrained, becomes steady upon the self alone, then he, being indifferent to all objects of desire, is said to be devoted. As a light standing in a windless place flickers not, that is declared to be the parallel for a devotee, whose mind is restrained, and who devotes his self to abstraction. That mental condition in which the mind restrained by practice of abstraction, ceases to work; in which too, one seeing the self by the self, is pleased in the self; in which one experiences that infinite happiness which transcends the senses, and which can be grasped by the understanding only; and adhering to which, one never swerves from the truth; acquiring which, one thinks no other acquisition higher than it; and adhering to which, one is not shaken off even by great misery; that should be understood to be called devotion in which there is a severance of all connexion with pain.

That devotion should be practised with steadiness and with an undesponding heart. Abandoning, without exception, all desires, which are produced from fancies, and restraining the senses on all sides by the mind only, one should by slow steps become quiescent, with a firm resolve coupled with courage; and fixing his mind upon the self, should think of nothing. Wherever the active and unsteady mind breaks forth, there one should ever restrain it, and fix it steadily on the self alone. The highest happiness comes to such a devotee whose mind is fully tranquil, in whom the quality of passion has been suppressed, who is free from sin, and who is become one with the Brahman. Thus constantly devoting his self to abstraction, a devotee, freed from sin, easily obtains that supreme happiness—contact with the Brahman. He who has devoted his self to abstraction, by devotion, looking alike on everything, sees the self abiding in all beings, and all beings in the self. To him who sees me in everything, and everything in me, I am never lost, and he is not lost to me. The devotee who worships me abiding in all beings, holding that all is one, lives in me, however he may be living. That devotee is deemed to be the best who looks alike on pleasure or pain, whatever it may be, in all creatures, comparing all with his own pleasure or pain.

ARJUNA: I cannot see how one could long sustain the existence of this devotion which you have declared—in consequence of man's fickleness. For, O Krishna, the mind is fickle, boisterous, strong, and obstinate; and I think that to restrain it is as difficult as to restrain the wind.

KRISHNA: Doubtless the mind is difficult to restrain, and fickle. Still it may be restrained by constant practice and by indifference to worldly objects. It is my belief that devotion is hard to obtain for one who does not restrain his self. But by one who is self-restrained and assiduous, it can be obtained through proper methods.

ARJUNA: What is the end of him who does not attain the consummation of his devotion, being not assiduous, and having a mind shaken off from devotion, though full of faith? Does he, fallen from both paths, go to ruin like a broken cloud, being without support, and deluded on the path leading to the Brahman? Be pleased to destroy this doubt of mine, for none else than you can destroy it.

KRISHNA: Neither in this world nor the next, is ruin for him; for, O dear friend, none who performs good deeds comes to an evil end. He who is fallen from devotion attains the worlds of those who perform meritorious acts, dwells there for many a year, and is afterwards born into a family of holy and illustrious men. Or he is even born into a family of talented devotees; and such a birth as that is difficult to obtain in this world. There he comes in contact with the knowledge which belonged to him in his former body, and then again, he works for perfection. For even though reluctant, he is led away by the self-same former practice, and although he only wishes to learn devotion, he rises above the fruits of action laid down in the divine word. But the devotee working with great efforts, and cleared of his sins, attains perfection after many births, and then reaches the supreme goal. The devotee is esteemed higher than the performers of penances, higher even than the men of knowledge, and the devotee is higher than the men of action; therefore, become a devotee. And even among all devotees, he who, being full of faith, worships me, with his inmost self intent on me, is esteemed by me to be the most devoted.

## THE WAY OF REALIZATION

### Chapter VII

KRISHNA: Now hear how you can without doubt know me fully, fixing your mind on me, and resting in me, and practising devotion. I will now tell you exhaustively about knowledge together with experience; that being known, there is nothing further left in this world to know. Among thousands of men, only some work for perfection; and even of those who have reached perfection, and who are assiduous, only some know me truly. Earth, water, fire, air, space, mind, understanding, and egoism, thus is my nature divided eightfold. But this is a lower form of my nature. Know that there is another form of my nature, higher than this, which is animate, and by which this universe is upheld. Know that all things have these for their source. I am the producer and the destroyer of the whole universe. There is nothing else higher than myself; all this is woven upon me, like numbers of pearls upon a thread. I am the taste in water. I am the light of the sun and moon. I am 'Om' in all the Vedas, sound in space, and manliness in human beings; I am the fragrant smell in the earth, refulgence in the fire; I am life in all beings, and penance in those who perform penance. Know me to be the eternal seed of all beings; I am the discernment of the discerning ones, and I the glory of the glorious. I am also the strength, unaccompanied by fondness or desire, of the strong. And I am love unopposed to piety among all divinities, observing various regulations, and controlled by their own natures.

Whichever form of deity any worshipper wishes to worship with faith, to that form I render his faith steady. Possessed of that faith, he seeks to propitiate the deity in that form, and obtains from it those beneficial things which he desires, and which are really given by me. But the fruit thus obtained by them who have little judgment is perishable. Those who worship the divinities go to the divinities, and my worshippers, too, go to me. The undiscerning ones, not knowing my transcendent and inexhaustible essence, than which there is nothing higher, think me, who am unperceived, to have become perceptible. Surrounded by the delusion of my mystic power, I am not manifest to all. This deluded world knows me not, unborn and inexhaustible. I know the things which have been, those which are, and those which are to be. But me nobody knows. All beings are deluded at the time of birth by the delusion caused by the pairs of opposites arising from desire and aversion. But the men of meritorious actions, whose sins have terminated, worship me, being released from the delusion caused by the pairs of opposites, and are firm in their beliefs. Those who, resting on me, work for release from old age and death, know the Brahman, the whole Adhyatma, and all action. And those who know me with the Adhibhuta, the Adhidaiva, and the Adhiyagna, having minds devoted to abstraction, know me at the time of departure from this world.

## The Way to the Imperishable Brahman

### Chapter VIII

ARJUNA: What is the Brahman? What the Adhyatma? And what is action? And what is called the Adhibhuta? And who is the Adhiyagna, and how in this body? And how, too, are you to be known at the time of departure from this world by those who restrain their selfs?

KRISHNA: The Brahman is the supreme, the indestructible. Its manifestation as an individual self is called the Adhyatma. The offering of an oblation to any divinity, which is the cause of the production and development of all things, is named action. The Adhibhuta is all perishable things. The Adhidaivata is the primal being. And the Adhiyagna is I myself in this body. And he who leaves this body and departs from this world remembering me in his last moments, comes into my essence. There is no doubt of that. Also whichever form of deity he remembers when he finally leaves this body, to that he goes, having been accustomed to ponder on it. Therefore, at all times remember me, and engage in battle. Fixing your mind and understanding on me, you will come to me, there is no doubt. He who thinks of the supreme divine Being, with a mind not running to other objects, and possessed of abstraction in the shape of continuous meditation about the supreme, goes to him. He who, possessed of reverence for the supreme Being with a steady mind, and with the power of devotion, properly concentrates the life-breath between the brows, and meditates on the ancient Seer, the ruler, more minute than the minutest atom, the supporter of all, who is of an unthinkable form, whose brilliance is like that of the sun, and who is beyond all darkness, he attains to that transcendent and divine Being.

I will tell you briefly about the state, which those who know the Vedas declare to be indestructible; which is entered by ascetics from whom all desires have departed; and wishing for which, people pursue the mode of life of Brahmakarins. He who leaves the body and departs from this world, stopping up all passages, and confining the mind within the heart, placing the life-breath in the head, and adhering to uninterrupted meditation, repeating the single syllable 'Om,' signifying the eternal Brahman, and meditating on me, he reaches the highest goal. To the devotee who constantly practises abstraction and who with a mind not turned to anything else, is ever and constantly meditating on me, I am easy of access. The high-souled ones, who achieve the highest perfection, attaining to me, do not again come to life, which is transient, a home of woes. All worlds up to the world of Brahman, are destined to return. But after attaining to me, there is no birth again. Those who know a day of Brahman to end after one thousand ages, and the night to terminate after one thousand ages, are the persons who know day and night. With the coming of day, all perceptible things are produced from the unperceived; and with the coming of night they dissolve in that same principle called the unperceived. This same assemblage of entities, being produced again and again, dissolves with the coming of night, and issues forth with the coming of day, with no will of its own.

But there is another entity, unperceived and eternal, and distinct from this unperceived principle, which is not destroyed when all entities are destroyed. It is called the unperceived, the indestructible; they call it the highest goal. Attaining to it, none returns. That is my supreme abode. That supreme Being, he in whom all these entities dwell, and by whom all this is permeated, is to be attained to by reverence. I will state the times at which devotees departing from this world go, never to return, or to return. The fire, the flame, the day, the bright fortnight, the six months of the northern solstice, departing from the world in these, those who know the Brahman go to the Brahman. Smoke, night, the dark fortnight, the six months of the southern solstice, dying in these, the devotee goes to the lunar light and returns. These two paths, bright and dark, are deemed to be eternal in this world. By the one a man goes never to return, by the other he comes back. Knowing these two paths no devotee is deluded. Therefore at all times be possessed of devotion. A devotee knowing all this, obtains all the holy fruit which is prescribed for study of the Vedas, for sacrifices, and also for penances and gifts, and he attains to the highest and primeval seat.

## The Way of Wisdom and Mystery

### Chapter IX

KRISHNA: Now I will speak to you, who are not given to carping, of that most mysterious knowledge, accompanied by experience, by knowing which you will be released from evil. It is the chief among the sciences, the chief among the mysteries. It is the best means of sanctification. It is imperishable, not opposed to the sacred law. It is to be apprehended directly, and is easy to practise. Those men who have no faith in this holy doctrine return to the path of this mortal world, without attaining to me. This whole universe is pervaded by me in an unperceived form. All entities live in me, but I do not live in them. Nor yet do all entities live in me. See my divine power.

Supporting all entities and producing all entities, my self lives not in those entities. As the great and ubiquitous atmosphere always remains in space, know that similarly all entities live in me. At the expiration of a Kalpa all entities enter my nature; and at the beginning of a Kalpa, I again bring them forth. Taking the control of my own nature, I bring forth again and again this whole collection of entities, without a will of its own, by the power of nature. But these actions do not fetter me, who remain like one unconcerned, and who am unattached to those actions. Nature gives birth to movables and immovables through me, the supervisor, and by reason of that the universe revolves. Deluded people of vain hopes, vain acts, vain knowledge, whose minds are disordered, and who are inclined to the delusive nature of Asuras and Rakshasas, not knowing my highest nature as great lord of all entities, disregard me as I have assumed a human body. But the high-souled ones who are inclined to the godlike nature, knowing me as the inexhaustible source of all entities, worship me with minds not turned elsewhere. Constantly glorifying me, and exerting themselves, firm in their vows, and saluting me with reverence, they worship me, being always devoted. And others again, offering up the sacrifice of knowledge, worship me as one, as distinct, and as all-pervading in numerous forms. I am the Kratu, I am the Yagna, I am the Svadha, I the product of the herbs. I am the sacred verse. I too am the sacrificial butter, and I the fire, I the offering. I am the father of this universe, the mother, the creator, the grandsire, the thing to be known, the means of sanctification, the syllable 'Om,' in Rik, Saman, and Yagus also; the goal, the sustainer, the lord, the supervisor, the residence, the asylum, the friend, the source, and that in which it merges, the support, the receptacle, and the inexhaustible seed. I cause heat and I send forth and stop showers. I am immortality and also death; and I am that which is and that which is not.

Those who know the three branches of knowledge, who drink the Soma juice, whose sins are washed away, offer sacrifices and pray to me for a passage into heaven; and reaching the holy world of the lord of gods, they enjoy in the celestial regions the celestial pleasures of the gods. And having enjoyed that great heavenly world, they enter the mortal world when their merit is exhausted. Thus those who wish for objects of desire, and resort to the ordinances of the three Vedas, obtain as the fruit death and rebirth. To those men who worship me, meditating on me and on no one else, and who are constantly devoted, I give new gifts and preserve what is acquired by them. Even those who, being devotees of other divinities, worship with faith, worship me only, but unknowingly. For I am the enjoyer as well as the lord of all sacrifices. But they know me not truly, therefore do they fall. Those who make vows to the gods go to the gods; those who make vows to the manes go to the manes; those who worship the Bhutas go to the Bhutas; and those likewise who worship me go to me. Whoever with devotion offers me leaf, flower, fruit, water, that, presented with devotion, I accept from him whose self is pure.

Whatever you do, whatever you eat, whatever sacrifice you make, whatever you give, whatever penance you perform, do that as offered to me. Thus will you be released from the bonds of action, the fruits of which are agreeable or disagreeable. And with your self possessed of this devotion, this renunciation, you will be released from the bonds of action and will come to me. I am alike to all beings; to me none is hateful, none dear. But those who worship me with devotion dwell in me, and I too in them. Even if an unrighteous man worships me, not worshipping any one else, he must be deemed to be good, for he has formed the right resolution. He soon becomes devout of heart, and obtains lasting tranquillity. You may affirm that my devotee is never ruined. For even those who are of sinful birth, women, Vaisyas, and Sudras likewise, resorting to me, attain the supreme goal. What then need be said of holy Brahmanas and royal saints who are my devotees? Having come into this transient unhappy world, worship me. Place your mind on me, become my devotee, my worshipper; reverence me, and thus, making me your highest goal, and devoting your self to abstraction, you will certainly come to me.

## The Divine Manifestations

### Chapter X

Krishna: Yet again, listen to my excellent words, which, out of a wish for your welfare, I speak to you who are delighted with them. Not the multitudes of gods, nor the great sages know my source; for I am in every way the origin of the gods and great sages. Of all mortals, he who knows me to be unborn, without beginning, the great lord of the world, being free from delusion, is released from all sins. Intelligence, knowledge, freedom from delusion, forgiveness, truth, restraint of the senses, tranquillity, pleasure, pain, birth, death, fear, and also security, harmlessness, equability, contentment, penance, making gifts, glory, disgrace, all these different tempers of living beings are from me alone. The seven great sages, and likewise the four ancient Manus, whose descendants are all the people in the world, were all born from my mind, partaking of my powers. Whoever correctly knows these powers and emanations of mine, becomes possessed of devotion free from indecision; of this there is no doubt. The wise, full of love, worship me, believing that I am the origin of all, and that all moves on through me. Placing their minds on me, offering their lives to me, instructing each other, and speaking about me, they are always contented and happy. To these, who are constantly devoted, and who worship with love, I give that knowledge by which they attain to me. And remaining in their hearts, I destroy, with the brilliant lamp of knowledge, the darkness born of ignorance in such men, out of compassion for them.

ARJUNA: You are the supreme Brahman, the supreme goal, the holiest of the holy. All sages, including Narada, Asita, Devala, and Vyasa, call you the eternal being, divine, the first god, the unborn, the all-pervading. And so, too, you tell me yourself. I believe all this that you tell me to be true; for neither the gods nor demons understand your manifestation. You alone know your self by your self. O best of beings! creator of all things! lord of all things! god of gods! lord of the universe! be pleased to declare without exception your divine emanations, by which emanations you pervade all these worlds. How shall I know you? And in what various entities should I meditate on you? Declare yet again your powers and emanations; because hearing this nectar, I still feel no satiety.

KRISHNA: Well then I will state to you my own divine emanations; but only the chief ones, for there is no end to the extent of my emanations. I am the self seated in the hearts of all beings. I am the beginning and the middle and the end also of all beings. I am Vishnu among the Adityas, the beaming sun among the shining bodies; I am Mariki among the Maruts, and the moon among the lunar mansions. Among the Vedas, I am the Sama-veda. I am Indra among the gods. And I am mind among the senses. I am consciousness in living beings. And I am Sankara among the Rudras, the lord of wealth among Yakshas and Rakshases. And I am fire among the Vasus, and Meru among the high-topped mountains. And know me to be Brihaspati, the chief among domestic priests. I am Skanda among generals. I am the ocean among reservoirs of water. I am Bhrigu among the great sages. I am the single syllable Om among words. Among sacrifices I am the Gapa sacrifice; the Himalaya among the firmly-fixed mountains; the Asvattha among all trees, and Narada among divine sages; Kitraratha among the heavenly choristers, the sage Kapila among the Siddhas. Among horses know me to be Ukkaissravas, brought forth by the labours for the nectar; and Airavata among the great elephants, and the ruler of men among men. I am the thunderbolt among weapons, the wish-giving cow among cows. And I am love which generates. Among serpents I am Vasuki. Among Naga snakes I am Ananta; I am Varuna among aquatic beings. And I am Aryaman among the manes, and Yama among rulers. Among demons, too, I am Pralhada. I am the king of death Kala. Among those who count, I am time. Among beasts I am the lord of beasts, and the son of Vinata among birds. I am the wind among those that blow. I am Rama among those that wield weapons. Among fishes I am Makara, and among streams, the Gahnavi. Of created things I am the beginning and the end and the middle also.

Among sciences, I am the science of the Adhyatma, and I am the argument of controversialists. Among letters I am the letter A, and among the group of compounds the copulative compound. I myself am time inexhaustible, and I the creator whose faces are in all directions. I am death who seizes all, and the source of what is to be. And among females, I am fame, fortune, speech, memory, intellect, courage, forgiveness. Likewise among Saman hymns, I am the Brihat-saman, and I the Gayatri among metres. I am Margasirsha among the months, the spring among the seasons; of cheats, I am the game of dice; I am the glory of the glorious; I am victory, I am industry, I am the goodness of the good. I am Vasudeva among the descendants of Vrishni, and Arjuna among the Pandavas. Among sages also, I am Vyasa; and among the discerning ones, I am the discerning Usanas. I am the rod of those that restrain, and the policy of those that desire victory. I am silence respecting secrets. I am the knowledge of those that have knowledge. And I am also that which is the seed of all things. There is nothing movable or immovable which can exist without me. There is no end to my divine emanations. Here I have declared the extent of those emanations only in part. Whatever thing there is of power, or glory, or splendour, know all that to be produced from portions of my energy. Or rather, what have you to do, knowing all this? I stand supporting all this by but a single portion of myself.

## The Universal Form

### Chapter XI

ARJUNA: In consequence of the excellent and mysterious words concerning the relation of the supreme and individual soul, which you have spoken for my welfare, this delusion of mine is gone. I have heard from you of the production and dissolution of things, and also of your inexhaustible greatness. What you have said about yourself is so. I wish to see your divine form. If you think that it is possible for me to look upon it, then show your inexhaustible form to me.

KRISHNA: In hundreds and in thousands see my forms, various, divine, and of various colours and shapes. See the Adityas, Vasus, Rudras, the two Asvins, and Maruts likewise. And see numerous wonders unseen before. Within my body see to-day the whole universe, including everything movable and immovable, all in one, and whatever else you wish to see. But you will not be able to see me with these eyes of yours. I give you an eye divine. Now see my divine power.

ARJUNA: O god! I see within your body the gods, as also all the groups of various beings; and the lord Brahman seated on his lotus seat, and all the sages and celestial snakes. I see you, who are of countless forms, possessed of many arms, stomachs, mouths, and eyes on all sides. And, O lord of the universe! O you of all forms! I do not see your end or middle or beginning. I see you bearing a coronet and a mace and a discus—a mass of glory, brilliant on all sides, difficult to look at, having on all sides the effulgence of a blazing fire or sun, and indefinable. You are indestructible, the supreme one to be known. You are the highest support of this universe. You are the inexhaustible protector of everlasting piety. I believe you to be the eternal being. I see you void of beginning, middle, end—of infinite power, of unnumbered arms, having the sun and moon for eyes, having a mouth like a blazing fire, and heating the universe with your radiance. This space between heaven and earth and all the quarters are pervaded by you alone.

Looking at this wonderful and terrible form of yours the three worlds are frightened. For groups of gods are entering into you. Some, being afraid, are praying with joined hands, and the groups of great sages and Siddhas are saying "Peace," praising you with hymns of praise. The Rudras, and Adityas, the Vasus, the Sadhyas, the Visvas, the two Asvins, the Maruts, and the Ushmapas, and the groups of Gandharvas, Yakshas, demons, and Siddhas are all looking at you amazed. Seeing your mighty form, with many mouths and eyes, with many arms, thighs, and feet, with many stomachs, and fearful with many jaws, all people, and I likewise, are much alarmed. Seeing you touching the skies, radiant, possessed of many hues, with a gaping mouth, and with large blazing eyes, I am much alarmed in my inmost self, and feel no courage, no tranquillity. And seeing your terrible mouths, resembling the fire of destruction, I cannot recognise the various directions; I feel no comfort. Be gracious, O lord of gods, who pervades the universe.

And all these sons of Dhritarashtra, together with all the bands of kings, and Bhishma and Drona, together with our principal warriors, are rapidly entering your mouths, fearful and horrible because of your jaws. And some with their heads smashed are seen to be stuck in the spaces between the teeth. As the many rapid currents of a river's waters run towards the sea alone, so do these heroes of the human world enter your blazing mouths. As butterflies, with increased velocity, enter a blazing fire to their destruction, so too do these people enter your mouths with increased velocity only to their destruction. Swallowing all these people, you are licking them over and over again from all sides, with your blazing mouths. Your fierce splendours fill the whole universe with their radiance and heat it. Tell me who you are in this fierce form. Be gracious. I wish to know you, the primeval one, for I do not understand your actions.

Krishna: I am death, the destroyer of the worlds, fully developed, and I am now active in overthrowing these men. Even without you, the warriors standing in the opposing hosts, shall all cease to be. Therefore, be up, obtain glory, and vanquishing your foes, enjoy a prosperous kingdom. All these have already been killed by me. Be only the instrument. Kill Drona, Bhishma, Gayadratha, and Karna, and other valiant warriors whom I have already killed. Be not alarmed. Fight. And in the battle you will conquer your foes.

Arjuna: It is proper that the universe is delighted and charmed by your renown, that the demons run away frightened in all directions, and that all the hosts of Siddhas bow down to you. And why should they not bow down to you who are greater than Brahman, and first cause? You are the indestructible, that which is, that which is not, and what is beyond them. You are the primal god, the ancient being; you are the highest support of this universe. You are that which has knowledge, that which is the object of knowledge; you are the highest goal. By you is this universe pervaded. You are the wind, Yama, fire, Varuna. the moon, you Pragapati, and the great grandsire. Obeisance to thee a thousand times, and again and again obeisance to thee! In front and from behind obeisance to thee! Obeisance be to thee from all sides, O you who are all! You are of infinite power, of unmeasured glory; you pervade all, and therefore you are all! Whatever I have said contemptuously,—for instance, 'O Krishna!' 'O Yadava!' 'O friend!'—thinking you to be my friend, and not knowing your greatness as shown in this universal form, or through friendliness, or incautiously; and whatever disrespect I have shown you for purposes of merriment, on occasions of play, sleep, dinner, or sitting together, whether alone or in the presence of friends,—for all that, I ask pardon of you who are indefinable. You are the father of the world—movable and immovable—you its great and venerable master; there is none equal to you. Therefore I bow and prostrate myself, and would propitiate you. Be pleased to pardon my guilt as a father that of his son, a friend that of his friend, or a husband that of his beloved. I am delighted at seeing what I had never seen before, but my heart is also troubled with fear. Show me that other form. Be gracious, O lord of gods. I wish to see you bearing the coronet and the mace, with the discus in hand, just the same as before. O you of thousand arms! O you of all forms! assume that same four-handed form.

KRISHNA: Being pleased with you, I have by my own mystic power shown you this supreme form, full of glory, universal, infinite, primeval, and which has not been seen before by any one else but you. I cannot be seen in this form by any one but you, even with the help of the study of the Vedas, or of sacrifices, or by gifts, or by actions, or by fierce penances. Be not alarmed, be not perplexed, at seeing this fearful form of mine. Free from fear and with delighted heart, see now again that other form of mine.

ARJUNA: Seeing this mild, human form of yours, I am now in my right mind, and have returned to my normal state.

KRISHNA: Even the gods are ever eager to see this form of mine, which it is difficult to get a sight of, and which you have seen. I cannot be seen, as you have seen me, by means of the Vedas, nor by penance, nor by gift, nor yet by sacrifice. But by devotion to me exclusively, I can in this form be truly known, seen, and assimilated with. He who performs acts for propitiating me, to whom I am the highest object, who is my devotee, who is free from attachment, and who has no enmity towards any being, he comes to me.

### The Way of Divine Love

### Chapter XII

Arjuna: Of the worshippers, who thus, constantly devoted, meditate on you, and those who meditate on the unperceived and indestructible, which best know devotion?

Krishna: Those who being constantly devoted, and possessed of the highest faith, worship me with a mind fixed on me, are deemed by me to be the most devoted. But those who, restraining all the senses, with a mind at all times equable, meditate on the indescribable, indestructible, unperceived principle which is all-pervading, unthinkable, indifferent, immovable, and constant, they, intent on the good of all beings, necessarily attain to me. For those whose minds are attached to the unperceived, the task is difficult, for the unperceived goal is obtained by embodied beings only with difficulty. As to those, however, who, dedicating all their actions to me, and holding me as their highest goal, worship me, meditating on me with a devotion towards none other, and whose minds are fixed on me, I come forward as their deliverer from the ocean of this world of death. Place your mind on me only; fix your understanding on me. In me you will dwell hereafter, there is no doubt. But if you are unable to fix your mind steadily on me, then, endeavour to obtain me by the abstraction of mind resulting from continuous meditation. If you are unequal even to continuous meditation, then let acts for propitiating me be your highest aim. Even performing actions for propitiating me, you will attain perfection. If you are unable to do even this, then resort to devotion to me, and, with self-restraint, abandon all fruit of action. For knowledge is better than continuous meditation; concentration is esteemed higher than knowledge; and the renunciation of fruit of action is better than concentration; from that renunciation, tranquillity results.

That devotee of mine, who hates no being, who is friendly and compassionate, who is free from egoism, and from the idea that this or that is mine, to whom happiness and misery are alike, who is forgiving, contented, constantly devoted, self-restrained, and firm in his determinations, and whose mind and understanding are devoted to me, he is dear to me. He by whom the world is not agitated, and who is not agitated by the world, who is free from joy and anger and fear and agitation, he too is dear to me. That devotee of mine, who is unconcerned, pure, assiduous, impartial, free from distress, who abandons all fruits of action, he is dear to me. He who is full of devotion to me, who feels no joy and no aversion, who does not grieve and does not desire, who abandons both what is agreeable and what is disagreeable, he is dear to me. He who is the same to friend and foe, the same in honour and dishonour, who is the same in cold and heat, pleasure and pain, who is free from attachments, to whom praise and blame are alike, who is taciturn, and contented with anything whatever that comes, who is homeless, and of a steady mind, and full of devotion, that man is dear to me. But those devotees who, imbued with faith, and regarding me as their highest goal, resort to this holy means for attaining immortality, they are extremely dear to me.

## The Way of Renunciation

### Chapter XVIII

Arjuna: I wish to know the truth about renunciation and abandonment and the distinction between them.

Krishna: By renunciation the sages understand the rejection of actions done as a result of desire. The wise call abandonment the renunciation of the fruit of all actions. Some wise men say, that action should be abandoned as being full of evil; and others, that the actions of sacrifice, gift, and penance should not be abandoned. As to that abandonment, listen to my decision; for abandonment is described to be threefold. The actions of sacrifice, gift, and penance should not be abandoned; they must be performed; for sacrifices, gifts, and penances are means whereby the wise are sanctified. But even these actions should be performed, abandoning attachment and fruit; such is my excellent and decided opinion. The renunciation of prescribed action is not proper. Its abandonment through delusion is described as of the quality of darkness. When a man abandons action, merely as being troublesome, through fear of bodily affliction, he does not obtain the fruit of abandonment. When prescribed action is performed, abandoning attachment and fruit also, merely because it ought to be performed, that is deemed to be a good abandonment. He who is possessed of abandonment, being full of goodness, and talented, and having his doubts destroyed, is not averse from unpleasant actions, is not attached to pleasant ones. Since no embodied being can abandon actions without exception, he is said to be possessed of abandonment who abandons the fruit of action.

The threefold fruit of action, agreeable, disagreeable, and mixed, accrues after death to those who are not possessed of abandonment, but never to renouncers. Learn from me these five causes of the completion of all actions, declared in the Sankhya system. The substratum, the agent likewise, the various sort of organs, and the various and distinct movements, and with these the deities, too, as the fifth. Whatever action, just or otherwise, a man performs with his body, speech, and mind, these five are its causes. That being so, the undiscerning man, who being of an unrefined understanding, sees the agent in the immaculate self, sees not rightly. He who has no feeling of egoism, and whose mind is not tainted, even though he kills all these people, kills not, is not fettered by the action. Knowledge, the object of knowledge, the knower—threefold is the prompting to action. The instrument, the action, the agent, thus in brief is action threefold. Knowledge and action and agent are declared in the enumeration of qualities to be of three classes only, according to the difference of qualities.

Know that knowledge to be good by which a man sees one entity, inexhaustible, and not different in all things apparently different from one another. Know that knowledge to be passionate which is based on distinctions between different entities, which sees in all things various entities of different kinds. And that is described as dark which clings to one created thing only as if it were everything, which is devoid of reason, devoid of real principle, and insignificant. That action is called good which is prescribed, which is devoid of attachment, which is not done from motives of affection or aversion, and which is done by one not wishing for the fruit. That is described as passionate which occasions much trouble, is performed by one who wishes for objects of desire, or one who is full of egotism. The action is called dark which is commenced through delusion, without regard to consequences, loss, injury, or strength. That agent is called good who has cast off attachment, who is free from egotistic talk, who is possessed of courage and energy, and unaffected by success or ill-success. That agent is called passionate who is full of affections, who wishes for the fruit of actions, who is covetous, cruel, and impure, and feels joy and sorrow. That agent is called dark who is without application, void of discernment, headstrong, crafty, malicious, lazy, melancholy, and slow.

Now hear the threefold division of intelligence and courage, according to qualities, which I am about to declare exhaustively and distinctly. That intelligence is good which understands action and inaction, what ought to be done and what ought not to be done, danger and the absence of danger, emancipation and bondage. That intelligence is passionate by which one imperfectly understands piety and impiety, what ought to be done and also what ought not to be done. That intelligence is dark which, shrouded by darkness, understands impiety to be piety, and understands all things incorrectly. That courage is good courage which is unswerving, and by which one controls the operations of the mind, breath, and senses, through abstraction. But that courage is passionate by which one adheres to piety, lust, and wealth, and through attachment wishes for the fruit. That courage is dark by which an undiscerning man does not give up sleep, fear, sorrow, despondency, and folly.

Now hear from me about the three sorts of happiness. That happiness is called good in which one is pleased after repetition of enjoyment, and reaches the close of all misery, which is like poison first and comparable to nectar in the long run, and which is produced from a clear knowledge of the self. That happiness is called passionate which flows from contact between the senses and their objects, and which is at first comparable to nectar and in the long run like poison. That happiness is described as dark which arises from sleep, laziness, heedlessness, which deludes the self, both at first and in its consequences. There is no entity either on earth or in heaven among the gods, which is free from these three qualities born of nature. The duties of Brahmanas, Kshatriyas, and Vaisyas, and of Sudras, too, are distinguished according to the qualities born of nature. Tranquillity, restraint of the senses, penance, purity, forgiveness, straightforwardness, also knowledge, experience, and belief in a future world, this is the natural duty of Brahmanas. Valour, glory, courage, dexterity, not slinking away from battle, gifts, exercise of lordly power, this is the natural duty of Kshatriyas. Agriculture, tending cattle, trade, this is the natural duty of Vaisyas. And the natural duty of Sudras, too, consists in service. Every man intent on his own respective duties obtains perfection. Listen, now, how one intent on one's own duty obtains perfection. Worshipping, by the performance of his own duty, him from whom all things proceed, and by whom all is permeated, a man obtains perfection. One's duty, though defective, is better than another's duty well performed. Performing the duty prescribed by nature, one does not incur sin. One should not abandon a natural duty though tainted with evil; for all actions are enveloped by evil, as fire by smoke. One who is self-restrained, whose understanding is unattached everywhere, from whom affections have departed, obtains the supreme perfection of freedom from action by renunciation.

Learn from me, only in brief, how one who has obtained perfection attains the Brahman, which is the highest culmination of knowledge. A man possessed of a pure understanding, controlling his self by courage, discarding sound and other objects of sense, casting off affection and aversion; who frequents clean places, who eats little, whose speech, body, and mind are restrained, who is always intent on meditation and mental abstraction, and has recourse to unconcern, who abandoning egoism, stubbornness, arrogance, desire, anger, and all belongings, has no thought that this or that is mine, and who is tranquil, becomes fit for assimilation with the Brahman. Thus reaching the Brahman, and with a tranquil self, he grieves not, wishes not; but being alike to all beings, obtains the highest devotion to me. By that devotion he truly understands who I am and how great. And then understanding me truly, he forthwith enters into my essence. Performing all actions, always depending on me, he, through my favour, obtains the imperishable and eternal seat. Dedicating in thought all actions to me, be constantly given up to me, placing your thoughts on me, through recourse to mental abstraction. Placing your thoughts on me, you will cross over all difficulties by my favour. But if you will not listen through egotism, you will be ruined. If entertaining egotism, you think that you may not fight, vain, indeed, is that resolution of yours. Nature will constrain you, for that which, through delusion, you do not wish to do, you will do involuntarily, tied down by your own duty, flowing from your nature. The lord is seated in the region of the heart of all beings, turning round all beings as though mounted on a machine, by his delusion. With him, seek shelter in every way; by his favour you will obtain the highest tranquillity, the eternal seat. Thus have I declared to you the knowledge more mysterious than any mystery. Ponder over it thoroughly, and then act as you like.

Once more, listen to my excellent words—most mysterious of all. I like you; therefore I will declare what is for your welfare. On me place your mind, become my devotee, sacrifice to me, reverence me and you will certainly come to me. I declare to you truly, you are dear to me. Forsaking all duties, come to me as your sole refuge. I will release you from all sins. Be not grieved. This you should never declare to one who performs no penance, who is not a devotee, nor to one who does not wait on some preceptor, nor yet to one who calumniates me. He who, with the highest devotion to me, will proclaim this supreme mystery among my devotees, will come to me, freed from all doubts. No one amongst men is superior to him in doing what is dear to me. And there will never be another on earth dearer to me than he. And he who will study this holy dialogue of ours, will, such is my opinion, have offered to me the sacrifice of knowledge. And the man, also, who with faith and without carping will listen to this will be freed from sin, and attain to the holy regions of those who perform pious acts. Have you listened to this with a mind fixed on this one point only? Has your delusion caused by ignorance been destroyed?

ARJUNA: Destroyed is my delusion; by your favour I now recollect myself. I stand freed from doubts. I will do your bidding.

## D. Selections from the Upanishads

*Translated by F. Max Müller*

### 1. CHANDOGYA-UPANISHAD

### Sixth Chapter

*Section One*

1. There lived once Svetaketu Aruneya (the grandson of Aruna). To him his father (Uddalaka, the son of Aruna) said: 'Svetaketu, go to school; for there is none belonging to our race, darling, who, not having studied (the Veda), is, as it were, a Brahmana by birth only.'

---

Reprinted from F. Max Müller, tr., *The Sacred Books of the East,* Vol. I (1879). Modified.

2. Having begun his apprenticeship (with a guru) when he was twelve years of age, Svetaketu returned to his father; when he was twenty-four, having then studied all the Vedas,—conceited, considering himself well-read, and stern.

3. His father said to him: 'Svetaketu, as you are so conceited, considering yourself so well-read, and so stern, my dear, have you ever asked for that instruction by which we hear what cannot be heard, by which we perceive what cannot be perceived, by which we know what cannot be known?'

4. 'What is that instruction, Sir?' he asked. The father replied: 'My dear, as by one clod of clay all that is made of clay is known, the difference being only a name, arising from speech, but the truth being that all is clay;

5. 'And as, my dear, by one nugget of gold all that is made of gold is known, the difference being only a name, arising from speech, but the truth being that all is gold;

6. 'And as by one pair of nail-scissors all that is made of iron is known, the difference being only a name, arising from speech, but the truth being that all is iron,—thus, my dear, is that instruction.'

7. The son said: 'Surely, those venerable men (my teachers) did not know that. For if they had known it, why should they not have told it to me? Do you, Sir, therefore tell me that.' 'Be it so,' said the father.

*Section Two*

1. 'In the beginning there was that only which is, one only, without a second. Others say, in the beginning there was that only which is not, one only, without a second; and from that which is not, that which is was born.

2. 'But how could it be thus?' the father continued. 'How could that which is, be born of that which is not? No, only that which is, was in the beginning, one only, without a second.

3. 'It thought, may I be many, may I grow forth. It sent forth fire. That fire thought, may I be many, may I grow forth. It sent forth water. And therefore whenever anybody anywhere is hot and perspires, water is produced on him from fire alone.

4. 'Water thought, may I be many, may I grow forth. It sent forth earth (food). Therefore whenever it rains anywhere, most food is then produced. From water alone is eatable food produced.

*Section Three*

1. 'Of all living things there are indeed three origins only, that which springs from an egg, that which springs from a living being, and that which springs from a germ.

2. 'That Being (i.e. the producer of fire, water, and earth) thought, let me now enter those three beings (fire, water, earth) with this living Self, and let me then reveal (develop) names and forms.

3. 'Then that Being having said, Let me make each of these three tripartite (so that fire, water, and earth should each have itself for its principal ingredient, besides an admixture of the other two) entered into those three beings with this living self only, and developed names and forms.

4. 'He made each of these tripartite; and how these three beings become each of them tripartite, that learn from me, my son.'

*Section Eight*

1. Uddalaka said to his son Svetaketu: 'Learn from me the true nature of sleep. When a man sleeps here, then he becomes united with the True, he is gone to his own (Self). Therefore they say he sleeps, because he is gone to his own.

2. 'As a bird when tied by a string flies first in every direction, and finding no rest anywhere, settles down at last on the

very place where it is fastened, exactly in the same manner, my son, that mind (the jiva, or living Self in the mind), after flying in every direction, and finding no rest anywhere, settles down on breath; for indeed, my son, mind is fastened to breath.

3. 'Learn from me, my son, what are hunger and thirst. When a man is thus said to be hungry, water is carrying away (digests) what has been eaten by him. Therefore as they speak of a cow-leader, a horse-leader, a man-leader, so they call water (which digests food and causes hunger) food-leader. Thus (by food digested, etc.) know this offshoot (the body) to be brought forth, for this body could not be without a root (cause).

4. 'And where could its cause be except in food (earth)? And in the same manner, my son, as food too is an offshoot, seek after its root, viz. water. And as water too is an offshoot, seek after its root, viz. fire. And as fire too is an offshoot, seek after its root, viz. the True. Yes, all these creatures have their root in the True, they dwell in the True, they rest in the True.

5. 'When a man is thus said to be thirsty, fire carries away what has been drunk by him. Therefore as they speak of a cow-leader, of a horse-leader, of a man-leader, so they call fire a water-leader. Thus (by water digested, etc.) know this offshoot (the body) to be brought forth: this body could not be without a root (cause).

6. 'And where could its root be except in water? As water is an offshoot, seek after its root, viz. fire. As fire is an offshoot, seek after its root, viz. the True. Yes, all these creatures have their root in the True, they dwell in the True, they rest in the True. And how these three things, fire, water, earth, when they reach man become each of them tripartite, has been said before. When a man departs from hence, his speech is merged in his mind, his mind in his breath, his breath in heat, heat in the Highest Being.

7. 'Now that which is that subtle essence (the root of all), in it all that exists has its self. It is the True. It is the Self, and

That Thou Art, Svetaketu.' 'Please inform me still more,' said the son. 'So be it,' said the father.

*Section Nine*

1. 'As the bees make honey by collecting the juices of distant trees, and reduce the juice into one form,

2. 'And as these juices have no discrimination, so that they might say, I am the juice of this tree or that, in the same manner, my son, all these creatures, when they have become merged in the True (either in deep sleep or in death), know not that they are merged in the True.

3. 'Whatever these creatures are here, whether a lion, or a wolf, or a boar, or a worm, or a midge, or a gnat, or a mosquito, that they become again and again.

4. 'Now that which is that subtle essence, in it all that exists has its self. It is the True. It is the Self, and That Thou Art, O Svetaketu.'

*Section Ten*

1. 'These rivers run, the eastern towards the east, the western towards the west. They go from sea to sea. They become indeed sea. And as those rivers, when they are in the sea, do not know, I am this or that river,

2. 'In the same manner, my son, all these creatures, when they have come back from the True, know not that they have come back from the True. Whatever these creatures are here, whether a lion, or a wolf, or a boar, or a worm, or a midge, or a gnat, or a mosquito, that they become again and again.

3. 'That which is that subtle essence, in it all that exists has its self. It is the True. It is the Self, and That Thou Art, O Svetaketu.

*Section Eleven*

1. 'If someone were to strike at the root of this large tree here, it would bleed, but live. If he were to strike at its stem, it would bleed, but live. If he were to strike at its top, it would bleed, but live. Pervaded by the living Self that tree stands firm, drinking in its nourishment and rejoicing;

2. 'But if the life (the living Self) leaves one of its branches, that branch withers; if it leaves a second, that branch withers; if it leaves a third, that branch withers. If it leaves the whole tree, the whole tree withers. In exactly the same manner, my son, know this.

3. 'This body indeed withers and dies when the living Self has left it; the living Self dies not. That which is that subtle essence, in it all that exists has its self. It is the True. It is the Self, and That Thou Art, O Svetaketu.

*Section Twelve*

1. 'Fetch me from thence a fruit of the Nyagrodha tree.'
'Here is one, Sir.'
'Break it.'
'It is broken, Sir.'
'What do you see there?'
'These seeds, almost infinitesimal.'
'Break one of them.'
'It is broken, Sir.'
'What do you see there?'
'Nothing, Sir.'

2. The father said: 'My son, that subtle essence which you do not perceive there, of that very essence this great Nyagrodha tree exists.

3. 'Believe it, my son. That which is the subtle essence, in it all that exists has its self. It is the True. It is the Self, and That Thou Art, O Svetaketu.

*Section Thirteen*

1. 'Place this salt in water, and then wait on me in the morning.' The son did as commanded. The father said, 'Bring me the salt, which you placed in the water last night.' The son looked for it but found it not for it had melted.

2. The father said, 'Taste it from the surface of the water. How is it?' The son replied, 'It is salt.' 'Taste it from the middle. How is it?' The son replied, 'It is salt.' 'Taste it from the bottom. How is it?' The son replied, 'It is salt.' The father said, 'Throw it away and then wait for me.' He did so; but salt exists for ever. Then the father said: 'Here also, in this body, forsooth, you do not perceive the True, my son; but indeed it is there.

3. 'That which is the subtle essence, in it all that exists has its self. It is the True. It is the Self, and That Thou Art.

*Section Fourteen*

1. 'As one might lead a person with his eyes covered away from the Gandharas, and leave him then in a place where there are no human beings; and as that person would turn towards the east, north, or the west and shout, "I have been brought here with my eyes covered, I have been left here with my eyes covered."

2. 'And as thereupon some one might loose his bandage and say to him, "Go in that direction, it is Gandhara, go in that direction"; and as thereupon, having been informed and being able to judge for himself, he would by asking his way from village to village arrive at last at Gandhara,—in exactly the same manner does a man, who meets with a teacher to inform him, obtain the true knowledge. For him there is only delay so long as he is not delivered (from the body); then he will be perfect.

3. 'That which is the subtle essence, in it all that exists has its self. It is the True. It is the Self, and That Thou Art, O Svetaketu.

*Section Fifteen*

1. 'If a man is ill, his relatives assemble around him and ask: "Dost thou know me? Dost thou know me?" Now as long as his speech is not merged in his mind, his mind in his breath, breath in heat, heat in the Highest Being, he knows them.

2. 'But when his speech is merged in his mind, his mind in breath, breath in heat, heat in the Highest Being, then he knows them not. That which is the subtle essence, in it all have their selves. It is the True. It is the Self, and That Thou Art, O Svetaketu.

*Section Sixteen*

1. 'They bring a man hither whom they have taken by the hand and they say: "He has taken something, he has committed a theft." (When he denies it, they say), "Heat the hatchet for him." If he committed the theft, then he makes himself to be what he is not. Then the false-minded, having covered his true Self by a falsehood, grasps the heated hatchet—he is burnt, and he is killed.

2. 'But if he did not commit the theft, then he makes himself to be what he is. Then the true-minded, having covered his true Self by truth, grasps the heated hatchet—he is not burnt, and he is delivered. As that truthful man is not burnt, thus has all that exists its self in That. It is the True. It is the Self, and That Thou Art.'

## 2. Kena-Upanishad

*Section One*

1. The pupil asks: 'At whose wish does the mind sent forth proceed on its errand? At whose command does the first breath

---

Reprinted from F. Max Müller, tr., *The Sacred Books of the East,* Vol. I (1879). Modified.

go forth? At whose wish do we utter this speech? What god directs the eye, or the ear?'

2. The teacher replies: 'It is the ear of the ear, the mind of the mind, the speech of the speech, the breath of the breath, and the eye of the eye. When freed from the senses, the wise, on departing this world, become immortal.

3. 'The eye does not go thither, nor speech, nor mind. We do not know, we do not understand, how anyone can teach it.

4. 'It is different from the known, it is also above the unknown, thus we have heard from those of old, who taught us this.

5. 'That which is not expressed by speech and by which speech is expressed, that alone know as Brahman, not that which people here adore.

6. 'That which does not think by mind, and by which, they say, mind is thought, that alone know as Brahman, not that which people here adore.

7. 'That which does not see by the eye, and by which one sees the work of the eyes, that alone know as Brahman, not that which people here adore.

8. 'That which does not hear by the ear, and by which the ear is heard, that alone know as Brahman, not that which people here adore.

9. 'That which does not breathe by breath, and by which breath is drawn, that alone know as Brahman, not that which people here adore.'

*Section Two*

1. The teacher says: 'If thou thinkest I know it well, then thou knowest surely but little, what is that form of Brahman known, it may be, to thee?'

2. The pupil says: 'I do not think I know it well, nor do I know that I do not know it. He among us who knows this, he knows it, nor does he know that he does not know it.

3. 'He by whom Brahman is not thought, by him it is thought; he by whom it is thought, knows it not. It is not understood by those who understand it, it is understood by those who do not understand it.

4. 'It is thought to be known as if by awakening, and then we obtain immortality indeed. By the Self we obtain strength, by knowledge we obtain immortality.

5. 'If a man know this here, that is the true end of life; if he does not know this here, then there is great destruction (new births). The wise who have thought on all things and recognize the Self in them become immortal, when they have departed from this world.'

*Section Three*

1. Brahman obtained the victory for the Devas. The Devas become elated by the victory of Brahman, and they thought, this victory is ours only, this greatness is ours only.

2. Brahman perceived this and appeared to them. But they did not know it, and said: 'What spirit is this?'

3. They said to Agni: 'Find out what spirit this is.'

4. Agni ran towards it, and Brahman said to him: "Who are you?' He replied: 'I am Agni, I am Gatavedas.'

5. Brahman said: 'What power is in you?' Agni replied: 'I could burn all whatever there is on earth.'

6. Brahman put a straw before him saying: 'Burn this.' He went towards it with all his might, but he could not burn it. Then he returned thence and said: 'I could not find out what spirit this is.'

7. Then they said to Vayu (air): 'O Vayu, find out what spirit this is.'

8. Vayu ran towards it, and Brahman said: 'Who are you?" He replied: 'I am Vayu, I am Matarisvan.'

9. Brahman said: 'What power is in you?' Vayu replied: 'I could take up all whatever there is on the earth.'

10. Brahman put a straw before him, saying: 'Take it up.' He went towards it with all his might, but he could not take it up. Then he returned and said: 'I could not find out what spirit this is.'

11. Then they said to Indra: 'O Maghavan, find out what spirit this is.' He went towards it, but it disappeared from before him.

12. Then in the same space, he came towards a woman, highly adorned: It was Uma, the daughter of Himavat. He said to her: 'Who is that spirit?'

*Section Four*

1. She replied: 'It is Brahman. It is through the victory of Brahman that you have thus become great.' After that he thought that it was Brahman.

2. Therefore, these Devas, viz. Agni, Vayu, and Indra, are, as it were, above the other gods, for they touched Brahman nearest.

3. And therefore Indra is, as it were, above the other gods, for he touched it nearest, he first knew it.

4. This is the teaching of Brahman, with regard to the mythological gods: It is that which now flashes forth in lightning, and now vanishes again.

5. And this is the teaching of Brahman, with regard to the body (psychological): It is that which seems to move as mind, and by it imagination remembers again and again.

6. That Brahman is called Tadvana ('the desire of it'), by the name of Tadvana it is to be meditated on. All beings have a desire for him who knows this.

7. The teacher: 'as you have asked me to tell you the Upanishad, the Upanishad has now been told you. We have told you the Brahmi Upanishad.'

8. The feet on which that Upanishad stands are penance, restraint, sacrifice; the Vedas are all its limbs, the True is its abode.

9. He who knows this Upanishad, and has shaken off all evil, stands in endless, unconquerable heaven, yea, in the world of heaven.

## 3. Brihadaranyaka-Upanishad

### Fourth Chapter

*Section Four*

1. Yâg*ñ*avalkya continued: 'Now when that Self, having sunk into weakness, sinks into unconsciousness, then gather those senses (prâ*n*as) around him, and he, taking with him those elements of light, descends into the heart. When that person in the eye turns away, then he ceases to know any forms.

2. ' "He has become one," they say, "he does not see." "He has become one," they say, "he does not smell." "He has become one," they say, "he does not taste." "He has become one," they say, "he does not speak." "He has become one," they say, "he does not hear." "He has become one," they say, "he does not think." "He has become one," they say, "he does not touch." "He has become one," they say, "he does not know." The point of his heart becomes lighted up, and by that light the Self departs, either through the eye, or through the skull, or through other places of the body. And when he thus departs, life (the

---

Reprinted from F. Max Müller, tr., *The Sacred Books of the East,* Vol. XV (1884).

chief prâ*n*a) departs after him, and when life thus departs, all the other vital spirits (prâ*n*as) depart after it. He is conscious, and being conscious he follows and departs.

'Then both his knowledge and his work take hold of him, and his acquaintance with former things.'

3. 'And as a caterpillar, after having reached the end of a blade of grass, and after having made another approach (to another blade), draws itself together towards it, thus does this Self, after having thrown off this body and dispelled all ignorance, and after making another approach (to another body), draw himself together towards it.

4. 'And as a goldsmith, taking a piece of gold, turns it into another, newer and more beautiful shape, so does this Self, after having thrown off this body and dispelled all ignorance, make unto himself another, newer and more beautiful shape, whether it be like the Fathers, or like the Gandharvas, or like the Devas, or like Pragâpati, or like Brahman, or like other beings.

5. 'That Self is indeed Brahman, consisting of knowledge, mind, life, sight, hearing, earth, water, wind, ether, light and no light, desire and no desire, anger and no anger, right or wrong, and all things. Now as a man is like this or like that, according as he acts and according as he behaves, so will he be:—a man of good acts will become good, a man of bad acts, bad. He becomes pure by pure deeds, bad by bad deeds.

'And here they say that a person consists of desires. And as is his desire, so is his will; and as is his will, so is his deed; and whatever deed he does, that he will reap.

6. 'And here there is this verse: "To whatever object a man's own mind is attached, to that he goes strenuously together with his deed; and having obtained the end (the last results) of whatever deed he does here on earth, he returns again from that world (which is the temporary reward of his deed) to this world of action."

'So much for the man who desires. But as to the man who does not desire, who, not desiring, freed from desires, is satisfied in his desires, or desires the Self only, his vital spirits do not depart elsewhere,—being Brahman, he goes to Brahman.

7. 'On this there is this verse: "When all desires which once entered his heart are undone, then does the mortal become immortal, then he obtains Brahman."

'And as the slough of a snake lies on an ant-hill, dead and cast away, thus lies this body; but that disembodied immortal spirit (prâ*n*a, life) is Brahman only, is only light.'

*G*anaka Vaideha said: 'Sir, I give you a thousand.'

8. 'On this there are these verses:

'The small, old path stretching far away has been found by me. On it sages who know Brahman move on to the Svarga-loka (heaven), and thence higher on, as entirely free.

9. 'On that path they say that there is white, or blue, or yellow, or green, or red; that path was found by Brahman, and on it goes whoever knows Brahman, and who has done good, and obtained splendour.

10. 'All who worship what is not knowledge (avidyâ) enter into blind darkness: those who delight in knowledge, enter, as it were, into greater darkness.

11. 'There are indeed those unblessed worlds, covered with blind darkness. Men who are ignorant and not enlightened go after death to those worlds.

12. 'If a man understands the Self, saying, "I am He," what could he wish or desire that he should pine after the body.[1]

13. 'Whoever has found and understood the Self that has entered into this patched-together hiding-place,[2] he indeed is the creator, for he is the maker of everything, his is the world, and he is the world itself.

14. 'While we are here, we may know this; if not, I am

[1] That he should be willing to suffer once more the pains inherent in the body.

[2] The body is meant.

ignorant, and there is great destruction. Those who know it, become immortal, but others suffer pain indeed.

15. 'If a man clearly beholds this Self as God, and as the lord of all that is and will be, then he is no more afraid.

16. 'He behind whom the year revolves with the days, him the gods worship as the light of lights, as immortal time.

17. 'He in whom the five beings and the ether rest, him alone I believe to be the Self,—I who know, believe him to be Brahman; I who am immortal, believe him to be immortal.

18. 'They who know the life of life, the eye of the eye, the ear of the ear, the mind of the mind, they have comprehended the ancient, primeval Brahman.

19. 'By the mind alone it is to be perceived, there is in it no diversity. He who perceives therein any diversity, goes from death to death.

20. 'This eternal being that can never be proved, is to be perceived in one way only; it is spotless, beyond the ether, the unborn Self, great and eternal.

21. 'Let a wise Brâhma*n*a, after he has discovered him, practise wisdom.[3] Let him not seek after many words, for that is mere weariness of the tongue.

22. 'And he is that great unborn Self, who consists of knowledge, is surrounded by the Prâ*n*as, the ether within the heart. In it there reposes the ruler of all, the lord of all, the king of all. He does not become greater by good works, nor smaller by evil works. He is the lord of all, the king of all things, the protector of all things. He is a bank and a boundary, so that these worlds may not be confounded. Brâhma*n*as seek to know him by the study of the Veda, by sacrifice, by gifts, by penance, by fasting, and he who knows him, becomes a Muni. Wishing for that world (for Brahman) only, mendicants leave their homes.

'Knowing this, the people of old did not wish for offspring.

[3] Let him practise abstinence, patience, &c., which are the means of knowledge.

What shall we do with offspring, they said, we who have this Self and this world (of Brahman)? And they, having risen above the desire for sons, wealth, and new worlds, wander about as mendicants. For desire for sons is desire for wealth, and desire for wealth is desire for worlds. Both these are indeed desires only. He, the Self, is to be described by No, no! He is incomprehensible, for he cannot be comprehended; he is imperishable, for he cannot perish; he is unattached, for he does not attach himself; unfettered, he does not suffer, he does not fail. Him (who knows), these two do not overcome, whether he says that for some reason he has done evil, or for some reason he has done good—he overcomes both, and neither what he has done, nor what he has omitted to do, burns (affects) him.

23. 'This has been told by a verse (*Rik*): "This eternal greatness of the Brâhma*n*a does not grow larger by work, nor does it grow smaller. Let man try to find (know) its trace, for having found (known) it, he is not sullied by any evil deed."

'He therefore that knows it, after having become quiet, subdued, satisfied, patient, and collected, sees self in Self, sees all as Self. Evil does not overcome him, he overcomes all evil. Evil does not burn him, he burns all evil. Free from evil, free from spots, free from doubt, he becomes a (true) Brâhma*n*a; this is the Brahma-world, O King,'—thus spoke Yâ*gñ*avalkya.

*G*anaka Vaideha said: 'Sir, I give you the Videhas, and also myself, to be together your slaves.'

24. This indeed is the great, the unborn Self, the strong, the giver of wealth. He who knows this obtains wealth.

25. This great, unborn Self, undecaying, undying, immortal, fearless, is indeed Brahman. Fearless is Brahman, and he who knows this becomes verily the fearless Brahman.

*Section Five*

1. Yâ*gñ*avalkya had two wives, Maitreyî and Kâtyâyanî. Of these Maitreyî was conversant with Brahman, but Kâtyâyanî

possessed such knowledge only as women possess. And Yâg*ñ*avalkya, when he wished to get ready for another state of life (when he wished to give up the state of a householder, and retire into the forest),

2. Said, 'Maitreyî, verily, I am going away from this my house (into the forest). Forsooth, let me make a settlement between thee and that Kâtyâyanî.'

3. Maitreyî said: 'My Lord, if this whole earth, full of wealth, belonged to me, tell me, should I be immortal by it, or no?'

'No,' replied Yâg*ñ*avalkya, 'like the life of rich people will be thy life. But there is no hope of immortality by wealth.'

4. And Maitreyî said: 'What should I do with that by which I do not become immortal? What my Lord knoweth (of immortality), tell that clearly to me.'

5. Yâg*ñ*avalkya replied: 'Thou who art truly dear to me, thou hast increased what is dear (to me in thee). Therefore, if you like, Lady, I will explain it to thee, and mark well what I say.'

6. And he said: 'Verily, a husband is not dear, that you may love the husband; but that you may love the Self, therefore a husband is dear.

'Verily, a wife is not dear, that you may love the wife; but that you may love the Self, therefore a wife is dear.

'Verily, sons are not dear, that you may love the sons; but that you may love the Self, therefore sons are dear.

'Verily, wealth is not dear, that you may love wealth; but that you may love the Self, therefore wealth is dear.

'Verily, cattle are not dear, that you may love cattle; but that you may love the Self, therefore cattle are dear.

'Verily, the Brahman-class is not dear, that you may love the Brahman-class; but that you may love the Self, therefore the Brahman-class is dear.

'Verily, the Kshatra-class is not dear, that you may love the

Kshatra-class; but that you may love the Self, therefore the Kshatra-class is dear.

'Verily, the worlds are not dear, that you may love the worlds; but that you may love the Self, therefore the worlds are dear.

'Verily, the Devas are not dear, that you may love the Devas; but that you may love the Self, therefore the Devas are dear.

'Verily, the Vedas are not dear, that you may love the Vedas; but that you may love the Self, therefore the Vedas are dear.

'Verily creatures are not dear, that you may love the creatures; but that you may love the Self, therefore are creatures dear.

'Verily, everything is not dear, that you may love everything; but that you may love the Self, therefore everything is dear.

'Verily, the Self is to be seen, to be heard, to be perceived, to be marked, O Maitreyî! When the Self has been seen, heard, perceived, and known, then all this is known.

7. 'Whosoever looks for the Brahman-class elsewhere than in the Self, was abandoned by the Brahman-class. Whosoever looks for the Kshatra-class elsewhere than in the Self, was abandoned by the Kshatra-class. Whosoever looks for the worlds elsewhere than in the Self, was abandoned by the worlds. Whosoever looks for the Devas elsewhere than in the Self, was abandoned by the Devas. Whosoever looks for the Vedas elsewhere than in the Self, was abandoned by the Vedas. Whosoever looks for the creatures elsewhere than in the Self, was abandoned by the creatures. Whosoever looks for anything elsewhere than in the Self, was abandoned by anything.

'This Brahman-class, this Kshatra-class, these worlds, these Devas, these Vedas, all these beings, this everything, all is that Self.

8. 'Now as the sounds of a drum, when beaten, cannot be seized externally (by themselves), but the sound is seized, when the drum is seized, or the beater of the drum;

9. 'And as the sounds of a conch-shell, when blown, cannot be seized externally (by themselves), but the sound is seized, when the shell is seized, or the blower of the shell;

10. 'And as the sounds of a lute, when played, cannot be seized externally (by themselves), but the sound is seized, when the lute is seized, or the player of the lute;

11. 'As clouds of smoke proceed by themselves out of lighted fire kindled with damp fuel, thus verily, O Maitreyî, has been breathed forth from this great Being what we have as *Ri*g-veda, Yagur-veda, Sâma-veda, Atharvâṅgirasas, Itihâsa, Purâ*n*a, Vidyâ, the Upanishads, *S*lokas, Sûtras, Anuvyâkhyânas, Vyâkhyânas, what is sacrificed, what is poured out, food, drink, this world and the other world, and all creatures. From him alone all these were breathed forth.

12. 'As all waters find their centre in the sea, all touches in the skin, all tastes in the tongue, all smells in the nose, all colours in the eye, all sounds in the ear, all percepts in the mind, all knowledge in the heart, all actions in the hands, all movements in the feet, and all the Vedas in speech,—

13. 'As a mass of salt has neither inside nor outside, but is altogether a mass of taste, thus indeed has that Self neither inside nor outside, but is altogether a mass of knowledge; and having risen from out these elements, vanishes again in them. When he has departed, there is no more knowledge (name), I say, O Maitreyî,'—thus spoke Yâ*gñ*avalkya.

14. Then Maitreyî said: 'Here, Sir, thou hast landed me in utter bewilderment. Indeed, I do not understand him.'

But he replied: 'O Maitreyî, I say nothing that is bewildering. Verily, beloved, that Self is imperishable, and of an indestructible nature.

15. 'For when there is as it were duality, then one sees the other, one smells the other, one tastes the other, one salutes the other, one hears the other, one perceives the other, one touches the other, one knows the other; but when the Self only is all this, how should he see another, how should he smell another, how should he taste another, how should he salute another, how should he hear another, how should he touch another, how should he know another? How should he know Him by whom

he knows all this? That Self is to be described by No, no! He is incomprehensible, for he cannot be comprehended; he is imperishable, for he cannot perish; he is unattached, for he does not attach himself; unfettered, he does not suffer, he does not fail. How, O beloved, should he know the Knower? Thus, O Maitreyî, thou hast been instructed. Thus far goes immortality.' Having said so, Yâg*ñ*avalkya went away (into the forest).

## 4. Katha-Upanishad

### First Chapter

*Section Two*

1. Death said: 'The good is one thing, the pleasant another; these two, having different objects, chain a man. It is well with him who clings to the good; he who chooses the pleasant, misses his end.'

2. 'The good and the pleasant approach man: the wise goes round about them and distinguishes them. Yea, the wise prefers the good to the pleasant, but the fool chooses the pleasant through greed and avarice.'

3. 'Thou, O Na*k*iketas, after pondering all pleasures that are or seem delightful, hast dismissed them all. Thou hast not gone into the road that leadeth to wealth, in which many men perish.'

4. 'Wide apart and leading to different points are these two, ignorance, and what is known as wisdom. I believe Na*k*iketas to be one who desires knowledge, for even many pleasures did not tear thee away.'

5. 'Fools dwelling in darkness, wise in their own conceit, and puffed up with vain knowledge, go round and round, staggering to and fro, like blind men led by the blind.'

6. 'The Hereafter never rises before the eyes of the careless

---

Reprinted from F. Max Müller, tr., *The Sacred Books of the East,* Vol. XV (1884).

child, deluded by the delusion of wealth. "This is the world," he thinks, "there is no other";—thus he falls again and again under my sway.'

7. 'He (the Self) of whom many are not even able to hear, whom many, even when they hear of him, do not comprehend; wonderful is a man, when found, who is able to teach him (the Self); wonderful is he who comprehends him, when taught by an able teacher.'[1]

8. 'That (Self), when taught by an inferior man, is not easy to be known, even though often thought upon; unless it be taught by another, there is no way to it, for it is inconceivably smaller than what is small.'[1]

9. 'That doctrine is not to be obtained by argument, but when it is declared by another, then, O dearest, it is easy to understand. Thou hast obtained it now; thou art truly a man of true resolve. May we have always an inquirer like thee!'

10. Na*k*iketas said: 'I know that what is called a treasure is transient, for that eternal is not obtained by things which are not eternal. Hence the Nâ*k*iketa fire (-sacrifice) has been laid by me (first); then, by means of transient things, I have obtained what is not transient (the teaching of Yama).' . . .

*Section Three*

1. 'There are the two,[2] drinking their reward in the world of their own works, entered into the cave (of the heart), dwelling

---

[1] Other interpretations: If it is taught by one who identified with the Self, then there is no uncertainty. If it has been taught as identical with ourselves, then there is no perception of anything else. If it has been taught by one who is identified with it, then there is no failure in understanding it (agati).

[2] The two are explained as the higher and lower Brahman, the former being the light, the latter the shadow. *Ri*ta is explained as reward, and connected with suk*ri*ta, lit. good deeds, but frequently used in the sense of svak*ri*ta, one's own good and evil deeds. The difficulty is, how the highest Brahman can be said to drink the reward (*ri*tapa) of former deeds, as it is above all works and above all rewards. The commentator explains it away as a metaphorical expression, as we often speak of many, when we mean one. (Cf. Mu*nd*. Up. III, 1, 1.) I have joined suk*ri*tasya with loke, loka meaning the world, i.e. the state, the environment, which we made to ourselves by our former deeds.

on the highest summit (the ether in the heart). Those who know Brahman call them shade and light; likewise, those householders who perform the Tri*n*â*k*iketa sacrifice.'

2. 'May we be able to master that Nâ*k*iketa rite which is a bridge for sacrificers; also that which is the highest, imperishable Brahman for those who wish to cross over to the fearless shore.'

3. 'Know the Self to be sitting in the chariot, the body to be the chariot, the intellect (buddhi) the charioteer, and the mind the reins.'

4. 'The senses they call the horses, the objects of the senses their roads. When he (the Highest Self) is in union with the body, the senses, and the mind, then wise people call him the Enjoyer.'

5. 'He who has no understanding and whose mind (the reins) is never firmly held, his senses (horses) are unmanageable, like vicious horses of a charioteer.'

6. 'But he who has understanding and whose mind is always firmly held, his senses are under control, like good horses of a charioteer.'

7. 'He who has no understanding, who is unmindful and always impure, never reaches that place, but enters into the round of births.'

8. 'But he who has understanding, who is mindful and always pure, reaches indeed that place, from whence he is not born again.'

9. 'But he who has understanding for his charioteer, and who holds the reins of the mind, he reaches the end of his journey, and that is the highest place of Vish*n*u.'

10. 'Beyond the senses there are the objects, beyond the objects there is the mind, beyond the mind there is the intellect, the Great Self is beyond the intellect.'

11. 'Beyond the Great there is the Undeveloped, beyond the

Undeveloped there is the Person (purusha). Beyond the Person there is nothing—this is the goal, the highest road.'

12. 'That Self is hidden in all beings and does not shine forth, but it is seen by subtle seers through their sharp and subtle intellect.'

13. 'A wise man should keep down speech and mind; he should keep them within the Self which is knowledge; he should keep knowledge within the Self which is the Great; and he should keep that (the Great) within the Self which is the Quiet.'

14. 'Rise, awake! having obtained your boons,[3] understand them! The sharp edge of a razor is difficult to pass over; thus the wise say the path (to the Self) is hard.'

15. 'He who has perceived that which is without sound, without touch, without form, without decay, without taste, eternal, without smell, without beginning, without end, beyond the Great, and unchangeable, is freed from the jaws of death.'

16. 'A wise man who has repeated or heard the ancient story of Na*k*iketas told by Death, is magnified in the world of Brahman.'

17. 'And he who repeats this greatest mystery in an assembly of Brâhmans, or full of devotion at the time of the *S*râddha sacrifice, obtains thereby infinite rewards.' . . .

## Second Chapter

*Section Fve*

1. 'There is a town with eleven gates belonging to the Unborn (Brahman), whose thoughts are never crooked. He who approaches it, grieves no more, and liberated (from all bonds of ignorance) becomes free. This is that.'

---

[3] Comm., excellent teachers.

2. 'He (Brahman) is the swan (sun), dwelling in the bright heaven; he is the Vasu (air), dwelling in the sky; he is the sacrificer (fire), dwelling on the hearth; he is the guest (Soma), dwelling in the sacrificial jar; he dwells in men, in gods (vara), in the sacrifice (*ri*ta), in heaven; he is born in the water, on earth, in the sacrifice (*ri*ta), on the mountains; he is the True and the Great.'

3. 'He (Brahman) it is who sends up the breath (prâ*n*a), and who throws back the breath (apâna). All the Devas (senses) worship him, the adorable (or the dwarf), who sits in the centre.'

4. 'When that incorporated (Brahman), who dwells in the body, is torn away and freed from the body, what remains then? This is that.'

5. 'No mortal lives by the breath that goes up and by the breath that goes down. We live by another, in whom these two repose.'

6. 'Well then, O Gautama, I shall tell thee this mystery, the old Brahman, and what happens to the Self, after reaching death.'

7. 'Some enter the womb in order to have a body, as organic beings, others go into inorganic matter, according to their work and according to their knowledge.'

8. 'He, the highest Person, who is awake in us while we are asleep, shaping one lovely sight after another, that indeed is the Bright, that is Brahman, that alone is called the Immortal. All worlds are contained in it, and no one goes beyond. This is that.'

9. 'As the one fire, after it has entered the world, though one, becomes different according to whatever it burns, thus the one Self within all things becomes different, according to whatever it enters, and exists also without.'

10. 'As the one air, after it has entered the world, though one, becomes different according to whatever it enters, thus the one Self within all things becomes different, according to whatever it enters, and exists also without.'

11. 'As the sun, the eye of the whole world, is not contaminated by the external impurities seen by the eyes, thus the one Self within all things is never contaminated by the misery of the world, being himself without.'

12. 'There is one ruler, the Self within all things, who makes the one form manifold. The wise who perceive him within their Self, to them belongs eternal happiness, not to others.'

13. 'There is one eternal thinker, thinking non-eternal thoughts, who, though one, fulfils the desires of many. The wise who perceive him within their Self, to them belongs eternal peace, not to others.'

14. 'They perceive that highest indescribable pleasure, saying, This is that. How then can I understand it? Has it its own light, or does it reflect light?'

15. 'The sun does not shine there, nor the moon and the stars, nor these lightnings, and much less this fire. When he shines, everything shines after him; by his light all this is lighted.'

## 5. Mundaka-Upanishad

### First Chapter

*Section Two*

1. This is the truth: the sacrificial works which they (the poets) saw in the hymns (of the Veda) have been performed in many ways in the Tretâ age. Practise them diligently, ye lovers of truth, this is your path that leads to the world of good works!

---

Reprinted from F. Max Müller, tr., *The Sacred Books of the East,* Vol. XV (1884).

2. When the fire is lighted and the flame flickers, let a man offer his oblations between the two portions of melted butter, as an offering with faith.

3. If a man's Agnihotra sacrifice is not followed by the new-moon and full-moon sacrifices, by the four-months' sacrifices, and by the harvest sacrifice, if it is unattended by guests, not offered at all, or without the Vai*s*vadeva ceremony, or not offered according to rule, then it destroys his seven worlds.[1]

4. Kâlî (black), Karâlî (terrific), Manogavâ (swift as thought), Sulohitâ (very red), Sudhûmravar*n*â (purple), Sphulinginî (sparkling), and the brilliant Vi*s*varûpî (having all forms), all these playing about are called the seven tongues (of fire).

5. If a man performs his sacred works when these flames are shining, and the oblations follow at the right time, then they lead him as sun-rays to where the one Lord of the Devas dwells.

6. Come hither, come hither! the brilliant oblations say to him, and carry the sacrificer on the rays of the sun, while they utter pleasant speech and praise him, saying: 'This is thy holy Brahma-world (Svarga), gained by thy good works.'

7. But frail, in truth, are those boats, the sacrifices, the eighteen, in which this lower ceremonial has been told. Fools who praise this as the highest good, are subject again and again to old age and death.

8. Fools dwelling in darkness, wise in their own conceit, and puffed up with vain knowledge, go round and round staggering to and fro, like blind men led by the blind.

9. Children, when they have long lived in ignorance, con-

---

[1] The seven worlds form the rewards of a pious sacrificer, the first is Bhu*h*, the last Satya. The seven worlds may also be explained as the worlds of the father, grandfather, and great-grandfather, of the son, the grandson, and great-grandson, and of the sacrificer himself.

sider themselves happy. Because those who depend on their good works are, owing to their passions, improvident, they fall and become miserable when their life (in the world which they had gained by their good works) is finished.

10. Considering sacrifice and good works as the best, these fools know no higher good, and having enjoyed (their reward) on the height of heaven, gained by good works, they enter again this world or a lower one.

11. But those who practise penance and faith in the forest, tranquil, wise, and living on alms, depart free from passion through the sun to where that immortal Person dwells whose nature is imperishable.

12. Let a Brâhma*n*a, after he has examined all these worlds which are gained by works, acquire freedom from all desires. Nothing that is eternal (not made) can be gained by what is not eternal (made). Let him, in order to understand this, take fuel in his hand and approach a Guru who is learned and dwells entirely in Brahman.

13. To that pupil who has approached him respectfully, whose thoughts are not troubled by any desires, and who has obtained perfect peace, the wise teacher truly told that knowledge of Brahman through which he knows the eternal and true Person. . . .

## Second Chapter

### *Section Two*

1. Manifest, near, moving in the cave (of the heart) is the great Being. In it everything is centred which ye know as moving, breathing, and blinking, as being and not-being, as adorable, as the best, that is beyond the understanding of creatures.

2. That which is brilliant, smaller than small, that on which the worlds are founded and their inhabitants, that is the in-

destructible Brahman, that is the breath, speech, mind; that is the true, that is the immortal. That is to be hit. Hit it, O friend!

3. Having taken the Upanishad as the bow, as the great weapon, let him place on it the arrow, sharpened by devotion! Then having drawn it with a thought directed to that which is, hit the mark, O friend, viz. that which is the Indestructible!

4. Om is the bow, the Self is the arrow, Brahman is called its aim. It is to be hit by a man who is not thoughtless; and then, as the arrow (becomes one with the target), he will become one with Brahman.

5. In him the heaven, the earth, and the sky are woven, the mind also with all the senses. Know him alone as the Self, and leave off other words! He is the bridge of the Immortal.

6. He moves about becoming manifold within the heart where the arteries meet, like spokes fastened to the nave. Meditate on the Self as Om! Hail to you, that you may cross beyond (the sea of) darkness!

7. He who understands all and who knows all, he to whom all this glory in the world belongs, the Self, is placed in the ether, in the heavenly city of Brahman (the heart). He assumes the nature of mind, and becomes the guide of the body of the senses. He subsists in food, in close proximity to the heart. The wise who understand this, behold the Immortal which shines forth full of bliss.

8. The fetter of the heart is broken, all doubts are solved, all his works (and their effects) perish when He has been beheld who is high and low (cause and effect).

9. In the highest golden sheath there is the Brahman without passions and without parts. That is pure, that is the light of lights, that is it which they know who know the Self.

10. The sun does not shine there, nor the moon and the stars,

nor these lightnings, and much less this fire. When he shines, everything shines after him; by his light all this is lighted.

11. That immortal Brahman is before, that Brahman is behind, that Brahman is right and left. It has gone forth below and above; Brahman alone is all this, it is the best. . .

## Third Chapter

*Section Two*

1. He (the knower of the Self) knows that highest home of Brahman, in which all is contained and shines brightly. The wise who, without desiring happiness, worship that Person, transcend this seed (they are not born again).

2. He who forms desires in his mind, is born again through his desires here and there. But to him whose desires are fulfilled and who is conscious of the true Self (within himself) all desires vanish, even here on earth.

3. That Self cannot be gained by the Veda, nor by understanding, nor by much learning. He whom the Self chooses, by him the Self can be gained. The Self chooses him (his body) as his own.

4. Nor is that Self to be gained by one who is destitute of strength, or without earnestness, or without right meditation. But if a wise man strives after it by those means (by strength, earnestness, and right meditation), then his Self enters the home of Brahman.

5. When they have reached him (the Self), the sages become satisfied through knowledge, they are conscious of their Self, their passions have passed away, and they are tranquil. The wise, having reached Him who is omnipresent everywhere, devoted to the Self, enter into him wholly.

6. Having well ascertained the object of the knowledge of the Vedânta, and having purified their nature by the Yoga[2] of re-

[2] By the Yoga system, which, through restraint (yoga), leads a man to true knowledge.

nunciation, all anchorites, enjoying the highest immortality, become free at the time of the great end (death) in the worlds of Brahmâ.

7. Their fifteen parts enter into their elements, their Devas (the senses) into their (corresponding) Devas. Their deeds and their Self with all his knowledge become all one in the highest Imperishable.

8. As the flowing rivers disappear in the sea, losing their name and their form, thus a wise man, freed from name and form, goes to the divine Person, who is greater than the great.[3]

9. He who knows that highest Brahman, becomes even Brahman. In his race no one is born ignorant of Brahman. He overcomes grief, he overcomes evil; free from the fetters of the heart, he becomes immortal.

10. And this is declared by the following *Rik*-verse: 'Let a man tell this science of Brahman to those only who have performed all (necessary) acts, who are versed in the Vedas, and firmly established in (the lower) Brahman, who themselves offer as an oblation the one *Ri*shi (Agni), full of faith, and by whom the rite of (carrying fire on) the head has been performed, according to the rule (of the Âtharva*n*as).'

11. The *Ri*shi Aṅgiras formerly told this true (science); a man who has not performed the (proper) rites, does not read it. Adoration to the highest *Ri*shis! Adoration to the highest *Ri*shis!

## 6. Svetasvatara-Upanishad

### Chapter 1

1. The Brahma-students say: Is Brahman the cause? Whence are we born? Whereby do we live, and whither do we go? O ye who know Brahman, (tell us) at whose command we abide, whether in pain or in pleasure?

---

[3] Greater than the conditioned Brahman. Comm.

Reprinted from F. Max Müller, tr., *The Sacred Books of the East,* Vol. XV (1884).

2. Should time, or nature, or necessity, or chance, or the elements be considered as the cause, or he who is called the person (purusha)? It cannot be their union either, because that is not self-dependent,[1] and the self also is powerless, because there is (independent of him) a cause of good and evil.[2]

3. The sages, devoted to meditation and concentration, have seen the power belonging to God himself,[3] hidden in its own qualities (gu*n*a). He, being one, superintends all those causes, time, self, and the rest.

4. We meditate on him who (like a wheel) has one felly with three tires, sixteen ends, fifty spokes, with twenty counter-spokes, and six sets of eight; whose one rope is manifold, who proceeds on three different roads, and whose illusion arises from two causes.

5.[4] We meditate on the river whose water consists of the five streams, which is wild and winding with its five springs, whose waves are the five vital breaths, whose fountain head is the

---

1 Union presupposes a uniter.

2 Âtmâ is explained by *S*añkara, the living self, and as that living self is in his present state determined by karman, work belonging to a former existence, it cannot be thought of as an independent cause.

3 Devâtma*s*akti is a very important term, differently explained by the commentators, but meaning a power belonging to the Deva, the Î*s*vara, the Lord, not independent of him, as the Sâñkhyas represent Prak*ri*ti or nature. Herein lies the important distinction between Vedânta and Sâñkhya.

4 Here again, where the î*s*vara is likened to a stream, the minute coincidences are explained by *S*añkara in accordance with certain systems of philosophy. The five streams are the five receptive organs, the five springs are the five elements, the five waves are the five active organs. The head is the manas, the mind, or common sensory, from which the perceptions of the five senses spring. The five whirlpools are the objects of the five senses, the five rapids are the five pains of being in the womb, being born, growing old, growing ill, and dying. The next adjective pa*ñk*â*s*adbhedâm is not fully explained by Sañkara. He only mentions the five divisions of the kle*s*a (see Yoga-sûtras II, 2), but does not show how their number is raised to fifty. Dr. Roer proposes to read pa*ñk*akle*s*a-bhedâm, but that would not agree with the metre. The five parvans or branches are not explained, and may refer to the fifty kinds of suffering (kle*s*a). The whole river, like the wheel in the preceding verse, is meant for the Brahman as kârya-kâra*n*âtmaka, in the form of cause and effect, as the phenomenal, not the absolutely real world.

mind, the course of the five kinds of perceptions. It has five whirlpools, its rapids are the five pains; it has fifty kinds of suffering, and five branches.

6. In that vast Brahma-wheel, in which all things live and rest, the bird flutters about, so long as he thinks that the self (in him) is different from the mover (the god, the lord). When he has been blessed by him, then he gains immortality.[5]

7. But what is praised (in the Upanishads) is the Highest Brahman, and in it there is the triad.[6] The Highest Brahman is the safe support, it is imperishable. The Brahma-students,[7] when they have known what is within this (world), are devoted and merged in the Brahman, free from birth.

8. The Lord (îsa) supports all this together, the perishable and the imperishable, the developed and the undeveloped. The (living) self, not being a lord, is bound, because he has to enjoy (the fruits of works); but when he has known the god (deva), he is freed from all fetters.

9. There are two, one knowing (îsvara), the other not-knowing (gîva), both unborn, one strong, the other weak; there is she, the unborn, through whom each man receives the recompense of his works; and there is the infinite Self (appearing) under all forms, but himself inactive. When a man finds out these three, that is Brahma.[8]

10. That which is perishable is the Pradhâna (the first), the immortal and imperishable is Hara. The one god rules the

---

[5] If he has been blessed by the Îsvara, i.e. when he has been accepted by the Lord, when he has discovered his own true self in the Lord. It must be remembered, however, that both the Îsvara, the Lord, and the purusha, the individual soul, are phenomenal only, and that the Brahma-wheel is meant for the prapañka, the manifest, but unreal world.

[6] The subject, the object, and the mover.

[7] Those who know the Vedas.

[8] The three are (1) the lord, the personal god, the creator and ruler; (2) the individual soul or souls; and (3) the power of creation. All three are contained in Brahman.

perishable (the pradhâna) and the (living) self.[9] From meditating on him, from joining him, from becoming one with him there is further cessation of all illusion in the end.

11. When that god is known, all fetters fall off, sufferings are destroyed, and birth and death cease. From meditating on him there arises, on the dissolution of the body, the third state, that of universal lordship[10]; but he only who is alone, is satisfied.[11]

12. This, which rests eternally within the self, should be known; and beyond this not anything has to be known. By knowing the enjoyer,[12] the enjoyed, and the ruler, everything has been declared to be threefold, and this is Brahman.

13. As the form of fire, while it exists in the under-wood, is not seen, nor is its seed destroyed, but it has to be seized again and again by means of the stick and the under-wood, so it is in both cases, and the Self has to be seized in the body by means of the pra*n*ava (the syllable Om).

14. By making his body the under-wood, and the syllable Om the upper-wood, man, after repeating the drill of meditation, will perceive the bright god, like the spark hidden in the wood.

15. As oil in seeds, as butter in cream, as water in (dry) river-beds, as fire in wood, so is the Self seized within the self, if man looks for him by truthfulness and penance;

16. (If he looks) for the Self that pervades everything, as butter is contained in milk, and the roots whereof are self-knowledge and penance. That is the Brahman taught by the Upanishad. . . .

---

9 The self, âtman, used here, as before, for purusha, the individual soul, or rather the individual souls.

10 A blissful state in the Brahma-world, which, however, is not yet perfect freedom, but may lead on to it.

11 This alone-ness, kevalatvam, is produced by the knowledge that the individual self is one with the divine self, and that both the individual and the divine self are only phenomenal forms of the true Self, the Brahman.

12 The enjoyer is the purusha, the individual soul, the subject; the enjoyed is prak*ri*ti, nature, the object; and the ruler is the îsvara, that is, Brahman, as god.

## Chapter 6

1. Some wise men, deluded, speak of Nature, and others of Time (as the cause of everything); but it is the greatness of God by which this Brahma-wheel is made to turn.

2. It is at the command of him who always covers this world, the knower, the time of time,[13] who assumes qualities and all knowledge, it is at his command that this work (creation) unfolds itself, which is called earth, water, fire, air, and ether;

3. He who, after he has done that work and rested again, and after he has brought together one essence (the self) with the other (matter), with one, two, three, or eight, with time also and with the subtile qualities of the mind,

4. Who, after starting the works endowed with (the three) qualities, can order all things, yet when, in the absence of all these, he has caused the destruction of the work, goes on, being in truth different (from all he has produced);

5. He is the beginning, producing the causes which unite (the soul with the body), and, being above the three kinds of time (past, present, future), he is seen as without parts, after we have first worshipped that adorable god, who has many forms, and who is the true source (of all things), as dwelling in our own mind.

6. He is beyond all the forms of the tree (of the world) and of time, he is the other, from whom this world moves round, when one has known him who brings good and removes evil, the lord of bliss, as dwelling within the self, the immortal, the support of all.

7. Let us know that highest great lord of lords, the highest deity of deities, the master of masters, the highest above, as god, the lord of the world, the adorable.

8. There is no effect and no cause known of him, no one is

---

[13] The destroyer of time.

seen like unto him or better; his high power is revealed as manifold, as inherent, acting as force and knowledge.

9. There is no master of his in the world, no ruler of his, not even a sign of him. He is the cause, the lord of the lords of the organs, and there is of him neither parent nor lord.

10. That only god who spontaneously covered himself, like a spider, with threads drawn from the first cause (pradhâna), grant us entrance into Brahman.

11. He is the one God, hidden in all beings, all-pervading, the self within all beings, watching over all works, dwelling in all beings, the witness, the perceiver, the only one, free from qualities.

12. He is the one ruler of many who (seem to act, but really do) not act; he makes the one seed manifold. The wise who perceive him within their self, to them belongs eternal happiness, not to others.

13. He is the eternal among eternals, the thinker among thinkers, who, though one, fulfils the desires of many. He who has known that cause which is to be apprehended by *S*âṅkhya (philosophy) and Yoga (religious discipline), he is freed from all fetters.

14. The sun does not shine there, nor the moon and the stars, nor these lightnings, and much less this fire. When he shines, everything shines after him; by his light all this is lightened.

15. He is the one bird in the midst of the world; he is also (like) the fire (of the sun) that has set in the ocean. A man who knows him truly, passes over death; there is no other path to go.

16. He makes all, he knows all, the self-caused, the knower, the time of time (destroyer of time), who assumes qualities and knows everything, the master of nature and of man, the lord

of the three qualities (gu*n*a), the cause of the bondage, the existence, and the liberation of the world.

17. He who has become that, he is the immortal, remaining the lord, the knower, the ever-present guardian of this world, who rules this world for ever, for no one else is able to rule it.

18. Seeking for freedom I go for refuge to that God who is the light of his own thoughts, he who first creates the priest and delivers the Vedas to him;

19. Who is without parts, without actions, tranquil, without fault, without taint, the highest bridge to immortality—like a fire that has consumed its fuel.

20. Only when men shall roll up the sky like a hide, will there be an end of misery, unless God has first been known.

21. Through the power of his penance and through the grace of God has the wise *S*vetâ*s*vatara truly proclaimed Brahman, the highest and holiest, to the best of ascetics, as approved by the company of *Ri*shis.

22. This highest mystery in the Vedânta, delivered in a former age, should not be given to one whose passions have not been subdued, nor to one who is not a son, or who is not a pupil.

23. If these truths have been told to a high-minded man, who feels the highest devotion for God, and for his Guru as for God, then they will shine forth,—then they will shine forth indeed.

CHAPTER III

# Two Representative Systems of Hindu Thought

## Samkhya-Yoga

*Mircea Eliade*

### Point of Departure

Four basic and interdependent concepts, four "kinetic ideas," bring us directly to the core of Indian spirituality. They are *karma, māyā, nirvāṇa,* and *yoga.* A coherent history of Indian thought could be written starting from any one of these basic concepts; the other three would inevitably have to be discussed. In terms of Western philosophy, we can say that, from the post-Vedic period on, India has above all sought to understand:

(1) The law of universal causality, which connects man with the cosmos and condemns him to transmigrate indefinitely. This is the law of *karma.*

(2) The mysterious process that engenders and maintains the cosmos and, in so doing, makes possible the "eternal return" of existences. This is *māyā,* cosmic illusion, endured (even worse—accorded validity) by man as long as he is blinded by ignorance (*avidyā*).

(3) Absolute reality, "situated" somewhere beyond the cosmic

---

Reprinted from Mircea Eliade, *Yoga: Immortality and Freedom,* translated by Williard R. Trask, pages 3–36. 

illusion woven by *māyā* and beyond human experience as conditioned by *karma*; pure Being, the Absolute, by whatever name it may be called—the Self (*ātman*), *brahman,* the unconditioned, the transcendent, the immortal, the indestructible, *nirvāṇa,* etc.

(4) The means of attaining to Being, the effectual techniques for gaining liberation. This corpus of means constitutes Yoga properly speaking.

With these four concepts in mind, we can understand how the fundamental problem of all philosophy, the search for truth, presents itself to Indian thought. For India, truth is not precious in itself; it becomes precious by virtue of its soteriological function, because knowledge of truth helps man to liberate himself. It is not the possession of truth that is the supreme end of the Indian sage; it is liberation, the conquest of absolute freedom. The sacrifices that the European philosopher is prepared to make to attain truth in and for itself: sacrifice of religious faith, of worldly ambitions, of wealth, personal freedom, and even life—to these the Indian sage consents only in order to conquer liberation. To "free oneself" is equivalent to forcing another plane of existence, to appropriating another *mode of being* transcending the human condition. This is as much as to say that, for India, not only is metaphysical knowledge translated into terms of *rupture* and *death* ("breaking" the human condition, one "dies" to all that was human); it also necessarily implies a consequence of a mystical nature: *rebirth to a nonconditioned mode of being.* And this is liberation, absolute freedom.

In studying the theories and practices of Yoga we shall have occasion to refer to all the other "kinetic ideas" of Indian thought. For the present, let us begin by defining the meaning of the term *yoga.* Etymologically, *yoga* derives from the root *yuj,* "to bind together," "hold fast," "yoke," which also governs Latin *jungere, jugum,* French *joug,* etc. The word *yoga* serves, in general, to designate any *ascetic technique* and any *method of meditation.* Naturally, these various asceticisms and meditations have been differently evaluated by the many Indian philosophical currents and mystical movements. As we shall soon see, there is a "classic" Yoga, a "system of philosophy" expounded by Patañjali in his celebrated *Yoga-sūtras*; and it is from the "system" that we must set out in order to understand the position of Yoga in the history of Indian thought. But, side by side with this "classic" Yoga, there are countless forms of "popular," nonsystematic yoga; there are also non-Brāhmanic yogas (Buddhist, Jainist); above all, there are yogas whose structures are "magical," "mystical," and so on. Basically it is the term *yoga* itself that has permitted this great variety of meanings, for if, etymologically, *yuj* means "to bind," it is nevertheless clear that the "bond" in which this action of binding is to result presupposes, at its preliminary condition, breaking the "bonds" that unite the spirit to the world. In other words, liberation cannot occur if one is not first "detached" from the world, if one has not begun by withdrawing from the cosmic circuit. For without doing so, one could never succeed in finding or mastering oneself. Even in its "mystical" acceptation—that is, as signifying *union*—Yoga implies a preliminary detachment from matter, emancipation with respect to the world. The emphasis is laid on man's *effort* ("to yoke"), on his self-discipline, by virtue of which he can obtain concentration of spirit even before asking (as in the mystical varieties of Yoga) for the aid of the divinity. "To bind together," "to hold fast," "to yoke"—the purpose of all this is to *unify* the spirit, to do away with the dispersion and automatism that characterize profane consciousness. For the "devotional" (mystical) schools of Yoga this "unification," of course, only precedes the true union, that of the human soul with God.

What characterizes Yoga is not only its *practical* side, but also its *initiatory* structure. One does not learn Yoga by oneself; the guidance of a master (*guru*) is necessary. Strictly speaking, all the other "systems of philosophy"—as, in fact, all traditional disciplines or crafts—are, in India, taught by masters and are thus initiations; for millenniums they have been transmitted orally, "from mouth to ear." But Yoga is even more markedly initiatory in character. For, as in other religious initiations, the yogin begins by forsaking the profane world (family, society) and, guided by his *guru,* applies himself to passing successively beyond the behavior patterns and values proper to the human condition. When we shall have seen to what a degree the yogin attempts to dissociate himself from the profane condition, we shall understand that he dreams of "dying to this life." We shall, in fact, witness a *death* followed by a *rebirth* to another mode of being—that represented by liberation. The analogy between Yoga and initiation becomes even more marked if we think of the initiatory rites—primitive or other—that pursue the creation of a "new body," a "mystical body" (symbolically assimilated, among the primitives, to the body of the newborn infant). Now, the "mystical body," which will allow the yogin to enter the transcendent mode of being, plays a considerable part in all forms of Yoga, and especially in tantrism and alchemy. From this point of view Yoga takes over and, on another plane, continues the archaic and universal symbolism of initiation—a symbolism that, it may be noted, is already documented in the Brāhmanic tradition (where the initiate is called the "twice-born"). The initiatory rebirth is defined, by all forms of Yoga, as access to a nonprofane and hardly describable mode of being, to which the Indian schools give various names: *mokṣa, nirvāṇa, asaṃskṛta,* etc.

Of all the meanings that the word *yoga* assumes in Indian literature, the most explicit is that which refers to the Yoga "philosophy" (*yoga-darśana*), particularly as set forth in Patañjali's *Yoga-sūtras* and in the commentaries on them. Certainly, a *darśana* is not a system of philosophy in the Western sense (*darśana* = view, vision, comprehension, point of view, doctrine, etc., from the root *dṛś* = to see, to contemplate, to comprehend, etc.). But it is none the less a system of coherent affirmations, coextensive with human experience, which it attempts to interpret in its entirety, and having as its aim the "liberation of man from ignorance" (however various the meanings that the word "ignorance" is made to express). Yoga is one of the six orthodox Indian "systems of philosophy" ("orthodox" here meaning "tolerated by Brāhmanism," in distinction from the "heretical" systems, such as Buddhism or Jainism). And this "classic" Yoga, as formulated by Patañjali and interpreted by his commentators, is also the best known in the West.

So we shall begin our investigation with a review of Yoga theories and practices as formulated by Patañjali. We have several reasons for adopting this procedure: first, because Patañjali's exposition is a "system of philosophy"; second, because a great many practical indications concerning ascetic techniques and contemplative methods are summarized in it—indications that other (the nonsystematic) varieties of Yoga distort or, rather, color in accordance with their particular conceptions; finally, because Patañjali's *Yoga-sūtras* are the result of an enormous effort not only to bring together and classify a series of ascetic practices and contemplative formulas that India had known from time immemorial, but also to validate them from a theoretical point of view by establishing their bases, justifying them, and incorporating them into a philosophy.

But Patañjali is not the creator of the Yoga "philosophy," just as he is not—and could not be—the inventor of yogic techniques. He admits himself that he is merely publishing and correcting (*atha yogānuśāsanam*) the doctrinal and technical traditions of Yoga. And in fact yogic practices were known in the esoteric circles of Indian ascetics and mystics long before Patañjali. Among the technical formulas preserved by tradition, he retained those which an experience of centuries had sufficiently tested. As to the theoretical framework and the metaphysical foundation that Patañjali provides for these practices, his personal contribution is of the smallest. He merely rehandles the Sāṃkhya philosophy in its broad outlines, adapting it to a rather superficial theism in which he exalts the practical value of meditation. The Yoga and Sāṃkhya systems are so much alike that most of the affirmations made by the one are valid for the other. The essential differences between them are few: (1) whereas Sāṃkhya is atheistic, Yoga is theistic, since it postulates the existence of a supreme God (Īśvara); (2) whereas, according to Sāmkhya, the only path to salvation is that of metaphysical knowledge, Yoga accords marked importance to techniques of meditation. In short, Patañjali's effort, properly speaking, was especially directed to co-ordinating philosophical material—borrowed from Sāṃkhya—around technical formulas for concentration, meditation, and ecstasy. Thanks to Patañjali, Yoga, which had been a "mystical" tradition, became a "system of philosophy." . . .

For Sāṃkhya and Yoga, the world is *real* (not illusory—as it is, for example, for Vedānta). Nevertheless, if the world *exists* and *endures,* it is because of the "ignorance" of spirit; the innumerable forms of the cosmos, as well as their process of manifestation and development, exist only in the measure to which the Self (*puruṣa*) is ignorant of itself and, by reason of this metaphysical ignorance, suffers and is enslaved. At the precise moment when the last Self shall have found its freedom, the creation in its totality will be reabsorbed into the primordial substance.

It is here, in this fundamental affirmation (more or less explicitly formulated) that the cosmos exists and endures because of man's lack of knowledge, that we can find the reason for the Indian depreciation of life and the cosmos—a depreciation that none of the great constructions of post-Vedic Indian thought attempted to hide. From the time of the Upaniṣads India rejects the world as it is and devaluates life as it reveals itself to the eyes of the sage—ephemeral, painful, illusory. Such a conception leads neither to nihilism nor to pessimism. *This* world is rejected, *this* life depreciated, because it is known that *something else* exists, beyond becoming, beyond temporality, beyond suffering. In religious terms, it could almost be said that India rejects the *profane* cosmos and *profane* life, because it thirsts for a *sacred* world and a *sacred* mode of being.

Again and again Indian texts repeat this thesis—that the cause of the soul's "enslavement" and, consequently, the source of its endless sufferings lie in *man's solidarity with the cosmos,* in his participation, active and passive, direct or indirect, in nature. Let us translate: solidarity with a *desacralized* world, participation in a *profane* nature. *Neti! neti!* cries the sage of the Upaniṣads: "No, no! thou art not *this*; nor art thou *that*!" In other words: you do not belong to the fallen cosmos, *as you see it now*; you are not necessarily engulfed in *this* creation; necessarily—that is to say, by virtue of the law of your own being. For *Being* can have no relation with *nonbeing*. Now, nature has no true ontological reality; it is, indeed, universal becoming. Every cosmic form, complex and majestic though it may be, ends by disintegrating; the universe itself is periodically reabsorbed by "great dissolutions" (*mahāpralāya*) into the primordial matrix (*prakṛti*). Now, whatever becomes, changes, dies, vanishes does not belong to the sphere of being—to translate once again, is not *sacred*. If solidarity with the cosmos is the consequence of a progressive desacralization of human existence, and hence a fall into ignorance and suffering, the road toward freedom necessarily leads to a desolidarization from the cosmos and profane life. (In some forms of tantric Yoga this desolidarization is followed by a desperate effort toward the resacralization of life.)

Yet the cosmos, life, have an ambivalent function. On the one hand, they fling man into suffering and, by virtue of *karma,* enmesh him in the infinite cycle of transmigrations; on the other hand, indirectly, they help him to seek and find "salvation" for his soul, autonomy, absolute freedom (*mokṣa, mukti*). For the more man suffers (that is, the greater is his solidarity with the cosmos), the more the desire for emancipation increases in him, the more intensely he thirsts for salvation. Thus the forms and illusions of the cosmos—and this by virtue of, not in spite of, their inherent magic, and by virtue of the suffering that their indefatigable becoming ceaselessly feeds—put themselves at the service of man, whose supreme end is emancipation, salvation. "From Brahman down to the blade of grass, the creation [*sṛṣti*] is for the benefit of the soul, until supreme knowledge is attained." Supreme knowledge—that is to say, emancipation not only from ignorance, but also, and indeed first of all, from pain, from suffering.

### The Equation Pain-Existence

"All is suffering for the sage" . . . , writes Patañjali. But Patañjali is neither the first nor the last to record this universal suffering. Long before him the Buddha had proclaimed: "All is pain, all is ephemeral." . . . It is leitmotiv of all post-Upaniṣadic Indian speculation. Soteriological techniques, as well as metaphysical doctrines, find their justification in this universal suffering, for they have no value save in the measure to which they free man from "pain." Human experience of whatever kind engenders suffering. "The body is pain, because it is the place of pain; the senses, objects, perceptions are suffering, because they lead to suffering; pleasure itself is suffering, because it is followed by suffering." And Īśvarakṛṣṇa, author of the earliest Sāṃkhya treatise, declares that the foundation stone of Sāṃkhya is man's desire to escape from the torture of the three sufferings—from celestial misery (provoked by the gods), from terrestrial misery (caused by nature), and from inner or organic misery.

Yet this universal suffering does not lead to a "philosophy of pessimism." No Indian philosophy or gnosis falls into despair. On the contrary, the revelation of "pain" as the law of existence can be regarded as the *conditio sine qua non* for emancipation. Intrinsically, then, this universal suffering has a positive, stimulating value. It perpetually reminds the sage and the ascetic that but one way remains for him to attain to freedom and bliss—withdrawal from the world, detachment from possessions and ambitions, radical isolation. Man, moreover, is not alone in suffering; pain is a cosmic necessity, an ontological modality to which every "form" that manifests itself as such is condemned. Whether one be a god or a tiny insect, the mere fact of existing in time, of having duration, implies pain. Unlike the gods and other living beings, man possesses the capability of passing beyond his condition and thus abolishing suffering. The certainty that there is a way to end suffering—a certainty shared by all Indian philosophies and mysticisms—can lead neither to "despair" nor to "pessimism." To be sure, suffering is universal; but if man knows how to set about emancipating himself from it, it is not final. For, if the human condition is condemned to pain for all eternity—since, like every condition, it is determined by *karma*—each individual who shares in it can pass beyond it, since each can annul the karmic forces by which it is governed.

To "emancipate" oneself from suffering—such is the goal of all Indian philosophies and all Indian mysticisms. Whether this deliverance is obtained directly through "knowledge" (according to the teaching of Vedānta and Sāṃkhya, for example) or by means of techniques (as Yoga and the majority of Buddhist schools hold), the fact remains that no knowledge has any value if it does not seek the "salvation" of man. "Save for that, nothing is worth knowing," says the *Śvetāśvatara Upaniṣad* (I, 12). And Bhoja, commenting on a text of the *Yoga-sūtras* (IV, 22), declares that any knowledge whose object is not deliverance is valueless. Vācaspatimiśra begins his commentary on Īśvarakṛṣṇa's treatise: "In this world, the audience listens only to the preacher who sets forth facts whose knowledge is necessary and desired. To those who set forth doctrines that no one desires, no one attends, as comes to pass with fools or with men of the herd, who are good in their practical affairs but ignorant of the sciences and arts." The same author, in his commentary on the *Vedānta-sūtra-bhāṣya,* specifies the necessary knowledge: "No lucid person desires to know what is devoid of all certainty or what is of no use . . . or of no importance."

In India metaphysical knowledge always has a soteriological purpose. Thus only metaphysical knowledge (*vidyā, jñāna, prajñā*)—that is, the knowledge of ultimate realities—is valued and sought, for it alone procures liberation. For it is by "knowledge" that man, casting off the illusions of the world of phenomena, "awakens." By knowledge—and that means: by practicing withdrawal, the effect of which will be to make him find his own center, to make him coincide with his "true spirit" (*puruṣa ātman*). Knowledge is transformed into a kind of meditation, and metaphysics becomes soteriology. In India not even "logic" is without a soteriological function in its beginnings. Manu uses the term *ānvkīṣaki* ("science of controversy," logic) as an equivalent to *ātmavidyā* ("knowledge of the soul," of the *ātman*)—that is, to metaphysics. Correct argumentation, in conformity with the norms, frees the soul—this is the point of departure of the Nyāya school. Moreover, the earliest logical controversies, from which the Nyāya *darśana* will later develop, were concerned precisely with sacred texts, with the different interpretations that could be put upon such and such an injunction in the Vedas; the purpose of all these controversies was to make possible the correct performance of a rite, in accordance with tradition. Now, this sacred tradition, of which the Vedas are the expression, is *revealed*. Under such conditions, to seek the meaning of words is to remain in permanent contact with the Logos, with the spiritual reality that is absolute, suprahuman, and suprahistorical. Just as the right pronunciation of the Vedic texts results in giving the ritual maximum efficacy, so *right comprehension* of a Vedic maxim results in purifying the intelligence and thus contributes to the spirit's liberation. All partial "ignorance," as it is abolished, carries man a step onward toward freedom and bliss.

The importance that all these Indian metaphysics, and even the ascetic technique and contemplative method that constitute Yoga, accord to "knowledge" is easily explained if we take into consideration the causes of human suffering. The wretchedness of human life is not owing to a divine punishment or to an original sin, but to *ignorance*. Not any and every kind of ignorance, but only ignorance of the true nature of *Spirit,* the ignorance that makes us confuse Spirit with our psychomental experience, that makes us attribute "qualities" and predicates to the eternal and autonomous principle that is Spirit—in short, a metaphysical ignorance. Hence it is natural that it should be a metaphysical knowledge that supervenes to end this ignorance. This metaphysical knowledge leads the disciple to the threshold of illumination—that is, to the true "Self." And it is this knowledge of one's Self—not in the profane sense of the term, but in its ascetic and spiritual sense—that is the end pursued by the majority of Indian speculative systems, though each of them indicates a different way of reaching it.

For Sāṃkhya and Yoga the problem is clearly defined. Since suffering has its origin in ignorance of "Spirit"—that is, in confusing "Spirit" with psychomental states—emancipation can be obtained only if the confusion is abolished. The differences between Sāṃkhya and Yoga on this point are insignificant. Only their methods differ: Sāṃkhya seeks to obtain liberation solely by *gnosis,* whereas for Yoga an *ascesis* and a *technique of meditation* are indispensable. In both *darśanas* human suffering is rooted in illusion, for man believes that his psychomental life—activity of the senses, feelings, thoughts, and volitions—is identical with Spirit, with the Self. He thus confuses two wholly autonomous and opposed realities, between which there is no real connection but only an illusory relation, for psychomental experience does not belong to Spirit, it belongs to nature (*prakṛti*); states of consciousness are the refined products of the same substance that is at the base of the physical world and the world of life. Between psychic states and inanimate objects or living beings, there are only differences of degree. But between psychic states and Spirit there is a difference of an ontological order; they belong to two different modes of being. "Liberation" occurs when one has understood this truth, and when the Spirit regains its original freedom. Thus, according to Sāṃkhya, he who would gain emancipation must begin by thoroughly knowing the essence and the forms of nature (*prakṛti*) and the laws that govern its evolution. For its part, Yoga also accepts this analysis of Substance, but finds value only in the practice of contemplation, which is alone capable of revealing the autonomy and omnipotence of Spirit experimentally. Hence, before expounding the methods and techniques of Yoga, we must see how the Sāṃkhya *darśana* conceives Substance and Spirit, together with the cause of their false solidarity; we must, in short, see in what the gnostic way advocated by this "philosophy" consists. We must also determine to what degree the Sāṃkhya and Yoga doctrines coincide, and distinguish, in the theoretical affirmations of the latter, those which are based on "mystical" experiences lacking in Sāṃkhya.

## The "Self"

Spirit ("soul")—as a transcendent and autonomous principle—is accepted by all Indian philosophies, except by the Buddhists and the materialists (the Lokāyatas). But it is by entirely different approaches that the various *darśanas* seek to prove its existence and explain its essence. For the Nyāya school, soul-spirit is an entity without qualities, absolute, unknowing. Vedānta, on the contrary, defines the *ātman* as being *saccidānanda* (*sat* = being; *cit* = consciousness; *ānanda* = bliss) and regards Spirit as a unique, universal, and eternal reality, dramatically enmeshed in the temporal illusion of creation (*māyā*). Sāṃkhya and Yoga deny Spirit (*puruṣa*) any attribute and any relation; according to these two "philosophies," all that can be affirmed of *puruṣa* is that it *is* and that it *knows* (its knowing **is**, of course, the metaphysical knowledge that results from its contemplation of its own mode of being).

Like the *ātman* of the Upaniṣads, *puruṣa* is inexpressible. Its "attributes" are negative. "Spirit is that which sees [*sākṣin* = witness], it is isolated [*kaivalyam*], indifferent, mere inactive spectator," writes Īśvarakṛṣṇa, and Guaḍapāda, in his commentary, insists on the eternal passivity of *puruṣa*. The autonomy and impassivity of Spirit are traditional epithets, as *Sāṃkhya-sūtras,* I, 147, attests; commenting on this text, Aniruddha cites the famous passage from the *Bṛhadāraṇyaka Upaniṣad* (IV, 3, 15), "This *puruṣa* is free" (*asaṅgo,* "without attachments"), and Vijñānabhikṣu refers to *Śvetāśvatara Upaniṣad,* VI, 2, and *Vedāntasāra,* 158. Being irreducible, without qualities (*nirguṇatvat*), *puruṣa* has no "intelligence" (*ciddharma*), for it is without desires. Desires are not eternal, hence they do not belong to Spirit. Spirit is eternally free, for states of consciousness, the flux of psychomental life, are foreign to it. If *puruṣa* nevertheless appears to us to be an "agent" (*kartṛ*), this is owing both to human illusion and to the unique correlation termed *yogyatā,* which designates a kind of pre-established harmony between the two essentially distinct realities constituted by Self (*puruṣa*) and intelligence (*buddhi*; the latter, as we shall see further on, being only a "more refined product" of the primordial matter or substance).

Patañjali's position is the same. In *Yoga-sūtras,* II, 5, he repeats the statement that ignorance (*avidyā*) consists in regarding what is ephemeral (*anitya*), impure (*aśuci*), painful (*duḥkha*), and non-Spirit (*anātma*) as being eternal (*nitya*), pure (*śuci*), bliss (*sukha*), and Spirit (*ātman*). Vyāsa reiterates that perception, memory, reasoning, etc., belong to the intelligence (*buddhi*) and that it is only by the effect of an illusion that these mental faculties are attributed to the *puruṣa*.

Now, this conception of *puruṣa* at once raises difficulties. For if Spirit is eternally pure, impassive, autonomous, and irreducible, how can it acquiesce in being accompanied by psychomental experience? And how is such a relation possible? We may profitably postpone an examination of the solution that Sāṃkhya and Yoga propose for this problem until we shall have become better acquainted with the possible relationships between the Self and nature. We shall then see that the effort of the two *darśanas* is principally applied to the problem of the true nature of this strange "relation" that links *puruṣa* to *prakṛti*. However, neither the *origin* nor the *cause* of this paradoxical situation has been the object of a formal discussion in Sāṃkhya-Yoga. Why, finally, did the Self acquiesce in being drawn into a foreign orbit, more particularly that of life—and thus in engendering man as such, concrete, historical man, condemned to every catastrophe, assailed by every suffering? *When,* and on what occasion, did this tragedy of the existence of man begin, if it is true that the ontological modality of Spirit is, as we have already seen, exactly opposite to the human condition, the Self being eternal, free, and passive?

The *cause* and the *origin* of this association between Spirit and experience—these are two aspects of a problem that Sāṃkhya and Yoga consider insoluble because it exceeds the present capacity of human comprehension. For man knows and comprehends by means of what Sāṃkhya-Yoga calls the "intellect," *buddhi.* But this intellect itself is only a product—an extremely refined product, to be sure—of matter, of the primordial substance (*prakṛti*). Being a product of nature, a "phenomenon," *buddhi* can enter into cognitional relations only with other phenomena (which, like it, belong to the infinite series of the creations of the primordial substance); under no circumstances could it know the Self, for it could by no possibility enter into any kind of relation with a transcendental reality. The cause and the origin of this paradoxical association between the Self and life (that is, "matter") could be understood only by an instrument of knowledge other than the *buddhi,* one in no way implying matter. Now, such knowledge is impossible in the present condition of humanity. It "reveals" itself only to him who, having broken his fetters, has passed beyond the human condition; "intellect" plays no part in this revelation, which is, rather, knowledge of one's Self, of the Self itself.

Sāṃkhya knows that the cause of "bondage"—that is, of the human condition, of suffering—is metaphysical ignorance, which, by force of the karmic law, is transmitted from generation to generation; but the historical moment at which this ignorance appeared cannot be established, just as it is impossible to determine the date of creation. The connection between the Self and life, and the resulting bondage (for the Self), have no history; they are beyond time, they are eternal. To insist upon finding a solution for these problems is vain, is childishness. They are problems wrongly posed; and in accordance with an old Brāhmanic practice, observed by Buddha himself on several occasions, the sage responds to a wrongly posed problem by silence. The only certainty attainable on the subject is that man has been in this condition since the dawn of time, and that the goal of knowledge is not a fruitless search for the first cause and historical origins of this condition, but liberation.

## SUBSTANCE

It is only in passing that Patañjali refers to *prakṛti* and its modalities, the *guṇas,* and only to define their relationships with psychomental life and the techniques of liberation. He assumes a knowledge of the analysis of Substance, laboriously pursued by Sāṃkhya authors. It is primarily to these authors that we shall have recourse in order to understand the structure and the procession of Substance.

*Prakṛti* is as real and as eternal as *puruṣa*; but unlike Spirit, it is dynamic and creative. Though perfectly homogeneous and inert, this primordial substance possesses, so to speak, three "modes of being," which permit it to manifest itself in three different ways, which are termed *guṇas*: (1) *sattva* (modality of luminosity and intelligence); (2) *rajas* (modality of motor energy and mental activity); (3) *tamas* (modality of static inertia and psychic obscurity). However, these *guṇas* must not be regarded as different from *prakṛti,* for they are never given separately; in every physical, biological, or psychomental phenomenon all three *guṇas* exist simultaneously, though in unequal proportions (indeed, it is this inequality that permits the appearance of a "phenomenon," of whatever kind; otherwise, the primordial equilibrium and homogeneity by virtue of which the *guṇas* were in perfect equilibrium would persist forever). It is clear, then, that the *guṇas* have a twofold character: objective on the one hand, since they constitute the phenomena of the external world, and, on the other hand, subjective, since they support, nourish, and condition psychomental life. (This is why *tamas* must be translated not only as "principle of the inertia of matter"—its objective meaning—but also as "darkness of consciousness," "obstacle created by the passions"—its psychophysiological meaning.)

As soon as *prakṛti* departs from its original state of perfect equilibrium (*aliṇga, avyakta*) and assumes specific characteristics conditioned by its "teleological instinct" (to which we shall return), it appears in the form of an energetic mass called *mahat* ("the great"). Drawn on by the force of evolution (*pariṇāma,* "development," "procession"), *prakṛti* passes from the state of *mahat* to that of *ahaṃkāra,* which means: uniform apperceptive mass, as yet without "personal" experience, but with the obscure consciousness of being an ego (hence the term *ahaṃkāra*; *aham* = ego). From this apperceptive mass, the process of "evolution" bifurcates in opposite directions, one of which leads to the world of objective phenomena and the other to that of subjective phenomena (sensible and psychomental). The *ahaṃkāra* has the ability to transform itself qualitatively in accordance with which of the three *guṇas* predominates in it. When *sattva* (the modality of luminosity, of purity and comprehension) is predominant in the *ahaṃkāra,* the five cognoscitive senses (*jñānendriya*), and *manas,* "the inner sense," make their appearance; the latter serves as liaison center between perceptive and motor activity; the base and receptacle of all impressions, it co-ordinates biological and psychic activities, particularly that of the subconscious. When, on the other hand, the equilibrium is dominated by *rajas* (the motor energy that makes all physical or cognoscitive experience possible), the five conative senses (*karmendriya*) appear. Finally, when *tamas* (inertia of matter, darkness of consciousness, the barrage of the passions) dominates, what appear are the five *tanmātras,* the five "subtle" (potential) elements, the genetic seeds of the physical world. By a process of condensation that tends to produce structures increasingly gross, these *tanmātras* give rise to atoms (*paramāṇu*) and molecules (*sthūlabhūtaṇi*; literally, "dense material particle"), which in turn give birth to vegetable organisms (*vrikṣa*) and animal organisms (*śarīra*). Thus man's body, as well as his "states of consciousness" and even his "intelligence," are all creations of one and the same substance.

It will be noted that, in accordance with Sāṃkhya and Yoga, the universe—objective or subjective—is only the evolution of an initial stage of nature (*ahaṃkāra*), that in which the homogeneous and energetic mass first gave birth to consciousness of individuality, to an apperception illuminated by the ego. By a twofold process of development and creation, the *ahaṃkāra* created a twofold universe—inner and outer—these two "worlds" having elective correspondences between them. Each sense corresponds to a specific atom, as each atom corresponds to a *tanmātra.* But each of these products contains the three *guṇas,* though in unequal proportions; each product is characterized by the supremacy of a particular *guṇa* or, in the last stages of creation, by the predominance of a particular *tanmātra.*

It is important that we understand the notion of evolution in Sāṃkhya. *Pariṇāma* signifies development of what exists, *in posse,* in the *mahat.* It is not a creation, nor a transcendence, nor the realization of new species of existence, but simply the realization of the potentialities that exist in *prakṛti* (under its living aspect, the *mahat*). To compare "evolution" in the Indian sense with Western evolutionism is to be guilty of great confusion. No new form, Sāṃkhya affirms, goes beyond the possibilities of existence that were already present in the universe. In fact, for Sāṃkhya, nothing is created, in the Western sense of the word. Creation exists from all eternity and can never be destroyed; but it will return to its original aspect of absolute equilibrium (in the great final resorption, *mahāpralāya*).

This conception of evolution is justified by a particular theory of causality. For if the effect exceeded the cause, there would be in the cause a nonexisting quantum, which would acquire existence in the effect. But, Sāṃkhya asks, how could this nonentity be the cause of an entity? How could *esse* come from *non esse*? Vācaspatimiśra says: "If one affirms the production of an entity by a nonentity, then the latter, existing everywhere and at every moment, should give birth everywhere and at every moment to any effect and all effects." And, commenting on *Sāṃkhya-kārikā,* 9, he adds: "The effect is an entity, that is to say, it exists before the causal operation." "If the effect were a nonentity before the causal operation, it could never be brought into existence."

Between the cause and the effect there exists a real and definite relation. But if the effect did not exist in the cause, how should a *relation* be possible between *ens* and *non ens*? How should an intimate connection be possible between *absence* and *presence*? "Under these conditions," says Īśvarakṛṣṇa, "all that can be brought about by the cause is the manifestation or the development of the pre-existing effect." To illustrate the theory of causality by an example, Vijñānabhikṣu writes: "Just as the statue, already existing in the block of stone, is only revealed by the sculptor, so the causal activity only engenders the action by which an effect manifests itself, giving the illusion that it exists only in the present moment."

Concerning the *ahaṃkāra,* Sāṃkhya texts give many details, but what is of interest to our brief exposition is that *ahaṃkāra* is defined as "self-knowledge." We should bear in mind that this entity, though "material," does not manifest itself in sensory, physical forms, but is homogeneous, a pure and energetic mass without structure. According to Sāṃkhya, the *ahaṃkāra* acquires consciousness of itself, and, through this process, reflects itself (*sarva,* "emanation") in the series of the eleven psychic principles (*manas,* or the inner sense, which co-ordinates the faculties of the soul; the five cognitive and the five conative senses) and in the series of physical powers (*tanmātra*).

We should note the capital importance that Sāmkhya, like almost all Indian systems, accords to the *principle of individuation through "consciousness of self."* We see that the genesis of the world is a psychic act, that it is from this self-knowledge (which, of course, is absolutely different from the "awakening" of the *puruṣa*) that the evolution of the physical world derives; and that objective and psychophysiological phenomena have a common matrix, the only difference between them being the *formula* of the *guṇas, sattva* predominating in psychic phenomena, *rajas* in psychophysiological phenomena (passion, activity of the senses, etc.), while the phenomena of "matter" are constituted by the increasingly inert and dense products of *tamas* (*tanmātra, aṇu, bhūtaṇi*).

Sāṃkhya-Yoga also provides a subjective interpretation of the three *guṇas* when it considers their psychic "aspects." When *sattva* predominates, consciousness is calm, clear, comprehensible, virtuous; dominated by *rajas,* it is agitated, uncertain, unstable; overwhelmed by *tamas,* it is dark, confused, passionate, bestial. But of course this subjective and human evaluation of the three cosmic modalities does not contradict their objective character—"outer" and "inner" being no more than verbal expressions.

With this physiological foundation, we can understand why Sāṃkhya-Yoga regarded all psychic experience as a simple "material" process. Ethics is affected—purity, goodness, is not a quality of spirit but a "purification" of the "subtle matter" represented by consciousness. The *guṇas* impregnate the whole universe and establish an organic sympathy between man and the cosmos, these two entities being pervaded by the same pain of existence and both serving the same absolute Self, which is foreign to the world and driven on by an unintelligible destiny. In fact, the difference between the cosmos and man is only a difference of degree, not of essence.

By virtue of *pariṇāma,* matter has produced an infinity of forms (*vikāra*), increasingly complex, increasingly varied. Sāṃkhya holds that such an immense creation, such a complicated edifice of forms and organisms, demands a justification and a signification outside of itself. A primordial, formless, and eternal *prakṛti* can have a meaning. But the world as we see it is not a homogeneous substance; on the contrary, it exhibits a number of distinct forms and structures. The complexity of the cosmos, the infinity of its "forms," are raised by Sāṃkhya to the rank of metaphysical arguments. The "creation" is, without any doubt, the product of our metaphysical ignorance; the existence of the universe and the polymorphism of life are owing to man's false opinion of himself, to the fact that he confuses the true Self with psychomental states. But, as we remarked above, it is impossible to know the origin and the cause of this false opinion. What we know, what we see, is that *prakṛti* has an extremely complicated evolution and that it is not simple but composite.

Now, common sense tells us that every compound exists in view of another. Thus, for example, a bed is a whole composed of various parts, but this provisional collaboration between the parts is not ordained for itself, it is in view of man. Sāṃkhya thus brings out the teleological nature of creation; for if the mission of creation were not to serve Spirit, it would be absurd, meaningless. Everything in nature is composite; everything, then, must have a "superintendent" (*adhyakṣah*), someone who can make use of these compounds. This "superintendent" cannot be mental activity, nor states of consciousness (themselves extremely complex products of *prakṛti*). There must, then, be an entity that transcends the categories of Substance (*guṇa*) and that exists in view of itself. Yet more: there must be a subject to which mental activity is subordinated, toward which "pleasure and pain" are oriented. For, Vācaspatimiśra adds, pleasure cannot be felt and distinguished by pleasure; and if it were felt by pain, it would no longer be an agreeable experience, but a painful one. Thus the two qualities (pain and pleasure) cannot exist, cannot be distinguished, save as oriented toward a single subject that transcends experience.

This represents the first proof found by Sāṃkhya for the existence of spirit: *saṃhataparārthatvat puruṣasya*—that is, "knowledge of the existence of spirit by combination for the profit of another"—an axiom abundantly repeated in Indian literature and adopted by Yoga. Vācaspatimiśra adds: if anyone objects that the evolution and heterogeneity of Substance are intended to serve other "compounds" (as is the case, for example, with a chair, a "compound" created to serve another "compound," the human body), we can answer him that these "compounds" too must, in turn, exist for other "compounds" to use; the series of interdependences would inevitably lead us to a *regressus ad infinitum*. "And since we can avoid this *regressus*," Vācaspatimiśra continues, "by postulating the existence of a rational Principle, it is obviously stupid to go on needlessly multiplying the series of relations between compounds." In accordance with this postulate, Spirit, the Self, is a simple and irreducible principle, autonomous, static, nonproductive, not implicated in mental or sensory activity, etc.

Although the Self (*puruṣa*) is veiled by the illusions and confusions of cosmic creation, *prakṛti* is dynamized by the "teleological instinct" that is wholly intent upon the "liberation" of *puruṣa*. Let us recall that "from Brahman down to the blade of grass, the creation is for the benefit of soul, until supreme knowledge is attained."

## The Relation Spirit-Nature

If the Sāṃkhya-Yoga philosophy explains neither the cause nor the origin of the strange association established between Spirit and experience, it nevertheless attempts to explain the nature of their association, to define the character of their mutual relations. They are not *real* relations, in the strict sense of the word—relations such as exist, for example, between external objects and perceptions. Real relations, of course, imply change and plurality;

now, these are modalities essentially opposed to the nature of Spirit.

"States of consciousness" are only products of *prakṛti* and can have no kind of relation with Spirit—the latter, by its very essence, being above all experience. However—and for Sāmkhya and Yoga this is the key to the paradoxical situation—the most subtle, most transparent part of mental life, that is, intelligence (*buddhi*) in its mode of pure luminosity (*sattva*), has a specific quality—that of reflecting Spirit. Comprehension of the external world is possible only by virtue of this reflection of *puruṣa* in intelligence. But the Self is not corrupted by this reflection and does not lose its ontological modalities (impassibility, eternity, etc.). The *Yoga-sūtras* (II, 20) say in substance: seeing (*draṣṭṛ*; i.e., *puruṣa*) is absolute consciousness ("sight par excellence") and, while remaining pure, it knows cognitions (it "looks at the ideas that are presented to it"). Vyāsa interprets: Spirit is reflected in intelligence (*buddhi*), but is neither like it nor different from it. It is not like intelligence because intelligence is modified by knowledge of objects, which knowledge is ever-changing—whereas *puruṣa* commands uninterrupted knowledge, in some sort it *is* knowledge. On the other hand, *puruṣa* is not completely different from *buddhi,* for, although it is pure, it knows knowledge. Patañjali employs a different image to define the relationship between Spirit and intelligence: just as a flower is reflected in a crystal, intelligence reflects *puruṣa.* But only ignorance can attribute to the crystal the qualities of the flower (form, dimensions, colors). When the object (the flower) moves, its image moves in the crystal, though the latter remains motionless. It is an illusion to believe that Spirit is dynamic because mental experience is so. In reality, there is here only an illusory relation (*upādhi*) owing to a "sympathetic correspondence" (*yogyatā*) between the Self and intelligence.

From all eternity, Spirit has found itself drawn into this illusory relation with psychomental life (that is, with "matter"). This is owing to ignorance (*avidyā*), and as long as *avidyā* persists, existence is present (by virtue of *karma*), and with it suffering. Let us dwell on this point a little. Illusion or ignorance consists in confusing the motionless and eternal *puruṣa* with the flux of psychomental life. To say "I suffer," "I want," "I hate," "I know," and to think that this "I" refers to Spirit, is to live in illusion and prolong it; for all our acts and intentions, by the simple fact that they are dependent upon *prakṛti,* upon "matter," are conditioned and governed by *karma.* This means that every action whose point of departure is illusion (that is, which is based on *ignorance,* the confusion between Spirit and non-Spirit) is either the consummation of a virtuality created by a preceding act or the projection of another force that in turn demands its actualization, its consummation, in the present existence or in an existence to come. When one sets up the equation, "I want" = "Spirit wants," either a certain force is set in motion or another force has been fertilized. For the confusion that this equation expresses is a "moment" in the eternal circuit of cosmic energies.

This is the law of existence; like every law, it is transsubjective, but its validity and universality are at the origin of the suffering by which existence is troubled. There is but one way to gain salvation—adequate knowledge of Spirit. Sāṃkhya only prolongs the tradition of the Upaniṣads: "He who knows the *ātman* crosses over [the ocean of suffering]." "Through knowledge, liberation; through ignorance, bondage." And the first stage of the conquest of this "knowledge" consists of one thing, in denying that Spirit has attributes—which is equivalent to denying suffering as something that concerns us, to regarding it as an objective fact, outside of Spirit, that is to say, *without value* and *without meaning* (since all "values" and all "meanings" are created by intelligence in so far as it reflects *puruṣa*). Pain exists only to the extent to which experience is referred to the human personality regarded as identical with *puruṣa,* with the Self. But since this relation is illusory, it can easily be abolished. When *puruṣa* is known, *values* are annulled; pain is no longer either pain or nonpain, but a simple *fact*; a fact that, while it preserves its sensory structure, loses its value, its meaning. This point should be thoroughly understood, for it is of capital importance in Sāṃkhya and Yoga and, in our opinion, has not been sufficiently emphasized. In order to deliver us from suffering, Sāṃkhya and Yoga *deny suffering as such,* thus doing away with all relation between suffering and the Self. From the moment we understand that the Self is free, eternal, and inactive, whatever happens to us—sufferings, feelings, volitions, thoughts, and so on—*no longer belongs to us.* All such things constitute a body of cosmic facts, which are conditioned by laws, and are certainly real, but whose reality has nothing in common with our *puruṣa.* Suffering is a cosmic fact, and man undergoes that fact, or contributes to its perpetuation, solely in so far as he allows himself to be seduced by an illusion.

Knowledge is a simple "awakening" that unveils the essence of the Self, of Spirit. Knowledge does not "produce" anything; it reveals reality immediately. This true and absolute knowledge —which must not be confused with intellectual activity, which is psychological in essence—is not obtained by experience but by a revelation. Nothing divine plays a part here, for Sāṃkhya denies the existence of God; Yoga accepts God, but we shall see that Patañjali does not accord him very much importance. The revelation is based on knowledge of the ultimate reality—that is, on an "awakening" in which object completely identifies itself with subject. (The "Self" "contemplates" itself; it does not "think" itself, for thought is itself an experience and, as such, belongs to *prakṛti.*)

For Sāṃkhya, there is no other way than this. Hope prolongs and even aggravates human misery; only he who has lost all hope is happy, "for hope is the greatest torture that exists, and despair the greatest happiness." Religious rites and practices have no value whatever, because they are founded on desires and cruelties. Every ritual act, by the very fact that it implies an effort, engenders a new karmic force. Morality itself leads to nothing decisive. Indifference (*vairāgya* = renunciation), orthodoxy (*śruti*), and meditation are only indirect instruments of salvation. For Sāṃkhya the only perfect and definitive means is metaphysical knowledge.

The cognitive process is naturally realized by the intellect; but intellect itself is a highly evolved form of "matter." How, then, can deliverance (*mukti*) be accomplished through the collaboration of *prakṛti*? Sāṃkhya answers with the teleological argument: matter (*prakṛti*) instinctively acts in view of the enfranchisement of the soul (*puruṣa*). Intellect (*buddhi*), being the most perfect manifestation of *prakṛti,* is able, because of its dynamic possibilities, to aid the process of deliverance by serving as the preliminary stage of revelation. Yoga takes exactly the same position: *prakṛti* makes experience possible and, at the same time, pursues the liberation of the Self. Commenting on this *sūtra,* Vyāsa adds an important detail; bondage, he says, is in fact only the situation of intelligence (*buddhi*) when the ultimate aim of the Self has not yet been attained, and liberation is only the state in which that end has been accomplished.

In the next chapter we shall see by what psychophysiological techniques one can, according to Yoga, attain this end. For Sāṃkhya, liberation is obtained almost automatically when intelligence (*buddhi*) leads man to the threshold of "awakening." As soon as this self-revelation is realized, intellect and all the other psychomental (hence material) elements that are wrongly attributed to *puruṣa* withdraw, detach themselves from Spirit, to be reabsorbed into *prakṛti,* like a "dancer who departs after having satisfied her master's desire." "Nothing is more sensitive than *prakṛti*; as soon as it has said to itself, 'I am recognized,' it no longer shows itself before the eyes of the Spirit." This is the state of the man who is "liberated in this life" (*jīvan-mukta*): the sage still lives, because his karmic residue remains to be consumed (just as the potter's wheel continues to turn from the velocity it has acquired, even though the pot is finished). But when, at the moment of death, he abandons the body, the *puruṣa* is completely "liberated."

## How Is Liberation Possible?

Sāṃkhya-Yoga has, then, understood that "Spirit [*puruṣa*] can be neither born nor destroyed, is neither bound nor active [actively seeking deliverance], neither thirsts for freedom nor is liberated." "Its mode is such that these two possibilities are excluded." The Self is pure, eternal, free; it cannot be bound because it cannot enter into relations with anything but itself. But man *believes* that *puruṣa* is bound and *thinks* that it can be liberated. These are illusions of our psychomental life. For, in fact, "bound" Spirit is free for all eternity. If its liberation seems to us a drama, it is because we place ourselves at a human point of view; Spirit is only spectator (*sākṣin*), just as liberation (*mukti*) is only a *becoming conscious* of its eternal freedom. *I* believe that I suffer, *I* believe that I am bound, *I* desire liberation. At the moment when—having "awakened"—I understand that this "I" (*asmitā*) is a product of matter (*prakṛti*), I at the same time understand that all existence has been only a chain of moments of suffering and that true Spirit "impassively contemplated" the drama of "personality." Thus, human personality does not exist as a final element; it is only a synthesis of psychomental experiences, and it is destroyed—in other words, ceases to act—as soon as revelation is an accomplished fact. Like all creations of the cosmic substance (*prakṛti*), the human personality (*asmitā*) also acted to bring about "awakening"; hence, once liberation is achieved, the personality is of no further use.

There is something of paradox in the way in which Sāṃkhya and Yoga conceive the situation of Spirit (*puruṣa*); though pure, eternal, and intangible, Spirit nevertheless consents to be associated, if only in an illusory manner, with matter; and, in order to acquire knowledge of its own mode of being and "liberate" itself, it is even obliged to make use of an instrument created by *prakṛti* (in this case, intelligence). Doubtless, if we view things in this way, human existence appears to be dramatic and even meaningless. If Spirit is free, why are men condemned to suffer in ignorance or to struggle for a freedom they already possess? If *puruṣa* is perfectly pure and static, why does it permit impurity, becoming, experience, pain, and history? Such questions could easily be multiplied. But Indian philosophy reminds us that we must not judge the Self from a logical or historical point of view—that is, by seeking the causes that have determined the present state of things. Reality must be accepted as it is.

It is nevertheless true that Sāṃkhya's position on this point is difficult to maintain. Hence, in order to avoid this paradox of a Self absolutely devoid of contact with nature and yet, in its own despite, the author of the human drama, Buddhism has entirely done away with the "soul-spirit," understood as an irreducible spiritual unity, and has replaced it by "states of consciousness." Vedānta, on the contrary, seeking to avoid the difficulty of the relations between the soul and the universe, denies the reality of the universe and regards it as *māyā,* illusion. Sāṃkhya and Yoga have been unwilling to deny ontological reality either to Spirit or to Substance. Hence Sāṃkhya has been attacked, principally because of this doctrine, by both Vedānta and Buddhism.

Vedānta also criticizes the concept of the plurality of "selves" (*puruṣa*), as formulated by Sāṃkhya and Yoga. For these two *darśanas* affirm that there are as many *puruṣas* as there are human beings. And each of these *puruṣas* is a monad, is completely isolated; for the Self can have no contact either with the world around it (derived from *prakṛti*) or with other spirits. The cosmos, then, is peopled with these eternal, free, unmoving *puruṣas*—monads between which no communication is possible. According to Vedānta, this conception is erroneous and the plurality of "selves" is an illusion. In any case, this is a tragic and paradoxical conception of Spirit, which is thus cut off not only from the world of phenomena but also from other liberated "selves." Nevertheless, Sāṃkhya and Yoga were obliged to postulate the multiplicity of *puruṣas*; for if there were but one Spirit, salvation would have been an infinitely simpler problem, the first man who should attain liberation would necessarily bring about that of the entire human race. If there had been but one universal Spirit, the concomitant existence of "liberated spirits" and "bound spirits" would have been impossible. Nor indeed, in such a case, could death, life, difference of sex, diversity in action, etc., have coexisted. The paradox is obvious: this doctrine reduces the infinite variety of phenomena to a single principle, matter (*prakṛti*); it sees the physical universe, life, and consciousness as derived from a single matrix—and yet it postulates the plurality of spirits, although by their nature these are essentially identical. Thus it unites what would appear to be so different—the physical, the biotic, and the mental—and isolates what, especially in India, seems so unique and universal—Spirit.

Let us more closely examine the conception of liberation (*mokṣa*) in the doctrines of Sāṃkhya and Yoga. As it is for most Indian schools of philosophy—except, of course, those influenced by mystical devotion (*bhakti*)—so here, too, liberation is in fact a liberation from the *idea of evil and pain*. It is only a becoming conscious of a situation that was already in existence but over which ignorance had cast its veils. Suffering ceases of itself as soon as we understand that it is *exterior to Spirit,* that it concerns only the human "personality" (*asmitā*). For let us imagine the life of a "liberated" person. He will continue to act, because the potentialities of his earlier lives, and those of his own life before his "awakening," demand their actualization and consummation, in accordance with the karmic law. But this activity is no longer *his*; it is objective, mechanical, disinterested—in short, it is not performed in view of its "fruit." When the "liberated" man acts, he is not conscious of an "I act" but of an "it acts"; in other words, he does not draw the Self into a psychophysical process. Since the force of ignorance no longer acts, new karmic nucleuses are no longer created. When all these "potentialities" are destroyed, liberation is absolute, final. It could even be said that the "liberated" man does not "experience" liberation. After his "awakening" he acts with indifference, and when the last psychic molecule detaches itself from him, he realizes a mode of being unknown to mortals, because absolute—a sort of Buddhist *nirvāṇa.*

Nevertheless, the "freedom" that the Indian gains through metaphysical knowledge or Yoga is real and concrete. It is not true that India has sought liberation only negatively, for it wishes to attain a positive realization of freedom. In fact, the man "liberated in this life" can extend the sphere of his action as far as he wishes; he has nothing to fear, for his acts no longer have any *consequences* for him and, hence, no *limits*. Since nothing can any longer bind him, the "liberated" man is free to do as he will, in any realm of activity; for he who acts is no longer *he,* as "Self," but a mere impersonal instrument. We shall see in later chapters how far the "situation of mere witness" in a transpersonal existence has been carried.

To us, Sāṃkhya's soteriological conception seems audacious. Starting from the original datum of every Indian philosophy, *suffering,* Sāṃkhya and Yoga, through promising to deliver *man* from suffering, are forced, at the end of their journey, to deny suffering as such, *human suffering.* Considered from the point of view of salvation, this road leads nowhere, since it starts from the axiom that Spirit is absolutely free—that is, not sullied by suffering—and arrives at the same axiom—that is, that the Self is only illusorily drawn into the drama of existence. The only term that matters in this equation—suffering—is left out of account. Sāṃkhya does not *do away* with human suffering; it *denies it as reality* by denying that it can have any real relationship with the Self. Suffering remains, because it is a cosmic fact, but it loses its significance. Suffering is done away with by *ignoring it as suffering.* Certainly, this suppression of suffering is not empirical (narcotics, suicide), for, from the Indian point of view, every empirical solution is illusory, since it is itself a karmic force. But Sāṃkhya's solution drives man outside of humanity, for it can be realized only through the destruction of the human personality. The Yoga practices proposed by Patañjali have the same goal.

These soteriological solutions may appear "pessimistic" to Westerners, for whom personality remains, in the last analysis, the foundation of all morality and all mysticism. But, for India, what matters most is not so much the salvation of the *personality* as obtaining *absolute freedom.* (We shall see later that the deep meaning of this freedom leaves the most extreme Western formulations far behind; what the Indian actually wants is, in a certain sense, to abolish creation by reincorporating all forms in the primordial Unity.) Once it is granted that this freedom cannot be gained in our present human condition and that personality is the vehicle of suffering and drama, it becomes clear that what must be sacrificed is the human condition and the "personality." And this sacrifice is lavishly compensated for by the conquest of absolute freedom, which it makes possible.

It could, obviously, be objected that the sacrifice demanded is too great for its fruits to be of any interest. For, after all, is not the human condition, whose suppression is demanded, man's sole patent of nobility? Sāṃkhya and Yoga answer this probable objection of the Westerner in advance when they affirm: as long as man has not risen above the level of psychomental life, he cannot but misjudge the transcendental "states" that will be the reward for the disappearance of normal consciousness; every value judgment in regard to these "states" is automatically invalidated by the mere fact that he who pronounces it is defined by his own condition, which is of an entirely different order from the condition upon which the value judgment is thought to bear.

# Vedanta

*Paul Deussen*

## Introduction

The fundamental idea of the Vedānta system, as most tersely expressed in the words of the Veda, "That art thou" (*tat tvam asi*), and "I am Brahman" (*aham brahma asmi*), is the identity of Brahman and the soul. This means that Brahman, that is, the eternal principle of all being, the power which creates all worlds, sustains them and again absorbs them, is identical with the Ātman, the self, or the soul; namely, with that in us which, when we judge rightly, we acknowledge as our own self, as our inner

Reprinted from Paul Deussen, *Outline of the Vedanta System of Philosophy According to Shankara*, translated by J. Woods and C. B. Runkle (Harvard University Press, 1906), pages 1–45.

and true essence. This soul in each one of us is not a part of Brahman nor an emanation from him, but it is, fully and entirely, the eternal indivisible Brahman itself.

2. This assertion contradicts experience, which presents not any such unity, but rather a multiplicity, a complex of names and forms, and as a part of these, our Self, incorporated in our body which has come into being and must in time be disintegrated.

3. No less the fundamental assumption of the Vedānta system contradicts the canon of the Vedic ritual: this indeed assumes a survival of the self beyond the body; but it also presupposes a multiplicity of individual souls discrete from Brahman. These souls, engaged in an endless round-of-rebirth, enter one body after another, the deeds done in each life necessarily determining the succeeding life and its quality.

4. Experience, as it is the result of our perceptive and cognitive faculties, and the Vedic ritual as well, with its commands and prohibitions, its promises and threats, both rest on a false cognition, an innate illusion, called *avidyā* or ignorance, the assertions of which, like apparitions in a dream, are true only till one awakes. On closer inquiry this innate *avidyā* is found to consist in the fact that the *ātman,* that is, the soul, the self, is not able to distinguish itself from the *upādhis* or limiting conditions with which it is invested. These limiting conditions include the body, the physical organs, and the deeds; and only a part of them, namely, the body, is destroyed at death, the rest accompanying the soul in its transmigrations. The converse of this *avidyā* is knowledge (*vidyā*), also called right cognition or universal cognition, by virtue of which the *ātman* distinguishes himself from the *upādhis,* and recognizes that the latter, resting on *avidyā,* are mere illusion or erroneous assumption, whereas he himself is identical with the one and only one, the all-embracing Brahman.

5. Universal cognition cannot be attained by means of worldly perceptive and cognitive faculties, nor can it be enjoined as a

duty by the canonical ordinances of the Veda, because both of these have their origin in *avidyā* and cannot lead beyond it.

The sole source of *vidyā* is rather revelation, *çruti* (or Scripture, as we not very appropriately translate it). By *çruti* is meant the Veda, both its "Work-section and Knowledge-section," the latter including several chapters scattered through the Mantras and Brāhmaṇas, and especially the concluding chapters of the Brāhmaṇas called the Veda-end (*Veda-anta,* that is, *Vedānta*) or Upanishads. The entire Veda, including both Work-section and Knowledge-section, the whole body of the Mantras (hymns and sacrificial formulas), the Brāhmaṇas (theological expositions), and the Upanishads, is of divine origin. It was "breathed forth" by Brahman, and only "seen" by the human authors, the inspired sages or Rishis. The world, including the gods, passes away, but the Veda is eternal; it survives the destruction of the universe and continues to exist in the soul of Brahman. In accordance with the word of the Veda which contains the eternal archetypes of all things, gods, men, animals, and so forth, are created anew by Brahman at the beginning of each world-cycle. The Veda is then revealed to them by the breath of Brahman. The Work-section is revealed as a code of conduct having happiness as its object; the Knowledge-section, as the source of right cognition, the one and only fruit of which is blessedness, that is, emancipation. Not by reflection is right cognition to be attained, nor yet through tradition or *smṛti*. Both reflection and tradition can only in a secondary sense be considered the source of truth, namely, in so far as, being based on the Veda, they attempt to interpret and supplement its revelation.

## Theology

6. The supreme aim of human beings is emancipation, that is, the cessation of the soul's transmigrations; but this emancipation of the soul from its transmigrations is brought about by the recognition of the individual self, as identical with the highest Self, namely, Brahman. The entire content of *vidyā* is, conse-

quently, knowledge of the *Ātman* or *Brahman,* for the two concepts are interchangeable.

There are, however, two kinds of knowledge in reference to Brahman, the higher and the lower knowledge. The higher knowledge has for its object right cognition, and its one and only fruit is emancipation; the lower knowledge does not aim at knowledge of Brahman, but at his worship, and has as its fruit, according to the grade of worship, success in undertakings, happiness, and finally progressive emancipation. The object of the higher knowledge is the higher Brahman; of the lower knowledge, the lower Brahman.

7. The Veda, then, distinguishes two forms of Brahman: the higher, attributeless Brahman; and the lower Brahman, possessing attributes. As to the former, the Veda teaches that Brahman is devoid of all attributes, distinctions, forms, and limiting conditions. To the latter, for purposes of worship, it ascribes various attributes, distinctions, forms, and conditions.

8. One and the same object cannot be with and without attributes, with and without form in itself. Brahman is without attributes, form, difference, and limitation, but becomes the lower Brahman when ignorance imposes on it, for the purpose of worship, the limiting conditions or *upādhis*. The imposition on Brahman of *upādhis* is only an illusion, just as it is an illusion to look upon a crystal as red when it reflects a red colour. As the transparency of the crystal is not affected by the red colour, so the essence of Brahman is not changed by the limiting conditions imposed upon it by *avidyā*.

9. The higher Brahman is, in essence, without attributes, formless, devoid of distinctions, and unconditioned. It is "not gross and not subtile, not short and not long," and so forth; "not to be heard, not to be touched, formless, imperishable"; it is "not so and not so," that is, no form and no representation can express its essence. It is therefore "different from that which we know and from that which we do not know"; words and thoughts turn back from it without finding it; and Bāhva, the sage, answered the question regarding its essence by silence.

10. The only thing that can be predicated of the attributeless Brahman is that it is not non-existent. It is therefore The Existent (*Sat*); but from the empirical point of view Brahman is rather the Non-Existent. The Scriptures still further define the essence of Brahman by declaring that, as a lump of salt has the taste of salt throughout, so Brahman is throughout pure intelligence. In these assertions, two attributes are not ascribed to Brahman, since both are identical; for the essence of being consists in intelligence; that of intelligence, in being. Bliss (*ānanda*) is occasionally acknowledged as a predicate of the attributeless Brahman, but it is not mentioned in the discussion of its essence, perhaps because it is considered a merely negative quality, that is, as freedom from pain. Of Brahman alone can freedom from pain be predicated; for the Scripture saith, "All that is different from Brahman,—*that* is subject to pain."

11. The impossibility of cognizing the attributeless Brahman rests on the fact that Brahman is the inner Self in everything that exists. As such it is more certain than anything else and cannot be denied by any one; but, on the other hand, it is impossible to cognize it, because in every act of cognition it is the knowing subject and therefore never an object. Brahman is, however, perceived by the sage in the state of *saṁrādhana,* complete satisfaction, which consists in the withdrawing the organs of sense from everything external, and in concentrating them upon one's own inner nature. In the consciousness that our inner Self is the attributeless Brahman, and in the accompanying conviction of the non-reality of the whole complex of names and forms, lies emancipation.

12. The higher Brahman is converted into the lower Brahman by imposing upon it pure or unsurpassable determinations. The lower Brahman is to be understood in all passages where the Scriptures ascribe any sort of determination, attribute, form, or distinguishing feature to Brahman. This is done not for the sake of cognition, but for purposes of worship, and the fruit of this worship, as well as that of works which belong to the same category, is not emancipation, but happiness, chiefly in heaven,

but nevertheless limited to the round-of-rebirths or *saṁsāra*. Heavenly glory, however, attained after death by way of the Path of the Gods, through worship of the lower Brahman, leads to full cognition and hence to complete emancipation. This is called progressive emancipation. Complete emancipation is not its immediate result, since the worshippers of the lower Brahman have not yet wholly burnt away their ignorance. For it is ignorance which determines the higher Brahman and thereby converts it into the lower Brahman. The nature of Brahman is as little changed by being thus determined (to use again the oft-cited simile) as the clearness of the crystal is affected by the colour by which it is tinged, or the sun by its reflections moving on the surface of a body of water, or space by bodies burnt in it or moving in it.

The elaborately developed conceptions of the lower Brahman may be divided into three groups according as it is conceived pantheistically as world-soul, psychologically as principle of the individual soul, or theistically as a personal God.

13. Several of the most important of the passages that constitute the first group may here be mentioned. At ChU. iii. 14, Brahman is called "all-effecting, all-wishing, all-smelling, all-tasting (that is, the principle of all action and sensuous perception), embracing the universe, silent, unperturbed."[1] Again, the moon and sun are called its eyes, the four quarters of the sky

[1] "Verily this universe is Brahman; in silence one should think it as beginning, ending, and breathing in him (the Brahman). Now man is formed out of will. According to what his will is in this world, so he will be when he has departed; let him then seek (the good) will. Spirit is his substance, life is his body, light is his form, his thoughts are truth, his self is infinity. All-effecting, all-wishing, all-smelling, all-tasting, embracing the universe, silent, unperturbed—this is myself in the inner heart, smaller than a kernel of rice, smaller than a grain of barley, smaller than a mustard seed, smaller than a grain of millet, even than a husked grain of millet—this is myself in the inner heart, greater than the earth, greater than the sky, greater than heaven, greater than all these worlds. The all-effecting, all-wishing, all-smelling, all-tasting, embracing the universe, silent, unperturbed—this is myself in the inner heart, this is the Brahman. When I shall depart from here I shall enter into it. He who knows this has no doubt. Thus spake Çāṇḍilya; thus spake Çāṇḍilya." This is the well-known doctrine of Çāṇḍilya in the Chāndogya-Upanishad, iii. 14.

its ears, the wind its breath, and so forth. To this class, also, belong such passages as represent Brahman as the source of all light; as the light beyond the heavens and in the heart; as the ether from which all creatures proceed, and which differentiates names and forms; as the vital principle from which all creatures spring, and in which the entire world moves trembling; as the inward ruler; as the principle of the world-order, the bridge which keeps these worlds asunder so that they are not confounded; and as the power by which sun and moon, heaven and earth, minutes, hours, years, and days remain discrete; finally as the world-destroyer who reabsorbs all created things.

14. Frequently contrasted with the vast spatial extent which the preceding conceptions suggest are the minute dimensions attributed to Brahman as psychical principle. As such it abides in the citadel of the body; in the lotus of the heart; as a dwarf; as tall as a single span; or an inch; smaller than a grain of millet; as big as the point of an awl; as vital principle; as spectator; also as the man in the eye. Illustrations of this sort might be multiplied.

15. These conceptions of the conditioned Brahman culminate in the conception of him as Īsvara, that is, as a personal God. In the Upanishads we find this view comparatively seldom and less fully developed, but in the Vedānta system it plays an important part. On Īsvara's consent depends the round-of-rebirths, and on his grace depends that true knowledge which brings emancipation. Just as rain develops each plant from seed, each after its own kind, so Īsvara, guided by the deeds done in the previous existence, and making the conditions of the new life to proceed from these deeds, decrees to souls both what they are to do and what they are to experience. It must be borne in mind, however, that the personification of Brahman as Īsvara, as Ruler, in contrast to the world over which he is to rule, is confined to the empirical point of view. This view, based on ignorance, has in the strict sense no reality.

## Cosmology

16. The duality of teachings in theology, and, as we shall see, in eschatology, corresponds to two different points of view, one view in the province of cosmology, and the other in that of psychology. The first of these, the empirical point of view,[2] teaches the creation of the world by Brahman and the transmigration of souls invested with the *upādhis* and thus made individual. The second, the metaphysical point of view,[3] maintains the identity of the soul and Brahman, denies all manifoldness, and in so doing denies not only the creation and existence of the world, but also individuality and transmigration of souls. Greatly to the detriment of clearness and consistency, this distinction is not everywhere strictly observed in the cosmology and in the psychology. The system is, in general, treated from the metaphysical point of view to the neglect of the empirical, without, however, denying, or being able to deny, to the latter its relative justification, since it is the necessary postulate of the *aparā vidyā* of the eschatology. In consequence of this, the creation of the world is treated at length and in very realistic fashion in the cosmology; but we are nevertheless constantly meeting with the assertion that this teaching of the Scriptures in regard to the creation is merely intended to enforce the doctrine of the Brahmanhood of the world, and that for this reason only has the conception of causality been substituted for that of identity. In the psychology, the metaphysical doctrine of the identity of Brahman and the world is maintained throughout, and is defended against the opposite empirical point of view presupposed in eschatology. At times, however, the metaphysical doctrine gives way before the empirical, as, for instance, in maintaining the coming into being of souls. Since, however, the arguments of the empirical point of view apply to a part of the exposition only, a clear presentation of the empirical psychology is lacking. Nevertheless, we may get a correct idea of this side of the system from the consideration of incidental and scattered remarks.

---

[2] Literally, point of view of practical life.

[3] Literally, point of view of highest reality.

17. The consistency of the system requires that the higher knowledge in theology and eschatology, together with the metaphysical point of view in cosmology and psychology, should make one inseparable metaphysical system. Also it requires that the lower knowledge of the theology and eschatology should unite with the empirical point of view of the cosmology and psychology to form a general presentation of metaphysics as it appears from the empirical point of view of *avidyā* (that is, realism), and that this empirical metaphysics should constitute a system of popular religion for the use of all those who cannot rise to the point of view of identity. Above all, it is plain that only the lower and not the higher Brahman can be conceived as the creator of the universe, chiefly because, for creation, as is repeatedly asserted, a multiplicity of faculties is needed. Such a multiplicity, however, is predicated only of the lower Brahman. And, indeed, the passage which enumerates such a multiplicity of creative faculties, "he is all-effecting, all-wishing, all-smelling, all-tasting," is by preference cited as a proof-text in favour of the doctrine of the lower Brahman.

18. According to the Upanishads, Brahman creates the world, and then enters it through the individual soul. There is no mention either of the existence of the individual soul before the creation of the world, or of a creation periodically repeated. In this conception, the germs of the empirical and of the metaphysical doctrines of the Vedānta system lie side by side as yet undeveloped. The metaphysical element is the identity of the soul and Brahman; the empirical element, the unfolding of the world of sense. In the Vedānta system these two doctrines are entirely separate. On the metaphysical side we have identity of the soul and Brahman, but no beginning nor persistence nor dissolution of the world. On the empirical side we have a creation of the universe, but no identity of Brahman and the soul; for the individual soul, with the *upādhis* which make it individual, exists from eternity, and transmigrates, except in case of emancipation, from one body to another for all eternity. The doctrine of the

creation of the universe is, however, transformed into a periodical and alternating unfolding of the world from Brahman and reabsorption of the same into Brahman, each cycle repeating itself not once, but countless times through all eternity.

The Souls, as well as the elements, at the reabsorption of the world into Brahman exist potentially as germs in latent power, and at each new creation come forth from him unchanged. In this new conception the original meaning of the doctrine of creation is entirely abandoned, but in the form just indicated the dogma is retained because the Veda teaches it. In the Vedānta system itself there is no motive for a creation of the universe, but rather for its existence from eternity; instead of this, in accordance with the authority of the Scriptures, we find a periodic creation and reabsorption, a cycle which must repeat itself without ceasing and without changing the stability of the universe. For the system demands the eternal existence of the world,—an existence depending, as we shall see, on a moral necessity.

19. The leading idea of the empirical cosmology and psychology is the existence from eternity of the round-of-rebirths. Without beginning there has existed, separately from Brahman, a multiplicity of individual souls. These souls are distinguished from Brahman, with whom metaphysically they are identical, by the *upādhis* in which they are enveloped. Among these *upādhis,* which together with the deeds adhere to the soul, must be counted the psychical organs of the subtile body which supports them, and also, occasionally, in a wider sense, the gross body and the external objects. Only the gross body is destroyed in death; the subtile body, with the psychical organs, has existed as the investment of the soul from eternity, and accompanies it in all its transmigrations. The transmigrating soul is also accompanied by the deeds, ritual and moral, which it has done during life, and these prevent the round-of-rebirths from coming to an end; for every deed, good as well as bad, demands in compensation reward or punishment, and this not only in another world, but in the form of a subsequent earthly existence. Without deeds

no human life is possible; hence no life is possible which is not followed by another as its atonement. Very good deeds produce existence as a god; very bad deeds produce existence as an animal or plant. Even if in this life the soul should not act at all, it would not thereby be preserved from subsequent rebirths, since deeds of remarkable goodness or badness demand several successive births as an atonement. This is the reason why the round-of-rebirths extends through all spheres of existence, from the gods down to plants, without beginning, and, unless the latent power of deeds is consumed by knowledge, also without end.

20. The unfolding of the perceptible world is, in its essence, nothing more than the fruit of deeds imposed upon the soul. The world is, as the common formula runs, "retribution of the deed visited upon the doer," it is "that which is to be enjoyed" (*bhogya*); whereas the soul in it is "the enjoyer" (*bhoktar*), and "the doer" (*kartar*), both of them corresponding necessarily and exactly to its "condition of being a doer," that is, to its *katṛtva* or to its activity in the previous existence. The connecting link between the deeds and their fruit—the latter comprising action and suffering in the subsequent existence—is not an invisible power or *adṛṣṭa* of deeds, reaching beyond existence, or at least not that alone; but it is rather the *Īsvara,* a personification of Brahman valid only for the empirical point of view, who retributes action and suffering to the soul in the new birth, according to the deeds done in the previous existence.

The recreation of the world after its absorption into Brahman depends each time upon the same necessity as the succession of rebirths. For souls, although absorbed into Brahman, still persist, together with their deeds, in a latent state as germs, and the latter demand for their atonement the repeated creation of the universe, that is, the unfolding of the elements from Brahman. We will now consider this process in detail.

21. At the time of creation, *sṛṣṭi,* which, according to the meaning of this word, must be conceived as an "outpouring" or emanation, the *ākāça* (the ether, or more correctly, the all-penetrating visible space conceived as a very subtile matter) comes

forth from Brahman first. From the ether comes wind; from wind comes fire; from fire comes water; from water comes earth. In this process the subsequent element is brought forth each time, not by means of the elements themselves, but by Brahman in the form of the elements. In reverse order, at the dissolution of the world earth merges into water, water into fire, fire into wind, wind into ether, ether into Brahman.

The ether is perceived through the sense of hearing; wind, through hearing and touch; fire, through hearing and touch and sight; water, through hearing and touch, sight and taste; and earth, through hearing and touch and sight and taste and smell. The elements, however, as they occur, are not the pure original elements, but a mixture of them, each with a preponderance of one or the other.

22. After Brahman has created the elements, he enters into them, according to the Upanishads, by means of individual souls; that is, according to the system which we are here considering, the transmigrating souls, which even after the dissolution of the world have persisted potentially, awake from this "deep sleep" which is part of the illusion of empirical reality, and receive, in accordance with their deeds in the previous existence, the body of a god or a human being or an animal or a plant. The process is as follows: the seed of the elements which souls carry with them in their transmigrations, in the form of the subtile body, grows through the accretion of similar particles proceeding from the gross elements to the gross body; at the same time the psychical organs, which were all implicated during the transmigration, unfold themselves.

The body is "the complex of organs of activity built up of names and forms"; it is, then, a complex of elements; the soul is the lord (*svāmin*) of this complex. The growth of the body arises from the elements of which three parts, gross, middle, and subtile, are distinguished. In correspondence with this tripartite division, faeces and flesh and *manas* come from the earth; urine and blood and *prāṇa* come from water; bones and marrow and speech come from fire. Since, however, according to this system, the soul has already brought its psychical organs with it, and among them, *manas* and *prāṇa* and speech, we must either admit an inconsistency, or else assume that the growing *manas* and *prāṇa* and speech bear the same relation to the innate psychical organs of like name that the gross body does to the subtile one. The evolution of these substances from nourishment is made possible by the fact that each body contains all the original elements of nature.

According to their origin, organisms are divided into those sprung from germs (plants), those sprung from moisture (insects), those born from an egg, and those born alive. Procreation takes place as follows: the soul of the child entering the father through the medium of nourishment remains in him only as a guest, and passing over through the medium of sperma to the body of the mother, develops, by the aid of her blood, the subtile body into the gross body. Death is the separation of the soul, together with its organs and with the subtile body, from the gross body; the organism is destroyed, and the soul proceeds on its further migration. The length of life is not a matter of chance, but is exactly predetermined by the quantity of deeds to be expiated, just as the nature of the life is predetermined by their quality. However, there are deeds which cannot be expiated in one life, but only by a series of births. Only such deeds, for instance, explain why a soul does not stop migrating when it enters a plant. Since each plant is an incarnated soul, and each incarnation serves the purpose of an expiation, the system proceeds logically in attributing sensation to plants also.

Although the life of the souls of plants and of animals and of human beings is of short duration, those souls which, by reason of superior achievements in a previous existence, have been born as gods are deathless, that is, they persist until the next dissolution of the world. Then they too revert to the round-of-rebirth, and the places of Indra and others may next time be filled by other souls.[4]

---

[4] The gods are mortal. The Vedas are eternal. The Vedas speak of the gods. Why then are not the gods eternal? The words of the Vedas are eternal; but the objects to which they refer are not the individual, but the species. The word

23. As all clay vessels are in reality clay, and as the conversion of clay into vessels, "depending on words only," is "but a name," so the whole universe is in fact only Brahman, and apart from Brahman has no existence; there is nothing separate from Brahman.

Here our system goes further than the Veda. The whole unfolding of names and forms, the whole complex of phenomena, when we regard it from the point of view of ultimate reality, is created, maintained, and imposed upon the soul by ignorance, springs from false cognition, and is mere false supposition which is to be disproved by complete cognition; just as the illusion that a rope is a snake, or that the trunk of a tree is a man, or that a mirage is an expanse of water, is disproved on closer examination and disappears. The whole world is only an illusion which Brahman as magician evolves from himself, and by which he is no more affected than is the magician by the illusion which he has produced. To use a variation of this simile, Brahman is made to appear multiplex by ignorance just as is the magician by his magic. Brahman is the cause of the persistence of the world just as the magician is the cause of the illusion which he produces; and he is the cause of the reabsorption of the world into himself just as, in similar fashion, the earth absorbs creatures into itself.

The variety of action during the persistence of the world, and the variety of potential existence before and after the world's phenomenal appearance, both rest on ignorance or false cognition. The conception of *avidyā* or *mithyā jñāna* bars the way to all further investigation. We cannot answer the question which is innate in all of us, the question, Whence arises this ignorance? The deepest explanation lies perhaps in the oft-recurring simile of a man who, through defective vision, sees two moons when in fact there is but one. In general, the non-existence of the universe is a relative non-existence only. The multiplex of phe-

---

"Indra" refers not to the individual, but to a particular position (*sthāna*). Whoever holds this position bears the name. The distinction is between the individual, the manifestation (*vyakti*), and the species, the form (*ākriti*). These species, like Plato's εἱδος, become powers (*çakti,* δύναμις). From them the worlds are recreated after a world-dissolution.

nomena, the universe of names and forms, the illusion (*māyā*), cannot be said to be the same as Brahman (*tat*), nor yet to be different (*anya*) from him. Like visions in a dream, the names and forms are true (*satya*) so long only as the dream lasts, and no longer true when the sleep comes to an end.

This idealism which we see first appearing in the Upanishads, the Vedānta tries to bring into agreement with the Vedic doctrine of creation, by maintaining that creation signifies only the identity of the universe and of Brahman; that the world is the effect and that Brahman is the cause, but that cause and effect are identical,—a thesis for the proof of which the persistence of substance in changes of its qualities serves as chief argument.

## Psychology

24. Although we are persuaded that all the complex of phenomena spread before us, all names and forms of which the world is composed, are an illusion resting on ignorance, comparable to the illusion of a dream, still there is one point in the universe where this view is not applicable. This point is our own soul, our true self.[5] This self cannot be demonstrated because it is the presupposition of every demonstration; but also it cannot be disproved because even the denial implies an affirmation of it.[6]

What now is the nature of this sole basis of all certainty, of the soul, of our inner self? How is it related to Brahman who comprehends all existence in himself?

25. The soul cannot be different from Brahman because there

---

[5] Or *ātman*.

[6] "If the Self were a modification of something else, it would be a mere effect. But just because it is the Self, it is impossible for us to entertain the idea of its being capable of refutation. For the knowledge of the Self is not adventitious, not established by any so-called means of right knowledge; it is rather self-established. The Self, the abode of the power which acts through the means of right knowledge, is established previously to that knowledge. And to refute such a self-established entity is impossible. An adventitious thing may be refuted, but not that which is the essential nature (of him who attempts the refutation); for it is the essential nature of him who refutes. The heat of the fire is not sublated by the fire itself."

This form of the *Cogito ergo sum* is found in Shankara on Vedānta Sūtra, ii. 3.7.

is nothing existing beyond Brahman. It is not, however, to be considered as a transformation of Brahman, because Brahman is unchangeable. Neither is it a part of Brahman, since Brahman has no parts. There remains then only the assumption that the soul is identical with Brahman; that each one of us is himself the whole, indivisible, immutable, all-pervading Brahman.

26. From this it follows that everything established in regard to the nature of the higher Brahman applies also to the soul. As Brahman is in essence pure intelligence, so is the soul also; and to it apply equally all those negative predicates the object of which is to keep away from Brahman all determinations which could limit his being. According to this, the soul is, like Brahman, omnipresent, or, as we might say, superspatial, all-knowing and all-powerful, neither acting nor enjoying nor suffering.

27. If this is the true nature of the soul, it follows that everything which is at variance with this nature is merely "attributed" to the soul through ignorance. To such attributes or *upādhis,* which depend on false cognition only and which include all physical existence, the following facts are due. First, that the soul while in the state of *saṁsāra* is not all-pervasive and omnipresent, but dwells in the limited space of the *manas* within the heart. Second, that it is not all-knowing and all-powerful, since through the *upādhis* its original omniscience and omnipotence become latent, just as light and heat of the fire are latent in wood. Finally, that through its union with the *upādhis,* the soul becomes an actor and enjoyer; and by these latter qualities its entanglement in the *saṁsāra* is necessitated; for the deeds of one life must be requited by enjoyment and action in the next succeeding life. The action, again, which forms a part of that requital, requires in turn a new requital, and so on to infinity.

28. This round-of-rebirth (*saṁsāra*), without beginning and without end, rests wholly on the fact that the soul's true nature is hidden from it by the limiting conditions (*upādhis*) imposed upon it by ignorance (*avidyā*). Among these *upādhis,* which convert Brahman into the individual soul together with the activities and sensations of the soul, the gross body, together with

all the things and relations of the external world, is not included. The gross body is resolved at death into the elements. The *upādhis* consist of the following:

First, the *manas* and the *indriya*;
Second, the *mukhya prāṇa*;
Third, the *sūkṣma çarīra.*

To this permanent psychical equipment, with which the soul remains endowed from eternity and until emancipation, there is added a fourth variable element which we may call the moral qualification. We will now consider these *upādhis* in detail.

29. Though the gross body and its organs, the eye, ear, hands, feet, and so forth, perish with death, the functions of these organs, conceived as self-existent essences, remain bound up with the soul for all time. These are the *indriya,* the senses, which the soul puts forth as tentacles during life and at death draws back into itself. Upon these depend the two sides of conscious life, perception and action. Corresponding to these two sides, the soul has five perceptive faculties, seeing, hearing, smelling, tasting, and touch; and five faculties relating to action, grasping, moving, speaking, generating, and voiding. These ten *indriya,* which are usually denoted by the names of the corresponding organs of the gross body, are governed by a central organ, the *manas,* which transforms into representations the data supplied by the perceptive faculties and effects the accomplishment of volitions through the faculties of action. It consequently represents both what we call understanding and what we call conscious will. The *indriya* permeate the whole body, but the *manas* dwells, "having the size of an awl's point," in the heart; and in the *manas,* filling it entirely and in closest union, to be sundered only by emancipation, dwells the soul,—the soul which only through the organs to which it is bound by ignorance becomes actor and enjoyer, but itself stands aloof from all the activity of the organs as pure perception, a passive spectator, so that in spite of its being plunged into the activities of daily life, it remains in its real essence untouched.

30. Less closely than to the *manas* and the *indriya,* the soul seems to be attached to the *mukhya prāṇa,* a term, which in the Upanishads, still denotes "breath in the mouth"; whereas in the Vedānta system it has come to mean "the chief breath of life." As the *manas* and the *indriya* are functions of perception and action hypostasized as special entities, so the *mukhya prāṇa,* on which they all depend, is a hypostasis of the physical life itself which is regulated through this *mukhya prāṇa* in its five branches, *prāṇa, apāna, vyāna, samāna, udāna.* Of these, *prāṇa* regulates expiration; *apāna* inspiration. *Vyāna* is that which maintains life while breathing is momentarily suspended: *samāna* is the digestive principle, and just as these four cause the persistence of life, so *udāna* causes its end by leading the soul out of the body at death through one of the one hundred and one principal veins. Along with the soul the *manas, indriya* and *mukhya prāṇa* leave the body. As during life they are the forces which govern the organs of the body, so after the death of the body they are the germ from which at each new birth the organs of the body grow anew.

31. As the soul carries with it the germ of the physical organs in the *indriya,* so it carries the germ of the body itself in the *sūkṣma çarīra,* or, as it is described more explicitly by Shankara, "the subtile parts of the elements forming the germ of the body." How these subtile parts of the elements are related to the gross body is not more definitely determined. The subtile body composed of them possesses materiality, but also transparency; hence it is not seen in the soul's migration. From it is derived animal warmth. The coldness of the dead body arises from the fact that the subtile body has left it at the same time as the other organs, to accompany the soul in its transmigrations.

32. To the psychical organism which adheres to the soul at all times in life and in death, and which appears always unchangeable, there is attached further, escorting the soul in its migration, a variable *upādhi.* This is the moral qualification consisting in the store of deeds collected during life. Besides the physical substrate, that is, the subtile body, this goes out with

the soul as a moral substrate and absolutely conditions the future existence in enjoyment and suffering as well as in action.

33. There are four states of the migratory soul: waking, dreaming, a state of deep sleep, and death. In the waking state, the soul, which in union with the *manas* dwells in the heart, rules the whole body, perceiving and acting through the medium of the *manas* and the *indriya*. In dreaming, the *indriya* are at rest, but the *manas* still remains active, and the soul, surrounded by the *manas* and the *indriya* which have entered the *manas*, circulates by means of the veins in the body, and while doing so sees dream-pictures built up of waking impressions. In deep sleep the connection of the soul with the *manas* is broken; the *manas* and *indriya,* having come to rest, enter the veins or the pericardium, and thence enter the *mukhya prāṇa,* the activity of which continues even in deep sleep. The soul, thus temporarily freed from all these *upādhis,* enters by means of the ether of the heart into Brahman. Since, apart from the *upādhis,* the soul is Brahman, this entrance into Brahman is merely another expression of complete emancipation from the *upādhis*. On waking, the soul goes forth from this temporary identification with Brahman with all its individual limitations, exactly as it was before.

### Migration of the Soul

34. At death, the *indriya* first enter the *manas*; the *manas* then enters the *mukhya prāṇa*; the *mukhya prāṇa* enters the soul to which is adhering the moral qualification; the soul then enters the *sūkṣma çarīra*. After all these have come together in the heart, the point of the heart becomes luminous in such wise as to light up the path, and the *udāna* escorts the soul with the *upādhis* from the body. From the body of those possessing the lower knowledge, the soul goes through the artery of the head; from the body of the ignorant, it goes through the hundred other principal veins of the body. The soul of a person possessing the higher knowledge, as we shall see, does not go out at all. Beginning at this point, the paths divide. The performer of pious works goes upon the path of the fathers (*pitṛyāna*); the man

possessing the lower knowledge, upon the path of the gods (*devayāna*); he who is without knowledge and without pious works, that is, the bad man, remains shut out from both these paths.

35. The path of the fathers, which is destined for those who possess neither the higher nor the lower knowledge of Brahman, but who have done good deeds, leads the soul in compensation up to the moon. The stations on this road are as follows: smoke; night; the part of the month in which the moon wanes; the part of the year in which the days shorten; the world of the fathers; the ether; the moon. In the heaven of the moon the souls enjoy intercourse with the gods as reward for their deeds. This intercourse lasts till the deeds are consumed. However, only a portion of deeds are thus rewarded by enjoyment on the moon; another portion is left over as a remainder, and finds its recompense in the succeeding birth. In which category any particular deed is to be classed is not made clear. After all the deeds which find their recompense on the moon are consumed, the soul descends again. As stations on the return there are named: ether; wind; smoke; clouds; rain; plants; the sperma; the womb. At all these stations the soul remains only temporarily, and must be distinguished from the elements and souls through which it passes. Finally, after it has arrived in the womb corresponding to its deeds, it comes forth to another life on earth.

36. The wicked, who have neither knowledge nor deeds, do not ascend to the moon. Their fate is not clearly traced, since Shankara in one place refers to a punishment in the seven hells of Yama; in another, to the "third place" in which these souls are born as lower animals. Although the wicked are excluded from life on the moon, not all souls which return from there obtain a happy life. Some, owing to good conduct, are destined to be born again in one of the three higher castes, but others, owing to bad conduct, enter the bodies of Caṇḍālas and animals. A reduction of these statements to a consistent whole, which could easily have been brought about by distinguishing different

grades in the good and bad deeds to be atoned for, is not made in the work of Shankara.

37. From those who perform religious works prescribed in the old Vedic sacrificial cult, must be distinguished those who adhere to the doctrine of Brahman, but nevertheless cannot raise themselves to a right knowledge of the dogma of identity, and accordingly know Brahman, not as their own soul, but as a god different from themselves whom they worship. These possessors of the lower knowledge, that is, worshippers of the lower, conditioned Brahman, all, with the exception of those who have worshipped him under a symbol (*pratīḳa*), go after death by the path of the gods into the lower Brahman. The stations of this path are differently designated in the different accounts. Shankara interweaves them into a whole. According to the Chāndogya Upanishad the following regions are traversed by the soul of the man possessing the lower knowledge after it has passed out of the body through the artery of the head: the flames of the fire; the day; the part of the month in which the moon waxes; the part of the year in which the days lengthen; the year; the sun; the moon; the lightning. These stations are not to be considered either as signposts or as places of enjoyment for the soul, but as guides which it needs because it cannot use its own organs, which are in an enveloped condition. The guides of the soul hitherto mentioned are to be understood as divine but anthropomorphic beings; later, however, after its entrance into the lightning, the soul is received by a "man who is not like a human being," and by him is escorted through Varuṇaloka, Indraloka, and Prajāpatiloka into Brahman. Nevertheless, by Brahman is here meant the lower, conditioned Brahman who has been born himself and hence, at the dissolution of the universe, perishes. In the world of this Brahman souls enjoy sovereignty, *āiçvarya,* which consists in an omnipotence like that of a god though restricted to fixed limits, and including the fulfilment of every wish. The *manas* serves as medium of enjoyment. Whether souls also make use of the *indriyas,* which also accompany them, is doubtful. Among their sovereign powers

belongs the ability to animate several bodies at once, and they divide themselves among these bodies by means of a division of their *upādhis*. Although for souls which have entered the lower Brahman by the *devayāna,* this *āiçvarya* is finite and lasts only till the dissolution of the universe, still Scripture says of them: "for such there is no return." We must therefore suppose that in the world of Brahman the higher knowledge of the *saṁyag-darçana* is revealed to them, and that at the end of the world, when the lower Brahman also perishes, they enter with him into "eternal and absolute *nirvāṇa*." This entrance is called progressive emancipation (*kramamukti*); it is performed in progression, or gradual emancipation, because it is obtained by the intermediate grades of heavenly sovereignty. Opposed to this stands the immediate emancipation of the knowing one, which is reached even here on earth, and which we have next to consider.

## Emancipation

38. The question of the possibility of emancipation from individual existence, which serves as the keystone of the Vedānta as of other Indian systems of philosophy, presupposes the pessimistic view that all individual existence is an evil. This thought finds occasional expression in the Veda as well as in the system under consideration, but it is not proclaimed with so much emphasis as we should expect.

How, then, is an emancipation from the bonds of existence possible? Not by works: for these, good as well as bad, demand their requital; necessitate accordingly a new existence, and are the cause of the continuance of the *saṁsāra*; not yet by (moral) purification, for this can take place only in an object capable of change, whereas the *ātman,* the soul, whose emancipation is concerned, is unchangeable. Emancipation therefore cannot consist in any development or in any activity, but only in the recognition of something already real, still concealed through ignorance. "From knowledge comes emancipation." When once the soul knows its identity with Brahman, this knowledge is emancipation. The individual soul on recognizing its identity with Brahman becomes by that concept the universal spirit.

39. The *ātman,* in the knowledge of which emancipation consists, is nothing else than the knowing subject in us. For this reason it is not knowable by the senses, "ne'er canst thou see the seer of seeing"; it cannot, like an object, be placed before us and examined; knowledge of it cannot be obtained at will, and even searching in the Scripture is not enough to attain this knowledge, but merely serves to remove obstacles. Whether the *ātman* is known or not depends, as does the perception of every object, on one fact, whether it manifests itself to us; depends consequently on the *ātman* itself. Hence in the lower knowledge, which opposes the *ātman* to our own self as a personal god and worships it, knowledge appears as the grace of God. In the higher knowledge, since the *ātman* is in reality not an object, the cause of its knowledge is not further explicable.

40. In spite of this, religious practice recognizes certain means by which knowledge of the *ātman* may be promoted. From the man who enters upon the pursuit of the higher knowledge there is demanded study of the Veda and the four requisites: distinguishing between eternal and perishable substance; renunciation of the enjoyment of reward here and hereafter; attainment of the six means; longing for emancipation. The six means are, tranquillity; control of passions; renunciation; patient endurance; concentration; and faith.

Besides these requisites, commonly enumerated in the instruction of the schools, two other means serve in a general way to promote knowledge: works and meditation.

Works, it is true, do not have a positive, but merely a negative value in the scheme of salvation. They cannot create knowledge, but they aid in acquiring it by destroying the barriers standing in the way of its acquisition. Among such barriers are enumerated various emotional disturbances, such as passionate love, hate, and so forth. The works which serve as a means in the acquisition of knowledge are useful partly in a remoter and partly in a closer sense. As remoter means are enumerated, study of the

Veda, sacrifice, almsgiving, penance, and fasting. These are to be pursued only till knowledge is attained. In distinction from these, the closer means are to be continued even after the attainment of knowledge. These are, tranquillity of spirit, control of the passions, renunciation, patience, and composedness.

Besides works, pious meditation serves as a means of acquiring knowledge. It consists in devout contemplation of words of Scripture, for example, the words *tat tvam asi,* and, like the process of threshing, is to be repeated until knowledge appears as its fruit. For this result a longer or a shorter time is required according as a person is subject to mental dullness or doubt. After the acquisition of the higher knowledge meditation is no longer needed since it has attained its end. On the other hand, meditations which are connected with works, as well as those practised in the lower knowledge, are to be continued till death, since the thoughts at the hour of death are of importance in shaping the destiny beyond. For meditation in the service of the higher knowledge the position of the body is of no importance; nor is it so for the performance of works. Meditation practised in the lower knowledge must be carried on not standing or lying, but sitting.

41. Knowledge consists in the immediate perception of the identity of the soul with Brahman. For the man who has attained to this perception, and with it to the conviction of the non-reality of the phenomenal world and of the round-of-rebirth, past deeds are annihilated. To him in the future deeds no longer cling. This annihilation, moreover, has reference to good as well as to bad deeds, since both require requital and both cease to exist when the *saṁsāra* ceases. The man possessing knowledge has arrived at the following judgement: "The Brahman who, instead of being in essence an actor and enjoyer, as I once thought him, is in truth in all the past, the present, and the future, a non-actor and a non-enjoyer, this Brahman am I; therefore neither was I formerly an actor and enjoyer, nor am I now, nor shall I ever be." With the recognition of the non-reality of being an actor, is recognized also the non-reality of one's own body, which exists as the fruit of action; hence the man possessing knowledge is as

little moved by pain in his own body as by that of another; and he who still feels pain has not yet attained perfect knowledge.

42. As for the man possessing knowledge there is no longer any world, any body, or any pain, so there are no longer any rules to direct his action. He will not, however, on that account, do evil, for in him has been destroyed that illusion which is the preliminary to all action good and bad alike. Whether he continues to act at all is unimportant, since his acts do not belong to him and do not cling to him any longer.

Opportune as it would have been to derive positive moral conduct from the condition just described of the man who knows himself to be the soul of the universe,—conduct expressing itself in works of justice and charity,—and though such a conduct may be derived from the Bhagavadgītā, yet Shankara does not touch this question.

43. Knowledge consumes the seed of deeds, so that there is no material left for another birth. On the other hand, knowledge cannot destroy deeds whose seed has already sprung up, namely, those which determine the present course of life. For this reason the body persists for a time even after the awakening has been accomplished, just as the potter's wheel continues to turn after the vessel is completed. Still this persistence is a mere illusion of which the enlightened Sage cannot, indeed, rid himself, but by which on the other hand he can no longer be deceived. Likewise the man with defective vision sees two moons, but knows that in fact there is only one.

44. When the deeds whose fruit has not yet begun to form, and when those whose fruit is the present existence, have been destroyed by knowledge, then, at the moment of death, complete and eternal emancipation begins for the enlightened sage: "his vital spirits do not depart, but he is Brahman, and in Brahman is he merged."

*As rivers run, and in the ocean*
*Renouncing name and form from vision vanish,*
*So names and forms the Enlightened Sage renouncing*
*Enters great Brahman, the all-embracing Spirit.*

## CHAPTER IV

# Jainism: A Heterodox System

### Historical Background

Of the two centuries spanning 800–600 B.C., our knowledge of developments in the religious life of India is principally confined to Brahministic sources. Some historians of religion have viewed this as the result of the fact that the Brahmins were the highest social class and, hence, the repository of religion and culture. But it is evident that the preeminent position of the Brahmins was not universally recognized or accepted. The Kshatriyas, or noblemen, frequently claimed a higher birth and exercised an equal power in the community (usually political, but sometimes even religious). The period 800–600 B.C. was one of relative peace in India. This circumstance permitted minor movement toward urbanization and a consolidation of the territorial boundaries of tribal chieftains. The aristocratic class, like the priestly class, was mostly hereditary and, as a result, faced the responsibility of preserving the continuity of their class both physically and culturally.

The ideal Brahminic life differed sharply from the ideal aristocratic life. Having completed his religious apprenticeship by intensive study of the Vedas and other oral traditions, the Brahmin settled down to a domestic existence in marriage and assumed his priestly responsibility of service to the community. Later in his life he could follow an existing tradition and abandon his home, to assume the life of a mendicant in the forest. There were, of course, a variety of roles and emphases that might shape a Brahmin's life of service as a professional religionist. Such nuances of role and emphasis resulted in extremes which ranged from priestly pedantry and superstition to serious theological activity and the most noble conduct.

The great unifying strength of the Brahmins had its source in their common adherence to and practice of Vedic beliefs and rites. Although the Brahmins were the dominant religious community during these two centuries, there were subcommunities and religious orders that stood in opposition to them. They constituted the repository of innovating religious and philosophical doctrines and of diverse codes of conduct. Such subcommunities are clearly distinguished from the Brahmins in early Jainist and Buddhist literature and are even mentioned in the earliest Upanishads. Probably, these communities were composed of the aristocrats, and they seemed to believe that no one caste or sacred literature possessed exclusive rights to religious knowledge. Most often they were pilgrims (unlike the generally sedentary Brahmins), and their reflections were frequently revolutionary and atheistic. They were manifestations of a tradition in the higher classes of that period of the wandering, religious life. Their speculations and religious practices were not, as yet, institutionalized, so that there existed very few literary sources and no established centers of religious thought and action. Evidently, a profound concern for speculative and theological questions was considered a profession in its own right. Thus we see the emergence in Indian religious history of the life of contemplation as a viable option for human commitment. The enormous commitment of aristocrats to this life of wandering search for truth and salvation led to the development of a pluralism in India's religious thought and life.

Out of this pluralism emerged two major religious movements which deserve special attention. Both Jainism and Buddhism are considered heterodox religions within Hinduism proper. Asceticism conjoined with the contemplative, wandering life seems to be the crucible out of which Jainism and early Buddhism were forged. These two traditions were considered by the Brahmins as unclassical and heretical. One ran a greater risk in encountering adherents to these faiths than if one encountered the dreaded tiger. After all, the tiger only consumed the body whereas these heresies corrupted the soul.

While Jainism and Buddhism were independent religious traditions, they shared much in common which distinguished them from classical Hinduism. They were united in denying the doctrinal authority of the Vedas and Upanishadic literature and, also, in their antagonism to the sacrificial and cultic practices of Brahminism. Their founders were of the Kshatriya caste, but their doctrines were put forth for all segments of society regardless of caste or sex. The numerous gods of the Hindu pantheon were recognized by both traditions, but their power was considered to be minimal. In the Buddhist and Jainist systems of thought, it was considered foolish to worship the gods and demigods of the Hindu pantheon, for such worship could not advance one along the path to salvation from the wheel of birth, suffering, death and rebirth. In spirit, they are atheistic, considering the gods as sharing in the human condition though on a higher plane of existence. Moreover, their atheism was not advanced in an apologetic fashion, but rather as a natural religious attitude.

Together they opposed the nature worship of Vedic religion and its highly systematized cultic forms. Upanishadic idealism was confronted in Jainism and early Buddhism with a thorough realism. This realistic bent made itself evident in all forms of Jainist and primitive Buddhist thought, e.g., in theory of knowledge, conceptions of reality, ethics, and doctrines of human nature. Since Jainism was the earlier of the two and is quite representative of the heterodox systems, let us consider its history and development.

### *Jainism*

Scholars in the West initially considered Mahavira, who died about 480 B.C. at the age of seventy-two, as the founder of the Jainist movement. More recent theories, based on the literature of the Jainist tradition, view Mahavira as the twenty-fourth in a series of Jainist prophets which stretches back into the mythological past. According to Jainist tradition, Mahavira is the consummation of a long line of Tirthankaras ("makers of the crossings"). Parsva, the twenty-third Jainist savior, probably was a historical person living approximately two hundred fifty years before Mahavira. Eighty-four thousand years separate Parsva from the twenty-second Tirthankara. As we descend into the mythological past, the temporal gap between the Jaina heroes widens in a mind-staggering fashion. Rishabha, the legendary first Jaina, lived approximately 8,400,000 years. His birth is presumed to have occurred one hundred billion *sagaras* of years ago. The *sagara* is considered to extend for 100,000,000,000 *palyas*. "A *palya* is a period in which a well a mile deep filled with fine hairs can be emptied if one hair is withdrawn every hundred years."[1] Both Jainist and Buddhist literature support the thesis that Mahavira was not the originator of the Jainist religion but rather its "historic" reviver and reformer. He is represented as lifting an ancient but established religious tradition out of the error and dissolution into which it had fallen.

Thus, Jainism represents itself as considerably older than the Vedic tradition. This tends to support the thesis advanced by some scholars that the Jainist faith has a non-Aryan origin accounting for its nonreliance upon the Vedas as the source of truth. Moreover, both Jainist and Buddhist scriptures insist upon the fact that the "conquerors" of Jainism are all of the aristocratic warrior caste and not of the Brahmins.

All Tirthankaras live completely beyond the body of the cosmos in a transcendent region at the very ceiling of the universe. In their transcendent purity and impassivity, they lie beyond the reach of human prayers and enter into no active relation with the struggling hordes of life-forms occupying the different areas of the universe's body. All qualities of perfection reside in them in their sublime state of complete luminosity and inaction, and, thus, they serve as models for all forms of life seeking liberation from the bondage of the conditioning factors in the world. The contemplation of their pristine purity coupled with

[1] Charles Eliot, *Hinduism and Buddhism: An Historical Sketch* (London: Routledge & Kegan Paul, Ltd., 1921), Vol. I, p. 110.

rigorous ascetic discipline leads the Jainist worshiper step by step through many lives until he achieves the absolute freedom which the "crossing makers" have manifested.

The unmitigated pessimism of Jainist religion astonishes even the most sober consciousness. No divine grace operates to assist men (and all living beings) in their struggles to escape the ineluctable operation of the karmic principle. Every life situation is a direct consequence of previous action either in the present existence or a prior one. Karmic law operates mechanically, materialistically, and inexorably. All life automatically binds itself to future life and suffering, through whatever action it takes. Violent deeds result in a massive influx of karmic matter of the darkest hue, weighing the soul (jiva) down further in the round of birth, suffering, and rebirth. Forms of the soul's life change according to the nature of the soul's action, but even these changes are destined by the sharply mechanical operation of the karmic principle. This cosmic mechanism which shapes the destiny of all living things has existed for all eternity, and one escapes entanglement in the perennial round of rebirth only by heroic self-abnegation. Yet even the achievement of complete liberation is effected only through the unfolding of eternal laws of the universe's mechanism.

Such unrelenting pessimism functions psychologically as an assault upon the will to live. It initiates a reorientation of human consciousness away from the world of earthly concerns, away from the hopes of achieving a heavenly existence. The gods of Jainism may enjoy a higher plane of existence due to meritorious action in a previous life, but they continue to live under the deluding spell of conditioned existence. For a brief duration, divine figures enjoy some measure of release from the typical enslavement of all living forms, but their respite is only temporary. They share the condition and destiny of the lowest form of the soul in the deepest hell residing within the body of the world. Hence, the proper orientation of all human effort is completely beyond good and evil, beyond the status of divine being toward an absolutely transcendent goal.

In this respect, Jainism is not a philosophy of life which aims at the enhancement or amelioration of human existence. The humanist ideal can find no place in a religious vision which seeks the dissolution of the will to live. Human activity of every sort brings about the recurring conditioning of life, and it is precisely this which must be shattered and transcended. All impetus to life must cease, whatever its form. No special dignity or value attaches to human life either individually or collectively. The highest value, which dissolves all life-oriented values, is the capacity man has to achieve the transcendence of all conditioning factors in life, even those which define him as a man.

Although karmic law was understood to operate inexorably, the Jainists believed that with the aid of proper vision and rigid ascetic practices one could accelerate the process of release from the cycle of life. Such heroic effort modeled itself upon the lives of the Jaina heroes, the victors. The path of release was mapped out in the historical and mythological biographies of the Tirthankaras. Their achievement of absolute liberation was a consequence of their knowledge of the immensity of the world's sorrow and the resulting practice by which they transcended the perennial cycle of rebirth. By sustained acts of self-renunciation, the conquerors created a path, a discipline by which enlightened Jains might make their own escapes from the nightmare of existence.

In the biography of Mahavira we can discover an example in knowledge and practice of how escape from bondage can be effected. Mahavira Vardhamana was a contemporary of Buddha and, like Buddha, was of the Kshatriya caste. Evidently, his parents were followers of the Jaina saint Parsva. When Mahavira was thirty-one, his parents (in the true Jaina spirit) voluntarily starved themselves to death (presumably in the hope of accelerating their release). Following this act, Mahavira renounced the world and wandered naked through western Bengal. At the conclusion of twelve years of intensive self-mortification, he achieved enlightenment (kevola). Having escaped the bonds of conditioned life, he continued to wander and teach for another thirty to forty years, collecting about him eleven disciples. He is reputed to have died at the age of seventy-two in Paua in the year 480 B.C. Most of his life had been spent in the northeastern section of India near his birthplace of Vaisali.

Following Mahavira's death a schism occurred in the Jainist faith. Even in the modern world Jainism is split into two sects which refuse to participate in social intercourse with each other, although they share principally the same beliefs and traditions. The *Svetambara* sect believes that dressing in plain white robes is not a hindrance to spiritual purity and also that women are capable of participating in the Jainist discipline. The *Digambaras* (clothed with air) at one time insisted that nudity is a fundamental prerequisite for attaining spiritual freedom. Moreover, the Digambaras maintained that women must await rebirth as males before undertaking Jainist discipline. In recent times, the Digambara sect has relaxed the principle of strict nudity (except in the most ascetic communities) and generally observe the dress code of their immediate community.

Jainism and Buddhism are the only two ancient heterodox religions which have survived in any significant fashion through the centuries. The survival of Jainism and its appearance in the modern world is a testimony to the heroic character of its tradition and followers. Throughout Indian history, Jainism has from time to time been a target of systematic religious and political persecution. An even greater pressure, however, failed to subdue or assimilate Jainist religion, and that pressure arose from the assimilative powers of Hinduism. The powers of Hinduism with respect to its absorption of heterodox or revolutionary movements is astonishing. Nevertheless, Jainism survives in India today, having approximately one and a quarter million adherents.

The special vows of right conduct observed by all Jainists throughout their history has determined in large measure the status of the Jainist in Indian society and history. In this respect, the primal importance of the doctrine of ahimsa (noninjury) to Jainist conduct cannot be underestimated. To the Jainist, the whole universe is alive, and as a consequence, everyone must strive to avoid injuring in any manner any living thing. The doctrine of ahimsa gave rise to a host of recommendations concerning how to avoid doing violence to living creatures, e.g., sweeping one's path to avoid stepping on small insects, kindling no fires, cutting hair without scissors (they frequently plucked it out), and extensive rules for housecleaning. Such practices shaped the ways in which the Jainist participated in Indian society. Because of their moral principles, the Jainists were excluded from any economic vocation which involved endangering life, such as agriculture, masonry, or any industry using sharp instruments. Moreover, the Jainists were enjoined by one of their vows of right conduct never to speak falsely. Hence, the Jainists were acknowledged throughout India for their honesty in all their business dealings. (Their exclusion from many normal vocations forced them into intensive activity in the spheres of trading and banking.)

A further injunction observed by all Jainists was the principle that there may be no unnecessary accumulation of wealth. This vow made the Jainists famous for their charity and philanthropic endeavors. The mere acquisition of wealth was not considered evil in itself; only the blind pursuit of wealth and the passionate attachment to riches were forbidden. Such factors governed the Jainists' participation in community life, guiding many into vocations involving exchange of goods and monies. They were widely respected for their veterinary hospitals and other charitable institutions serving all forms of suffering life. Their almost puritan ethic has made them into an industrious people with a significant social conscience.

Because the laity in Jainism is enjoined not to possess wealth beyond necessity, they have throughout their history contributed elaborate proportions of their riches to the construction of religious temples and artifacts. The traditional feeling, in this respect, seems to be that the most meritorious work that a layman can do is to multiply religious iconography and shrines. Since the laity of Jainism have prospered in their economic professions, they have committed their financial resources to the support of large communities of ascetic monks and have also contributed substantially to the survival of Jainism in art and architecture.

Throughout the ages, Indian religious thought seems to have been dominated by two fundamentally different world views. One we find systematically explicated in the Vedanta system. In its purest form, Vedanta maintains that the soul and absolute reality are identical, in some sense, and that the external world is maya (illusion). The other world view, expressed in Samkhya-Yoga and in Jainism, is dualistic. It insists that both matter and souls are primordial, uncreated and eternal. The similarity between the doctrines and practices of Samkhya-Yoga and of Jainism should be carefully considered. Such close similarity would suggest a unitary mythological or speculative source. The contrast between the radical dualism of Samkhya-Yoga and Jainism and the nondualism of Vedanta is striking. Yet, as we shall see, subtle, but interesting, differences emerge between Samkhya-Yoga and Jainism at crucial points. For example, in the Samkhya system, man's bondage to the conditions of life is a product of the distracted, ignorant condition of his consciousness. This bondage is explained psychologically, whereas in Jainism man's enslavement to life is the result of a *material* contamination of his soul.

The Jainist believes that the faithful seeker actually cleanses a soul darkened by the murky influx of karmic matter. Samkhya-Yoga teaches that the cleansing process is entirely psychological (remarkably akin to psychoanalytic technique). It involves a reorientation of consciousness so that an actual state which has never been lost may be consciously regained. It is avidya, a psychological condition, which requires therapy, and not a material condition of the soul as in Jainism. Further, there is a significant contrast between Samkhya-Yoga's conception of release ("isolation") and that of the Jainists. In the Jainist view, *kaivalya* ("restoration of integration") is for the released life-monad a state of pure luminosity, perfect consciousness, and knowledge. In the Samkhya-Yoga view, the purified purusa, having achieved a final liberation from the instrumentalities of consciousness, resides in a state of eternal unawareness. In spite of these significant differences, there are adequate grounds for considering Samkhya-Yoga and Jainism as part of a family of religions sharing basic presuppositions and world views.

## On Jainism

*Heinrich Zimmer*

### The Makers of the Crossing

Jainism denies the authority of the Vedas and the orthodox traditions of Hinduism. Therefore it is reckoned as a heterodox Indian religion. It does not derive from Brāhman-Āryan sources, but reflects the cosmology and anthropology of a much older, pre-Āryan upper class of northeastern India—being rooted in the same subsoil of archaic metaphysical speculation as Yoga, Sāṅkhya, and Buddhism, the other non-Vedic Indian systems. . . .

This is a philosophy of the profoundest pessimism. The round of rebirths in the world is endless, full of suffering, and of no avail. Of and in itself it can yield no release, no divine redeeming grace; the very gods are subject to its deluding spell. Therefore, ascent to heaven is no less a mere phase or stage of delusion than descent to the purgatorial hells. As a result of meritorious conduct, one is reborn a god among the gods; as a result of evil conduct, a being among the beings of hell or an animal among the beasts; but there is no escape, either way, from this perennial circulation. One will continue to revolve forever through the various spheres of inconsequential pleasures and unbearable pains unless one can manage somehow to

Reprinted from Heinrich Zimmer, *Philosophies of India,* edited by Joseph Campbell (Bollingen Series XXVI, Princeton University Press, 1967), pages 217, 227–240, 248–262. 

release *oneself*. But this can be accomplished only by heroic effort—a long, really dreadful ordeal of austerities and progressive self-abnegation.

## The Qualities of Matter

According to Jaina cosmology, the universe is a living organism, made animate throughout by life-monads which circulate through its limbs and spheres; and this organism will never die. We ourselves, furthermore—i.e., the life-monads contained within and constituting the very substance of the imperishable great body—are imperishable too. We ascend and descend through various states of being, now human, now divine, now animal; the bodies seem to die and to be born, but the chain is continuous, the transformations endless, and all we do is pass from one state to the next. The manner in which the indestructible life-monads circulate is disclosed to the inward eye of the enlightened Jaina saint and seer.

The life-monads enjoying the highest states of being, i.e., those temporarily human or divine, are possessed of five sense faculties, as well as of a thinking faculty (*manas*) and span of life (*āyus*), physical strength (*kāya-bala*), power of speech (*vacana-bala*), and the power of respiration (*śvāsocchvāsa-bala*). In the classic Indian philosophies of Sāṅkhya, Yoga, and Vedānta, the same five sense faculties appear as in the Jaina formula (namely touch, smell, taste, hearing, and sight); however, there have been added the so-called "five faculties of action." These begin with speech (*vāc,* corresponding to the Jaina *vacana-bala*), but then go on to grasping (*pāṇi,* the hand), locomotion (*pāda,* the feet), evacuation (*pāyu,* the anus), and reproduction (*upastha,* the organ of generation). *Manas* (the thinking faculty) is retained, but is linked to further functions of the psyche, namely *buddhi* (intuitive intelligence) and *ahaṅkāra* (ego-consciousness). Also added are the five *prāṇas,* or "life breaths."[1]

---

[1] In Jainism the term *prāṇa* is used in the sense not of "life breath" but of "bodily power," and refers to the ten faculties above noted. Dr. Zimmer is sug-

Apparently the Jaina categories represent a comparatively primitive, archaic analysis and description of human nature, many of the details of which underlie and remain incorporated in the later, classic Indian view.

Frogs, fish, and other animals not born from the womb are without a thinking faculty (*manas*)—they are called, therefore, *a-sañjñin* ("insensible"); whereas elephants, lions, tigers, goats, cows, and the rest of the mammals, since they have a thinking faculty, are *sañjñin*. The various beings in the hells, and the lower gods, as well as human beings, also are *sañjñin*.

In contrast to those views that represent the soul as being minute, like an atom (*aṇu*), or of the size of a thumb, and dwelling in the heart, Jainism regards the life-monad (*jīva*) as pervading the whole organism; the body constitutes, as it were, its garb; the life-monad is the body's animating principle. And the subtle substance of this life-monad is mingled with particles of karma, like water with milk, or like fire with iron in a red-hot, glowing iron ball. Moreover, the karmic matter communicates colors (*leśyā*) to the life-monad; and these colors are six in number. Hence there are said to be six types of life-monad, in ascending series, each with its color, smell, taste, and quality of tangibility, as follows:

6. white (*śukla*)
5. yellow, or rose (*padma,* like a lotus)

4. flaming red (*tejas*)
3. dove-grey (*kapota*)

2. dark blue (*nīla*)
1. black (*kṛṣṇa*)

These six types fall into three groups of two, each pair corresponding precisely to one of the three *guṇas,* or "natural quali-

gesting that the analysis of the psyche that prevailed in the classic period of Indian philosophy, in the synthesis of the so-called "Six Systems," was originally not a Brāhman contribution but non-Āryan, having come in through Sāṅkhya and Yoga, and that its categories are prefigured in the Jaina view. For the Six Systems, cf. Appendix A.

ties," of the classic Sāṅkhya and Vedāntic writings.[2] The Jaina leśyās 1 and 2 are dark; they correspond to the guṇa *tamas,* "darkness." Leśyā 3 is smoky grey while 4 is of the red of flame; both pertain to fire, and thus correspond to the guṇa *rajas* (fire = *rajas,* "red color"; cf. *rañj,* "to tinge red"; *rakta,* "red"). Leśyās 5 and 6, finally, are clear and luminous, being states of comparative purity, and thus are the Jaina counterparts of the classic guṇa *sattva:* "virtue, goodness, excellence, clarity; ideal being; the supreme state of matter." In sum, the six Jaina leśyās seem to represent some system of archaic prototypes from which the basic elements of the vastly influential later theory of the guṇas was evolved.

Black is the characteristic color of merciless, cruel, raw people, who harm and torture other beings. Dark-blue characters are roguish and venal, covetous, greedy, sensual, and fickle. Dove-grey typifies the reckless, thoughtless, uncontrolled, and irascible; whereas the prudent, honest, magnanimous, and devout are fiery red. Yellow shows compassion, consideration, unselfishness, nonviolence, and self-control; while the white souls are dispassionate, absolutely disinterested, and impartial.

As water flows into a pond through channels, so karmic matter of the six colors flows into the monad through the physical organs. Sinful acts cause an "influx of evil karma" (*pāpa-āsrava*), and this increases the dark matter in the monad; virtuous acts, on the other hand, bring an "influx of good or holy karma" (*puṇya-āsrava*), which tends to make the monad white. But even this holy karma keeps the life-monad linked to the world.[3] By

---

[2] Editor's Note: Here again Dr. Zimmer is pointing to the prefigurement in Jainism of the classic Indian categories. It can be stated that according to the classic Indian view, matter (*prakṛti*) is characterized by the three qualities (*guṇas*) of inertia (*tamas*), activity (*rajas*), and tension or harmony (*sattva*). These are not merely qualities, but the very substance of the matter of the universe, which is said to be constituted of the guṇas, as a rope of three twisted strands—*tamas guṇa* being, as it were, black, *rajas* red, and *sattva* white. A predominance of *tamas guṇa* in an individual's disposition makes him dull, sluggish, and resentful, *rajas* makes him aggressive, heroic, and proud, while *sattva* conduces to illuminated repose, benignity, and understanding.

[3] Compare *Bhagavad Gītā* 14, 5–9. "The guṇas—sattva, rajas, and tamas—which are born of matter, bind the immortal dweller-in-the-body fast in the

increasing the yellow and white karmic matter, virtuous acts produce the gentler, more savory ties—but these are ties, even so; they do not suffice to consummate release. "Influx" (*āsrava*) of every type has to be blocked if nirvāṇa is to be attained, and this arrestment of life can be affected only by abstention from action —all action whatsoever, whether good or bad.[4]

A basic fact generally disregarded by those who "go in" for Indian wisdom is this one of the total rejection of every last value of humanity by the Indian teachers and winners of redemption from the bondages of the world. "Humanity" (the phenomenon of the human being, the ideal of its perfection, and the ideal of the perfected human society) was the paramount concern of Greek idealism, as it is today of Western Christianity in its modern form; but for the Indian sages and ascetics, the Mahātmas and enlightened Saviors, "humanity" was no more than the shell to be pierced, shattered, and dismissed. For perfect non-activity, in thought, speech, and deed, is possible only when one has become dead to *every* concern of life: dead to pain and enjoyment as well as to every impulse to power, dead to the interests of intellectual pursuit, dead to all social and political affairs—deeply,

---

body. Sattva, being stainless, is luminous and of the nature of peace and serenity; it binds by creating attachment to happiness and to knowledge. Rajas, the essence of passion, is the cause of thirst and fascination; it binds the dweller-in-the-body by attachment to action. Tamas, finally, is born of ignorance, and bewilders all embodied beings; it binds by inadvertence, indolence, and sleep. Thus, while tamas darkens judgment and attaches to miscomprehension, rajas attaches to action, and sattva to happiness."

[4] The Jaina Tīrthaṅkara, by virtue of his boundless intuition, or omniscience, which is based on the crystal purity and infinite radiance of the life-monad released from its karmic matter, directly perceives, in the case of each and all, the precise color, taste, fragrance, and quality of the matter infecting the life-monad; he knows exactly the degree of pollution, obscurity, or brightness of every individual that he sees. For the luminosity of the monad pervades the whole organism, and is thought of as emanating even beyond the strict circumference of the bodily frame, in such a way as to form around it a subtle halo, invisible to the average mortal but clearly perceptible to the enlightened saint. Here we have the archaic background of the halo—the "aura" of the Theosophists—which encompasses every living form, and which, through its shadings, darkness, or radiance, betrays the status of the soul, showing whether one is steeped in obscuring animal passions and bedimming ego-propensities, or advanced along the path toward purification and release from the bondages of universal matter.

absolutely, and immovably uninterested in one's character as a human being. The sublime and gentle final fetter, virtue, is thus itself something to be severed. It cannot be regarded as the goal, but only as the beginning of the great spiritual adventure of the "Crossing-Maker," a stepping place to the superhuman sphere. That sphere, moreover, is not only superhuman but even super-divine—beyond the gods, their heavens, their delights, and their cosmic powers. "Humanity," consequently, whether in the individual or in the collective aspect, can no longer be of concern to anyone seriously striving for perfection along the way of the ultimate Indian wisdom. Humanity and its problems belong to the philosophies of life that we discussed above: the philosophies of success (*artha*), pleasure (*kāma*), and duty (*dharma*); these can be of no interest to one who has literally died to time—for whom life is death. "Let the dead bury their dead": that is the thought. This is something that makes it very difficult for us of the modern Christian West to appreciate and assimilate the traditional message of India.

The sentimental or heroic divinization of man along the lines of the classic and modern humanitarian ideals is something totally foreign to the Indian mind. From the Indian point of view, the special dignity of the human being consists solely in the fact that he is capable of becoming enlightened, free from bondage, and therewith competent, ultimately, for the role of the supreme teacher and savior of all beings, including the beasts and the gods. The life-monad mature enough for this super-godly task descends to earth from the high realm of heavenly beatitude, as did the monad of the Jaina Savior, Pārśvanātha, the temporary delights and powers of the gods having become meaningless for his ripened insight. And then, in a final existence among men, the savior himself achieves perfect enlightenment and therewith release, and by his teaching renews the timeless doctrine of the way to reach this goal.

This amazing ideal, expressed in the legendary biographies of the Buddhas and Tīrthaṅkaras, was taken seriously and literally as an ideal for all. It was actually regarded as open to man, and steps were taken to realize it. Apparently, it was a non-Brāhman, pre-Āryan vision of man's role in the cosmos native to the Indian sub-continent. The way of perfectibility taught was that of yogic asceticism and self-abnegation, while the image constantly held before the mind's eye was that of the human savior as the redeemer even of the gods.

In the West such thinking has been suppressed systematically as heresy—a heresy of titanism. Already for the Greeks, it was the classic fault of the suffering hero, the ὕβϱις of the anti-gods or titans, while in the Christian Church such presumption has been mocked as simply incredible. Nevertheless, in our modern Western Christian poetry there can be pointed out at least one great instance of the idea of the coming of a human being to the rescue of God. For when Parsifal, in the third act of Wagner's opera, brings back the holy spear, cures Amfortas, the sick guardian of the holy grail, and restores the grail itself to its beneficent function, the voices of the angels sing out from on high: "Redemption to the Redeemer." The sacred blood of Christ, that is to say, has been redeemed from the curse or spell that was nullifying its operation. And again, in Wagner's cycle of the *Ring of the Nibelung,* a pagan parallel to this motif is developed in almost identical terms. Brünnhilde quiets Wotan's sufferings, putting to rest the All-Father of the universe, when she returns the Ring to the primeval waters and sings to Wotan: *"Ruhe nun, ruhe, du Gott!"*—"Rest now, rest, thou God!" The enlightened individual, perfected through suffering, all-knowing through compassion, self-detached through having conquered ego, redeems the divine principle, which is incapable, alone, of disengaging itself from its own fascination with the cosmic play.

### The Mask of the Personality

Ulysses, in the Homeric epic, descended to the netherworld to seek counsel of the departed, and there found, in the murky twilight land of Pluto and Persephone, the shades of his former companions and friends who had been killed at the siege of Troy or had passed away during the years following the conquest of the town. They were but shadows in that dim realm; yet each could be recognized immediately, for all preserved the features that had been theirs on earth. Achilles declared that he would prefer the hard and joyless life of an obscure peasant in the broad daylight of the living to the melancholy monotony of his present half-existence as the greatest of the heroes among the dead; nevertheless, he was still perfectly himself. The physiognomy, the mask of the personality, had survived the separation from the body and the long exile from the human sphere on the surface of the land.

Nowhere in the Greek epic do we find the idea of the dead hero being divested of his identity with his former, temporal being. The possibility of losing one's personality through death, the slow dissolution, melting away, and final fading out of the historic individuality, was something not considered by the Greeks of Homer's time. Nor did it dawn on the medieval Christian mind. Dante, like Ulysses, was a wayfarer in the world beyond the grave; conducted by Virgil through the circles of hell and purgatory, he ascended to the spheres; and everywhere, throughout the length of his journey, he beheld and conversed with personal friends and enemies, mythical heroes, and the great figures of history. All were recognizable immediately, and all satisfied his insatiable curiosity by recounting their biographies, dwelling at greath length, in spun-out tales and arguments, upon the minute details of their trifling, short-lived individual existences. Their personalities of yore seem to have been only too well preserved through the long wandering in the vastness of eternity. Though definitely and forever severed from the brief moments of their lifetimes on earth, they were still preoccupied with the problems and vexations of their biographies and haunted by their guilt, which clung to them in the symbolic forms of their peculiar punishments. Personality held all in its clutches—the glorified saints in heaven as well as the tortured, suffering inmates of hell; for personality, according to the medieval Christians, was not to be lost in death, or purged away by the after-death experiences. Rather, life beyond the grave was to be but a second manifestation and experience of the very essence of the personality, only realized on a broader scale and in a freer style, and with a more striking display of the nature and implications of the virtues and the vices.

For the Western mind, the personality is eternal. It is indestructible, not to be dissolved. This is the basic idea in the Christian doctrine of the resurrection of the body, the resurrection being our regaining of our cherished personality in a purified form, worthy to fare before the majesty of the Almighty. That personality is thought to go on forever—even though, by a curious inconsistency, it is not believed to have existed anywhere, in any state or form, previous to the carnal birth of the mortal individual. The personality did not exist in extra-human spheres, from all eternity, before its temporal earthly manifestation. It is declared to have come into being with the mortal act of procreation, and yet is supposed to go on after the demise of the procreated mortal frame: temporal in its beginning, immortal in its end.

The term "personality" is derived from the Latin *persona. Persona,* literally, means the mask that is worn over the face by the actor on the Greek or Roman stage; the mask "through" (*per*) which he "sounds" (*sonat*) his part. The mask is what bears the features or make-up of the role, the traits of hero or heroine, servant or messenger, while the actor himself behind it remains anonymous, an unknown being intrinsically aloof from the play, constitutionally unconcerned with the enacted sufferings and passions. Originally, the term *persona* in the sense of "personality" must have implied that people are only impersonating what they seem to be. The word connotes that the personality is but the mask of one's part in the comedy or tragedy of life and not to be identified with the actor. It is not a manifestation of his true nature, but a veil. And yet the Western outlook—which originated with the Greeks themselves and was then developed in Christian philosophy—has annulled the distinction, implied in the term, between the mask and the actor whose face it hides. The two have become, as it were, identical. When the play is over the *persona* cannot be taken off; it clings through death and into the life beyond. The Occidental actor, having wholly identified himself with the enacted personality during his moment on the stage of the world, is unable to take it off when the time comes for departure, and so keeps it on indefinitely, for millenniums—even eternities—after the play is over. To lose his *persona* would mean for him to lose every hope for a future beyond death. The mask has become for him fused, and confused, with his essence.

Indian philosophy, on the other hand, insists upon the difference, stressing the distinction between the actor and the role. It continually emphasizes the contrast between the displayed existence of the individual and the real being of the anonymous actor, concealed, shrouded, and veiled in the costumes of the play. Indeed, one of the dominant endeavors of Indian thought throughout the ages has been to develop a dependable technique for keeping the line clear between the two. A meticulous defining of their interrelationships and their modes of collaboration, as well as a practical, systematic, and courageously enforced effort to break from the confines of the one into the unfathomed reaches of the other, has been carried on for ages—primarily through the numerous introspective processes of yoga. Piercing and dissolving all the layers of the manifest personality, the relentlessly introverted consciousness cuts through the mask, and, at last discarding it in all of its stratifications, arrives at the anonymous and strangely unconcerned actor of our life.

Although in the Hindu and Buddhist texts vivid descriptions of the traditional hells or purgatories are to be found, where appalling details are dwelt upon minutely, never is the situation quite the same as that of the afterworlds of Dante and Ulysses, filled with celebrities long dead who still retain all of the characteristics of their personal masks. For in the Oriental hells, though multitudes of suffering beings are depicted in their agonies, none retain the traits of their earthly individualities. Some can remember having once been elsewhere and know what the deed was through which the present punishment was incurred, nevertheless, in general, all are steeped and lost in their present misery. Just as any dog is absorbed in the state of being precisely whatever dog it happens to be, fascinated by the details of its present life—and as we ourselves are in general spellbound by our present personal existences—so are the beings in the Hindu, Jaina, and Buddhist hells. They are unable to remember any former state, any costume worn in a previous existence, but identify themselves exclusively with that which they now are. And this, of course, is why they are in hell.

Once this Indian idea has struck the mind, then the question immediately presents itself: Why am I bound to be what I am? Why have I to wear the mask of this personality, which I think and feel myself to be? Why must I endure its destiny, the limitations, delusions, and ambitions of this peculiar part that I am being driven to enact? Or why, if I have left one mask behind me, am I now back again in the limelight in another, enacting another role and in a different setting? What is compelling me to go on this way, being always something particular—an individual, with all of these particular shortcomings and experiences? Where and how am I ever to attain to another state—that of not being something particular, beset by limitations and qualities that obstruct my pure, unbounded being?

Can one grow into something devoid of any specificity of shade and color, undefined by shape, unlimited by qualities: something unspecific and therefore not liable to any specific life?

These are the questions that lead to the experiment of asceticism and yoga practice. They arise out of a melancholy weariness of the will to live—the will grown tired, as it were, of the prospect of this endless before and after, as though an actor should become suddenly bored with his career. The doom of this timeless course of transmigration: forgotten past and aimless future! Why do I bother being what I am: man, woman, peasant, artist, rich or poor? Since I have impersonated, without remembering, all of the possible attitudes and roles—time and time again, in the lost past, in the worlds that have dissolved—why do I keep going on?

One might very well come to loathe the hackneyed comedy of life if one were no longer blinded, fascinated, and deluded by the details of one's own specific part. If one were no longer spellbound by the plot of the play in which one happened to be caught for the present, one might very well decide to resign—

give up the mask, the costume, the lines, and the whole affair. It is not difficult to imagine why, for some, it might become simply a bore to go on with this permanent engagement, enacting character after character in this interminable stock company of life. When the feeling comes of being bored with it or nauseated (as it has come, time and time again, in the long history of India) then life revolts, rebels against its own most elementary task or duty of automatically carrying on. Growing from an individual to a collective urge, this leads to the founding of ascetic orders, such as those of the Jaina and the Buddhist communities of homeless monks: troops of renegade actors, heroic deserters, footloose and self-exiled from the universal farce of the force of life.

The argument—if the renegades would bother to justify themselves—would run like this:

"Why should we care what we are? What real concern have we with all those parts that people are continually forced to play? Not to know that one has already enacted every sort of role, time and time again—beggar, king, animal, god—and that the actor's career is no better in one than in another, is truly a pitiable state of mind; for the most obvious fact about the timeless engagement is that all the objects and situations of the plot have been offered and endured in endless repetition through the millenniums. People must be completely blind to go on submitting to the spell of the same old allurements; enthralled by the deluding enticements that have seduced every being that ever lived; hailing with expectation, as a new and thrilling adventure, the same trite deceptions of desire as have been experienced endlessly; clinging now to this, now to that illusion—all resulting only in the fact that the actor goes on acting roles, each seemingly new yet already rendered many times, though in slightly differing costumes and with other casts. Obviously, this is a ridiculous impasse. The mind has been bewitched, trapped by the pressures of a blind life-force that whirls creatures along in a cycling, never-ending stream. And why? Who or what is doing this? Who is the fool that keeps this dim-witted entertainment on the boards?"

The answer that would have to be given to you should you be unable to find it for yourself would be simply—Man: Man himself: each individual. And the answer is obvious. For each goes on doing what has always been done, continually imagining himself to be doing something different. His brain, his tongue, his organs of action, are incorrigibly possessed by a drive to be doing something—and he does it. That is how he builds up new tasks for himself, contaminating himself every minute with new particles of karmic matter, which enter into his nature, flow into his life-monad, sully its essence, and bedim its light. These involvements fetter him to an existence murky with desire and ignorance; and here he treasures his transitory personality as though it were something substantial—clings to the short spell of confused life which is the only thing of which he is aware, cherishes the brief passage of individual existence between birth and the funeral pyre—and thus unconsciously prolongs the period of his own bondage indefinitely into the future. By being active in the pursuit of what he conceives to be his own or someone else's welfare and happiness, he only makes his own bonds, as well as everyone else's, the tighter. . . .

## The Jaina Doctrine of Bondage

Every thought and act, according to the pessimistic philosophy of the Jainas, entails an accumulation of fresh karmic substance. To go on living means to go on being active—in speech, in body, or in mind; it means to go on doing something every day. And this results in the storing up involuntarily of the "seeds" of future action, which grow and ripen into the "fruits" of our coming sufferings, joys, situations, and existences. Such "seeds" are represented as entering and lodging in the life-monad, where, in due time, they become transformed into the circumstances of life, producing success and calamity and weaving the mask—the physiognomy and character—of a developing individual. The process of life itself consumes the karmic substance, burning it up like fuel, but at the same time attracts fresh material to the burning center of vital operations. Thus the life-monad is reinfected by karma. New seeds of future fruits pour in. Two contradictory yet exactly complementary processes are kept, in this way, in operation. The seeds, the karmic materials, are being exhausted rapidly all the time through the unconscious as well as the conscious actions of the psychosomatic system, and yet through those identical actions the karmic storage bins are being continually re-stocked. Hence the conflagration that is one's life goes crackling on.

This self-supporting, continuous, dual process (the karmic seed-substance of the six colorings burning itself out into events that themselves replenish it) is regarded as taking place—in a very literal, physical sense—in the subtle sphere or body of the life-monad (*jīva*). The continuous influx (*āsrava*) of subtle matter into the life-monad is pictured as a kind of pouring in of liquid colorings, which then tinge it; for the life-monad is a subtle crystal, which, in its pristine state, untinged by karmic matter, is stainless, devoid of color, and perfectly transparent; the flow entering the clear body darkens it, infecting it with the color (*leśyā*) corresponding to the moral character of the committed act. Virtuous acts and the lighter, venial offenses impart comparatively light, less obscuring leśyās (mild whitish shades, through yellow and violent red, down to smoky tones—as we have already seen) whereas major sins bring in much darker stains (dark blue and black). The worst offense possible, according to the Jaina view, is the killing or injuring of a living being: *hiṁsā,* "the intent to kill" (from the verbal root *han,* "to kill"). *Ahiṁsā,* "non-injury," correspondingly (i.e., the infliction of no harm on *any* creature), is the primary Jaina rule of virtue.

This clean-cut principle is based on the belief that all life-monads are fundamentally fellow creatures—and by "all" is meant not only human beings, but also animals and plants, and even the indwelling molecules or atoms of matter. The killing even accidentally of such a fellow being darkens the crystal of the life-monad with a dye of deepest hue. That is why animals of prey, which feed on creatures that they have killed, are always infected with leśyās very dark in shade. So also men who engage in killing professionally—butchers, hunters, warriors, etc.: their life-monads are completely without light.

The color of the monad-crystal indicates the realm of the universe, whether high or low, which the individual is to inhabit. Gods and celestial beings are of the brighter hues; animals and the tortured inmates of hell are dark. And during the course of a lifetime the color of the crystal continually changes according to the moral conduct of the living being. In merciful, unselfish people, inclined toward purity, self-abnegation, enlightenment, and release, the crystal continually brightens, the lighter colorings coming finally to prevail, whereas in the selfish, heedless, and reckless—those doomed to sink in their following birth either to the tortures of hell or to the lower realms of the animal world where they will feed upon each other—the darkness of the crystal thickens into black. And according to its color, the life-monad ascends or falls (quite literally) in the body of the Universal Being.

This literal-minded, gentle doctrine of universal vice and virtue was evolved by an ascetic, self-denying, saintly group of renegades from the struggle for life, and accepted by a peaceful, vegetarian bourgeoisie—merchants, money-dealers, and artisans. Apparently, it goes back to the deepest Indian past. The theory of the karmic colors (*leśyās*) is not peculiar to the Jainas, but seems to have been part of the general pre-Āryan inheritance that was preserved in Magadha (northeastern India), and there restated in the fifth century B.C. by a number of non-Brāhman teachers. It is an archaic bit of naïvely materialistic psychology diametrically opposed to the main tenets of the Vedic tradition. And yet, the vivid metaphor of the tainted crystal has been carried on in the composite stream of classical Indian teaching, which developed when the ancient Brāhman orthodoxy and the no less ancient non-Āryan traditions at last became synthesized. In the Sāṅkhya system it figures conspicuously, where it is used to illustrate the relationship between the life-monad and the context of bondage in which the monad is held until discriminating knowledge finally dawns and the bonds are dissolved. From the Sāṅkhya it passed then into Buddhist and Brāhman thought.

As represented by the Jainas, the advance of the individual toward perfection and emancipation is the result of an actual physical process of cleansing taking place in the sphere of subtle matter—literally, a cleansing of the crystal-like life-monad. When the latter is freed completely of all coloring karmic contamination it literally shines with a transparent lucidity; for the crystal of the life-monad, in itself, is absolutely diaphanous. Moreover, when made clean it is immediately capable of mirroring the highest truth of man and the universe, reflecting reality as it really is. The instant the karmic darkening substance of the six colorings is removed, therefore, non-knowing too is gone. Omniscience, that is to say, is co-existent with the supreme state of the absolute clarity of the life-monad, and this, precisely, is release. No longer is the monad dimmed with beclouding passions, but open—free—unlimited by the particularizing qualities that constitute individuality. No longer is there felt the otherwise universal compulsion to keep on wearing the mask of some bewildered personality, the mask of man, beast, tortured soul, or god.

## The Jaina Doctrine of Release

The transcendental wisdom that confers, and is identical with, release from the round of rebirths is regarded as a secret doctrine in the Brāhmanic tradition, into which it was introduced as a new disclosure in the comparatively late period of the Upaniṣads. The Āryan sages of the Vedic Age knew nothing of transmigration; nor was the doctrine alluded to in the complete course of orthodox Vedic studies that was communicated centuries later by the Brāhman sage Āruṇi to his son Śvetaketu. The idea of the sorrowful round really belongs to the non-Āryan, aboriginal inheritance of those noble clans that in Mahāvīra's and the Buddha's time were challenging the somewhat narrow views of Brāhman orthodoxy; and it was imparted freely to spiritually qualified Brāhmans when those haughty conquerors finally condescended to ask for it. For the wisdom of the non-Āryan sages had never been exclusive in quite the same way as that of the Vedic Brāhmans. The Jaina, Buddhist, and other related heterodox Indian teachings are not kept secret like the powerful formulae of the Brāhman families. They are regarded as belonging to all—the only prerequisite to their communication being that the candidate should have adopted an ascetic way of life after fulfilling the preliminary disciplines of his normal secular duties; that is to say, they are exclusive only in a spiritual, not in a genealogical way.

In Vedic Brāhmanism the domestic cult serves the departed Fathers sent ahead to the Father-world, who require ancestral offerings lest destruction in the form of absolute dissolution (*nivṛtti*) should overtake them. The cult, in other words, serves the end of continued life, defending the dead against the terrible "dying again" (*punar-mṛtyu*) through which their existence would be brought to its final term. This is in diametrical contrast to the chief concern of aboriginal, pre-Āryan India, which was, as we have seen, lest life in its painful round should *not* end. The rituals of the secular cult here were practiced not for the continuance, but for the amelioration, of existence—the averting of ill-fortune and sufferings during the present life, as well as the avoidance of descent to the painful purgatories or rebirth in the kingdom of the beasts. Celestial bliss was desired as infinitely preferable to the agonies of the lower realms, but beyond that, there was the still higher good known to the one who would never again be involved in any form at all.

*Omnis determinatio est negatio*: all determination of the life-monad through the karmic influx that makes for individualization detracts from its infinite power and negates its highest possibilities. Hence the proper goal is *restitutio in integrum,* restitution of the life-monad to its innate ideal state. This is what is known in Sanskrit as *kaivalya,* "integration," the restoration of the faculties that have been temporarily lost through being obscured. All entities as we see them in the world are in varying degrees imperfect, yet capable of perfection through proper effort and the consequent insight. All beings are intended to be omniscient, omnipotent, unlimited, and unfettered; that is what constitutes their secret veiled dignity. Potentially they partake of the plenitude of life, which is divine; essentially they are constituents of the abundance and fullness of blissful energy. And yet they dwell in sorrow. The aim of men must be to make manifest the power that is latent within them by removing whatever hindrances may be standing in the way.

Although this conception was certainly not native to the Āryan religion of the Vedic gods, and was in fact diametrically opposed to its conception of the nature and destiny of man, it became fused with it during the first millennium B.C., and since that time has stood as one of the basic doctrines of classical Indian philosophy. It pervades the whole texture of Brāhmanic thought throughout the period of the Upaniṣads, where the realization of the divine Self within is proclaimed as the sole pursuit worthy of one endowed with human birth. And yet it is important to note that between the Jaina view and that of the Brāhmanic development of the first millennium (as represented, typically, in the Upaniṣads) there is no less difference than resemblance: also the Buddhist doctrine is very different; for whereas the Jaina philosophy is characterized by a strictly mechanical materialism with respect to the subtle substantiality of the life-monad and the karmic influx, as well as with respect to the state of the released, both in the Upaniṣads and in the Buddhistic writings an immaterial, psychological outlook on the same questions is presented. And this fundamental difference touches every detail, not only of the cosmologies and metaphysics in question, but also of the related moral codes.

For example, if a Jaina monk swallows a morsel of meat inadvertently while eating the food that has collected in his alms-bowl during his daily begging-tour (at the doors of whatever town or village he may happen to be traversing in the course of his aimless, homeless pilgrimage), the crystal of his life-monad becomes automatically stained by a dark influx, in mechanical consequence of the fact that he has shared in the flesh of some slaughtered being. And wherever the Jaina ascetic walks, he has to sweep the way before his feet with a little broom, so that no minute living thing may be crushed by his heel. The Buddhist monk, on the contrary, goes without a broom. He is taught to be constantly watchful not so much of where he steps as of his feelings and intentions. He is to be "fully conscious and full of self-control" (*smṛtimant samprajānan*), mindful, attentive, and with his sense of responsibility constantly alert. With respect to meat, he is guilty only if he longs for it, or if the animal has been killed expressly for him and he knows it. Should he merely happen to receive some scraps along with the rice that he is offered, he can swallow these with the rest of the dish without becoming polluted.

The Buddhist idea of the progress to purity, self-detachment, and final enlightenment is based on a principle of basically moral watchfulness over one's feelings and propensities. Not the fact but the attitude toward it is the thing that counts. The Buddhist way, in other words, is a discipline of psychological control; and so there will be found no theories about either the subtle karmic influx or the subtle imperishable crystal of the life-monad in the Buddhist doctrine. Both of these ideas are discarded as materialistic errors, caused by primitive ignorance and not verified by inner experience. They are regarded as belonging to that vast morass of abstract metaphysical and biological lore which serves only to involve and trap the human mind—notions that rather fetter one to, than release one from, the spheres of pain and birth. For the outlook on psychic reality of the practicing Buddhist is based on the actual experiences of his own yoga-practice (the techniques of dismissing or doing away with every kind of fixed notion and attitude of mind), and these lead inevitably to a complete spiritualization not only of the idea of release but also of that of bondage. The accomplished Buddhist clings, in the end, to no notion whatsoever, not even that of the Buddha, that of the path of the doctrine, or that of the goal to be attained.

Jainism, on the other hand, is naïvely materialistic in its direct and simple view of the universe, the hosts of monads that fill matter as its elementary living molecules, and the problem of gaining release. The crystal of the life-monad, according to this system of archaic positivism, is actually (i.e., physically) stained and darkened by the various colors of the karmic influx; and this, moreover, has been its condition since immemorial times. To bring the monad to its proper state, every door through which new karmic substance might enter into it must be tightly closed and kept that way, so that the process of the automatic "influx of the six colorings" (*āsrava*) will be blocked. To close the gates means to abstain from action, action of every sort. The beclouding matter already present within will then slowly dwindle, transforming itself automatically into the natural events of the biological life-process. The present karmic seeds will grow and yield their inevitable fruits in the form of sufferings and physical experiences, and so the discoloration will gradually disappear. Then at last, if no fresh particles are permitted to enter, the translucent purity of the life-monad will be automatically attained.

The Jaina monk does not permit himself to respond in any manner whatsoever to the events that afflict his person or take place within his ken. He subjects his physique and psyche to a terrific training in ascetic aloofness, and actually becomes unassailably indifferent to pleasure and pain, and to all objects, whether desirable, repugnant, or even dangerous. An incessant cleansing process is kept in operation, a severe and difficult physical and mental discipline of interior concentration, which burns up with its heat (*tapas*) the karmic seeds already present. Thus the life-monad gradually clears, and attains its intrinsic crystal clarity, while the actor obdurately refuses to participate any longer in the play on the stage of life. His goal is to achieve a state of intentional psychic paralysis. Rejecting every kind of mask and holding with a sublime stubbornness to his invincible state of non-co-operation, finally he wins. The busy host of players who fill the universe, still enchanted by their roles and eager to go on contending with each other for the limelight, changing masks and lines from life to life, enacting all the sufferings, achievements, and surprises of their biographies, simply turn from him and let him go. He has escaped. So far as the world is concerned, he is a useless fool.

The final state to which the Jaina monk thus wins is termed, as we have said, *ḳaivalya,* "isolation," "completeness through integration"—which means absolute release; for when every particle of karmic substance has been burnt out, no influx of new seeds having been permitted, there remains no longer any possibility of maturing a new experience. Even the danger of becoming a celestial being has been overcome—a king of gods, an Indra, wielding the thunderbolt and enjoying in domains of heavenly bliss, for periods of numerous oceans of time, the delectable fruits of virtuous conduct in former lives. All the ties that ever fettered the life-monad, whether to higher or to lower realms of being, have been dissolved away. No coloring remains as a hue of kinship to prompt one to assume the garb of some element, plant, animal, human or superhuman being; no hue of ignorance to make one move. And though the body may remain intact for a few more days, until its metabolism has completely ceased, the center of attraction of the life-monad has already lifted far beyond this mortal coil.

For karmic matter, subtle though it is, is a weight that pulls the monad down, retaining it in one or another of the spheres of ignorant action, the precise placement of the monad in these spheres being dependent upon its density or specific gravity—which is indicated by its hue. The darker leśyās—deep blue or black—hold the monad in the lower storeys of the universe, the subterranean chambers of hell or the worlds of mineral and plant existence, whereas when the hue brightens the monad is relieved somewhat of weight and mounts to one or another of the more elevated spheres, ascending perhaps to the human kingdom—which is situated on the surface of the earth, the middle plane of the numerously stratified universe—or even to the higher, supernal abodes of the godly beings. When, however, the supreme state of isolation (*kaivalya*) has been attained and the monad has been purged absolutely, relieved of every ounce of karmic ballast, then it lifts itself with unresisted buoyancy beyond all the strata of the six colors to the zenith, like a bubble of air, destitute of weight. There it abides above the cycling flow of the currents of life that agitate, one way or another, all the realms below. It has left permanently behind the active theater of the continually changing masks.

The metaphor of the bubble is one that is used frequently in the Jaina texts. The life-monad rises, passing through the celestial regions of the gods where radiant beings still burdened by the weight of virtuous karma enjoy the fruits of former lives of benignant thought and action. Self-luminous, transparent, the balloon ascends to the dome of the world—that highest sphere, called "slightly inclined" (*iṣat-prāgbhāra*), which is whiter than milk and pearls, more resplendent than gold and crystal, and has the shape of a divine umbrella. Another metaphor compares the life-monad to a gourd that has been made into a flask or bottle; its marrow has been removed and its surface covered with layers of clay to render it the more solid. Such an empty vessel if placed in the water will sink to the bottom because of the weight of the clay; but as the covering slowly dissolves, the gourd regains its natural lightness, and since it is filled with air it becomes lighter than the water, rising automatically from the bottom to the surface of the pond. With just such an automatic movement, the life-monad, once rid of karmic substance, rises from the depths of its imprisonment—this submarine world of the coating layers and masks of individual existence. Divested of the characteristic features of this or that particular existence-form—the nature of this or that man, woman, animal, or divine being—it becomes anonymous, absolutely buoyant, and absolutely free.

The universe through which the bubble or gourd ascends is pictured in the form of a colossal human being: a prodigious male or female, whose macrocosmic organism comprises the celestial, earthly, and infernal regions, all of which are peopled by innumerable beings. The male colossus appeals to the manly asceticism of the Jaina monks and saints, while the female reflects an old pre-Āryan concept of the Universal Mother. The cult of the Mother Goddess goes back to the Neolithic Age, when it was distributed throughout western Asia and the lands surrounding the Mediterranean. Images of this goddess have been found even from the Paleolithic period. And to this day her worship survives in popular Hinduism. The Jaina conception is of a prodigious human form, male or female, the bounds of which constitute the limits of the universe. The surface of the earth, the playground of the human race, is regarded as situated at the level of the waist. The regions of the hells are beneath this plane, in the pelvic cavity, thighs, legs, and feet, while those of celestial beatitude, stratified one above the other, fill the chest, shoulders, neck, and head. The region of supreme isolation (*kaivalya*) is at the crown of the dome inside the hollow of the skull.

After its pilgrimage of innumerable existences in the various inferior stratifications, the life-monad rises to the cranial zone of the macrocosmic being, purged of the weight of the subtle karmic particles that formerly held it down. Nothing can happen to it any more; for it has put aside the traits of ignorance, those heavy veils of individuality that are the precipitating causes of biographical event. Decisively, once and for all, it has broken free from the vortex. It is now deathless, birthless, suspended beyond the cyclic law of karmic causation, like a distilled drop of water clinging to a ceiling or to the underside of the lid of a boiling pot. There, among all the other released life-monads clinging to the interior of the dome of the divine World Being, it remains forever—and the monads in that state, of course, are all as alike as so many drops. For they are pure particles, serene existences, purged of those imperfections that make for individuality. The masks, the former personal features, were distilled away, together with the seed-stuff that would have ripened into future experiences. Sterilized of coloring, flavor, and weight, the sublime crystals now are absolutely pure —like the drops of rain that descend from a clear sky, tasteless and immaculate.

Furthermore, since they have been relieved of the faculties of sensation that are inherent in all organisms (those that render sound, sight, smell, taste, and touch), the released life-monads are beyond the bounds of conditioned understanding which determine the modes of being of the various human, animal, plant, and even inorganic species. They neither perceive nor think, but are aware of everything directly. They know Truth precisely as it is. They are omniscient, as the sheer life-force itself would be if it could be relieved of the modifying darknesses of specific organisms, each with its limited range of sense and thinking faculties. For the moment the limitations that make particular experiences possible are eliminated, the perfect intuition of everything knowable is immediately attained. The need of experience is dissolved in infinite knowledge.—This is the *positive* meaning of the term and state of *kaivalya.*

One is reminded of the protest of the modern French poet and philosopher, Paul Valéry, in his novel, *Monsieur Teste.* "There are people," he writes, "who feel that their organs of sense are cutting them off from reality and essence. This feeling then *poisons* all their sense perceptions. What I see blinds me. What I hear makes me deaf. What I know makes me unknowing. In so far and inasmuch as I know, I am ignorant. This light before me is no more than a kind of blindfold and conceals either a darkness or a light that is more. . . . More what? Here the circle closes with a strange reversal: knowledge, a cloud obscuring the essence of being; the shining moon, like darkness or a cataract on the eye! Take it all away, so that I may see!" This outcry, together with the modern theory of knowledge from which it arises, is remarkably close to the old idea to which Jainism holds: that of the limiting force of our various faculties of human understanding.

But the Tīrthaṅkaras have lost even the faculty of feeling; for this too belongs but to the texture of the flesh, the suffering garment of blood and nerves. Hence they are completely indifferent to what goes on in the stratified worlds that they have left beneath them. They are not touched by any prayer, nor moved by any act of worship. Neither do they ever descend to intervene in the course of the universal round as does, for example, the supreme divinity of the Hindus, Viṣṇu, when he sends down periodically a particle of his transcendent essence as an Incarnation to restore the divine order of the universe upset by reckless tyrants and selfish demons. The Jaina Tīrthaṅkaras are absolutely cut off. Nevertheless, the Jaina devotee pays them unceasing worship, concentrating his pious attention upon their images, as a means to his own progress in inner purification. And they are sometimes even celebrated side by side with the popular Hindu household and village gods; but never in the same spirit. For what the gods provide is temporal well-being, warding away the demons of disease and disaster, whereas the worship of the Tīrthaṅkaras—the "Victors," the "Heroes," the "Makers of the Crossing"—moves the mind to its highest good, which is eternal peace beyond the joys as well as the sorrows of the universal round.

## Selections from Jaina Sutras

*Translated by Herman Jacobi*

### A. Uttaradhyayana

### Lecture 28

### The Road to Final Deliverance

Learn the true road leading to final deliverance, which the Jinas have taught; it depends on four causes and is characterised by right knowledge and faith.

I. Right knowledge; II. Faith; III. Conduct; and IV. Austerities; this is the road taught by the Jinas who possess the best knowledge.

Right knowledge, faith, conduct, and austerities; beings who follow this road, will obtain beatitude.

I. Knowledge is fivefold: 1. knowledge derived from the sacred books; 2. perception; 3. supernatural knowledge; 4. knowledge of the thoughts of other people; 5. Kêvala, the highest, unlimited knowledge.

---

Uttaradhyayana selections reprinted from Herman Jacobi, tr., *Jaina Sutras* (Part II), in *The Sacred Books of the East,* Vol. XLV (1895), pages 152–173. Modified.

This is the fivefold knowledge. The wise ones have taught the knowledge of substances, qualities, and all developments.

Substance is the substrate of qualities; the qualities are inherent in one substance; but the characteristic of developments is that they inhere in either (viz. substances or qualities).

Dharma, Adharma, space, time, matter, and souls are the six kinds of substances; they make up this world, as has been taught by the Jinas who possess the best knowledge.

Dharma, Adharma, and space are each one substance only; but time, matter, and souls are an infinite number of substances.

The characteristic of Dharma is motion, that of Adharma immobility, and that of space, which contains all other substances, is to make room for everything.

The characteristic of time is duration, that of soul the realisation of knowledge, faith, happiness, and misery.

The characteristic of Soul is knowledge, faith, conduct, austerities, energy, and realisation of its developments.

The characteristic of matter is sound, darkness, lustre (of jewels, &c.), light, shade, sunshine; colour, taste, smell, and touch.

The characteristic of development is singleness, separateness, number, form, conjunction, and disjunction.

1. jiva, Soul; 2. ajiva, the inanimate things; 3. bandha, the binding of the soul by Karma; 4. pu*n*ya, merit; 5. pâpa, demerit; 6. âsrava, that which causes the soul to be affected by sins; 7. sa*m*vara, the prevention of âsrava by watchfulness; 8. the annihilation of Karma; 9. final deliverance: these are the nine truths (or categories).

He who verily believes the true teaching of the above nine fundamental truths, possesses righteousness.

II. Faith is produced by 1. nature; 2. instruction; 3. command; 4. study of the sûtras; 5. suggestion; 6. comprehension of the meaning of the sacred lore; 7. complete course of study; 8. religious exercise; 9. brief exposition; 10. dharma, the Law.

1. He who truly comprehends, by a spontaneous effort of his mind, the nature of soul, inanimate things, merit, and demerit, and who puts an end to sinful influences, believes by nature.

He who spontaneously believes the four truths explicitly mentioned in the last verse, which the Jinas have taught, thinking they are of this and not of a different nature, believes by nature.

2. But he who believes these truths, having learned them from somebody else, either a *Kh*admastha[1] or a Jina, believes by instruction.

3. He who has got rid of love, hate, delusion, and ignorance, and believes because he is told to do so, believes by command.

4. He who obtains righteousness by the study of the Sûtras, either Aṅgas or other works, believes by the study of Sûtras.

5. He who by correctly comprehending one truth arrives at the comprehension of more—just as a drop of oil expands on the surface of water—believes by suggestion.

6. He who truly knows the sacred lore, viz. the eleven Aṅgas, the Prakîr*n*as, and the D*r*ish*t*ivâda, believes by the comprehension of the sacred lore.

7. He who understands the true nature of all substances by means of all proofs, believes by a complete course of study.

8. He who sincerely performs all duties implied by right knowledge, faith, and conduct, by asceticism and discipline, and by all Samitis and Guptis, believes by religious exercise.

9. He who though not versed in the sacred doctrines nor acquainted with other systems, holds no wrong doctrines, believes by brief exposition.

10. He who believes in the truth of the realities, the Sûtras, and conduct, as it has been explained by the Jinas, believes by the Law.

Right belief depends on the acquaintance with truth, on the devotion to those who know the truth, and on the avoiding of schismatical and heretical tenets.

There is no right conduct without right belief, and it must be cultivated for obtaining right faith; righteousness and conduct originate together, or righteousness precedes conduct.

Without right faith there is no right knowledge, without right knowledge there is no virtuous conduct, without virtues

---

[1] A *kh*admastha is one who has not yet obtained Kêvala, or the highest knowledge.

there is no deliverance, and without deliverance there is no perfection.

The excellence of faith depends on the following eight points: 1. that one has no doubts about the truth of the tenets; 2. that one has no preference for heterodox tenets; 3. that one does not doubt its saving qualities; 4. that one is not shaken in the right belief because heretical sects are more prosperous; 5. that one praises the pious; 6. that one encourages weak brethren; 7. that one supports or loves the confessors of the Law; 8. that one endeavours to exalt it.

III. Conduct, which produces the destruction of all Karma, is 1. the avoidance of everything sinful; 2. the initiation of a novice; 3. purity produced by peculiar austerities; 4. reduction of desire; 5. annihilation of sinfulness according to the precepts of the Arhats, as well in the case of a *Kh*admastha as of a Jina.

IV. Austerities are twofold: external and internal; both external and internal austerities are sixfold.

By knowledge one knows things, by faith one believes in them, by conduct one gets freedom from Karma, and by austerities one reaches purity.

Having by control and austerities destroyed their Karma, great sages, whose purpose is to get rid of all misery, proceed to perfection. . . .

## Lecture 29

. . . 1. Sir, what does the soul obtain by the longing for liberation? By the longing for liberation the soul obtains an intense desire of the Law; by an intense desire of the Law he quickly arrives at an increased longing for liberation; he destroys anger, pride, deceit, and greed, which reproduce themselves infinitely; he acquires no bad Karma, and ridding himself of wrong belief which is the consequence of the latter, he becomes possessed of right faith; by the purity of faith some will reach perfection after one birth; nobody, however, who has got this purity, will be born more than thrice before he reaches perfection.

2. Sir, what does the soul obtain by disregard of worldly

objects? By disregard of worldly objects the soul quickly feels disgust for pleasures enjoyed by gods, men, and animals; he becomes indifferent to all objects; thereby he ceases to engage in any undertakings, in consequence of which he leaves the road of Sa*m*sâra and enters the road to perfection.

3. Sir, what does the soul obtain by the desire of the Law? By the desire of the Law the soul becomes indifferent to pleasures and happiness to which he was attached; he abandons the life of householders, and as a houseless monk he puts an end to all pains of body and mind, which consist in the suffering of cutting, piercing, union with unpleasant things, etc; and he obtains unchecked happiness.

4. By obedience to co-religionists and to the Guru the soul obtains discipline (vinaya). By discipline and avoidance of misconduct towards the teacher he avoids being reborn as a denizen of hell, an animal, a low man, or a bad god; by zealous praise of, devotion to, and respect for the Guru he obtains birth as a good man or god, gains perfection and beatitude, does all praiseworthy actions prescribed by discipline, and prevails upon others to adopt discipline.

5. By confession of sins before the Guru the soul gets rid of the thorns, as it were, of deceit, misapplied austerities, and wrong belief, which obstruct the way to final liberation and cause an endless migration of the soul; he obtains simplicity, whereby the soul which is free from deceit does not acquire that Karma which results in his having a carnal desire for a woman or eunuch, and annihilates such Karma as he had acquired before.

6. By repenting of one's sins to oneself the soul obtains repentance, and becoming indifferent by repentance he prepares for himself an ascending scale of virtues, by which he destroys the Karma resulting from delusion.

7. By repenting of one's sins before the Guru the soul obtains humiliation; feeling humiliated, he will leave off all blameable occupations, and apply himself to praiseworthy occupations, whereby a houseless monk will stop infinite disabling developments.

8. By moral and intellectual purity (literally, equilibrium) the soul ceases from sinful occupations.

9. By the adoration of the twenty-four Jinas the soul arrives at purity of faith.

10. By paying reverence to the Guru the soul destroys such Karma as leads to birth in low families, and acquires such Karma as leads to birth in noble families; he wins the affection of people, which results in his being looked upon as an authority, and he brings about general goodwill.

11. By expiation of sins he obviates transgressions of the vows; thereby he stops the Âsravas, preserves a pure conduct, practises the eight articles, does not neglect the practice of control, and pays great attention to it.

12. By Kâyôtsarga he gets rid of past and present transgressions which require Prâya*sk*itta[2]; thereby his mind is set at ease like a porter who is eased of his burden; and engaging in praiseworthy contemplation he enjoys happiness.

13. By self-denial he shuts, as it were, the doors of the Âsravas; by self-denial he prevents desires rising in him; by prevention of desires he becomes, as it were, indifferent and cool towards all objects.

14. By praises and hymns he obtains the wisdom consisting in knowledge, faith, and conduct; thereby he gains such improvement, that he will put an end to his worldly existence, or be born afterwards in one of the Kalpas and Vimânas.

15. By keeping the right time he destroys the Karma which obstructs right knowledge.

16. By practising Prâya*sk*itta he gets rid of sins, and commits no transgressions; he who correctly practises Prâya*sk*itta, gains the road and the reward of the road,[3] he wins the reward of good conduct.

17. By begging forgiveness he obtains happiness of mind; thereby he acquires a kind disposition towards all kinds of liv-

---

[2] Expiatory rites.

[3] By road is meant the means of acquiring right knowledge, and by the reward of the road, right knowledge. The reward of good conduct is mukti.

ing beings; by this kind disposition he obtains purity of character and freedom from fear.

18. By study he destroys the Karma which obstructs right knowledge.

19. By the recital of the sacred texts he obtains destruction of Karma, and contributes to preserve the sacred lore, whereby he acquires the Law of the Tîrtha, which again leads him to the complete destruction of Karma, and to the final annihilation of worldly existence.

20. By questioning he arrives at a correct comprehension of the Sûtra and its meaning, and he puts an end to the Karma which produces doubts and delusion.

21. By repetition he reproduces the sounds (i.e. syllables) and commits them to memory.

22. By pondering (on what he has learned) he loosens the firm hold which the seven kinds of Karma, except the Âyushka[4] (have upon the soul); he shortens their duration when it was to be a long one; he mitigates their power when it was intense; (he reduces their sphere of action when it was a wide one); he may either acquire Âyushka-karma or not, but he no more accumulates Karma which produces unpleasant feelings, and he quickly crosses the very large forest of the fourfold Sa*m*sâra, which is without beginning and end.

23. By religious discourses he obtains destruction of the Karma; by religious discourses he exalts the creed, and by exalting the creed he acquires Karma, which secures, for the future, permanent bliss.

24. By acquisition of sacred knowledge he destroys ignorance, and will not be corrupted by worldliness.

25. By concentration of his thoughts he obtains stability of the mind.

26. By control he obtains freedom from sins.

27. By austerities he cuts off the Karma.

28. By cutting off the Karma he obtains the fourth stage of

[4] Âyushka is that Karma which determines the length of time which one is to live.

pure meditation characterised by freedom from actions, by doing no actions he will obtain perfection, enlightenment, deliverance, and final beatitude, and will put an end to all misery.

29. By renouncing pleasures he obtains freedom from false longing, whereby he becomes compassionate, humble, free from sorrow, and destroys the Karma produced by delusion regarding conduct.

30. By mental independence he gets rid of attachment, whereby he will concentrate his thoughts on the Law, and will for ever be without attachment and fondness for worldly things.

31. By using unfrequented lodgings and beds he obtains the Gupti of conduct, whereby he will use allowed food, be steady in his conduct, be exclusively delighted with control, obtain a yearning for deliverance, and cut off the tie of the eightfold Karma.

32. By turning from the world he will strive to do no bad actions, and will eliminate his already acquired Karma by its destruction; then he will cross the forest of the fourfold Sa*m*sâra.

33. By renouncing collection of alms in one district only he overcomes obstacles; unchecked by them he exerts himself to attain liberation; he is content with the alms he gets, and does not hope for, care for, wish, desire, or covet those of a fellow-monk; not envying other monks he takes up a separate, agreeable lodging.

34. By renouncing articles of use he obtains successful study; without articles of use he becomes exempt from desires, and does not suffer misery.

35. By renouncing forbidden food he ceases to act for the sustenance of his life; ceasing to act for the sustenance of his life he does not suffer misery when without food.

36. By conquering his passions he becomes free from passions; thereby he becomes indifferent to happiness and pains.

37. By renouncing activity he obtains inactivity, by ceasing to act he acquires no new Karma, and destroys the Karma he had acquired before.

38. By renouncing his body he acquires the pre-eminent vir-

tues of the Siddhas, by the possession of which he goes to the highest region of the universe, and becomes absolutely happy.

39. By renouncing company he obtains singleness; being single and concentrating his mind, he avoids disputes, quarrels, passions, and censoriousness, and he acquires a high degree of control, of Sa*m*vara, and of carefulness.

40. By renouncing all food he prevents his being born again many hundreds of times.

41. By perfect renunciation he enters the final (fourth stage of pure meditation), whence there is no return; a monk who is in that state, destroys the four remnants of Karma which even a Kêvalin possesses, and then he will put an end to all misery.

42. By conforming to the standard of monks he obtains ease, thereby he will be careful, wear openly the excellent badges of the order, be of perfect righteousness, possess firmness and the Samitis, inspire all beings with confidence, mind but few things, subdue his senses, and practise, in a high degree, the Samitis and austerities.

43. By doing service he acquires the Karma which brings about for him the name and rank of a Tîrthakara.

44. By fulfilling all virtues he secures that he will not be born again; thereby he will become exempt from pains of the body and mind.

45. By freedom from passion he cuts off the ties of attachment and desire; thereby he becomes indifferent to all agreeable and disagreeable sounds, touches, colours, and smells.

46. By patience he overcomes troubles.

47. By freedom from greed he obtains voluntary poverty, whereby he will become inaccessible to desire for property.

48. By simplicity he will become upright in actions, thoughts, and speech, and he will become veracious; thereby he will truly practise the Law.

49. By humility he will acquire freedom from self-conceit; thereby he will become of a kind and meek disposition, and avoid the eight kinds of pride.

50. By sincerity of mind he obtains purity of mind, which

will cause him to exert himself for the fulfilment of the Law which the Jinas have proclaimed; and he will practise the Law in the next world too.

51. By sincerity in religious practice he obtains proficiency in it; being proficient in it he will act up to his words.

52. By sincerity of acting he will become pure in his actions.

53. By watchfulness of the mind he concentrates his thoughts; thereby he truly practises control.

54. By watchfulness of speech he keeps free from prevarication; thereby he enables his mind to act properly.

55. By watchfulness of the body he obtains Sa*m*vara; thereby he prevents sinful Âsravas.

56. By discipline of the mind he obtains concentration of his thoughts; thereby he obtains development of knowledge, which produces righteousness and annihilates wrong belief.

57. By discipline of the speech he obtains development of faith, whereby he acquires facility of becoming enlightened, and destroys preventing causes.

58. By discipline of the body he obtains development of conduct, which causes him to conduct himself according to the regulation; thereby he destroys the four remnants of Karma which even a Kêvalin possesses; after that he obtains perfection, enlightenment, deliverance, and final beatitude, and he puts an end to all misery.

59. By possession of knowledge he acquires an understanding of words and their meaning; thereby he will not perish in the forest of the fourfold Sa*m*sâra; as a needle with its thread will not be lost, thus the soul possessing the sacred lore will not be lost in the Sa*m*sâra; he performs all prescribed actions relating to knowledge, discipline, austerities, and conduct, and well versed in his own and in heterodox creeds he will become invincible.

60. By possession of faith he annihilates wrong belief which is the cause of worldly existence, and he will not lose his inner light; but he endues his Self with the highest knowledge and faith, and purifies it.

61. By possession of conduct he obtains a stability like that of the king of mountains whereby a houseless monk destroys the four remnants of Karma which even a Kêvalin possesses; after that he obtains perfection, enlightenment, deliverance, and final beatitude, and puts an end to all misery.

62. By subduing the organ of hearing he overcomes his delight with or aversion to all pleasant or unpleasant sounds, he acquires no Karma produced thereby, and destroys the Karma he had acquired before. . . .

71. By conquering love, hate, and wrong belief he exerts himself for right knowledge, faith, and conduct, then he will cut off the fetters of the eightfold Karma; he will first destroy the twenty-eight kinds of Karma, which are productive of delusion; then the five kinds of obstruction to right knowledge, the nine kinds of obstruction to right faith, and the five kinds of obstacles: the last three remnants of Karma he destroys simultaneously; afterwards he obtains absolute knowledge and faith, which is supreme, full, complete, unchecked, clear, faultless, and giving light (or penetrating) the whole universe; and while he still acts, he acquires but such Karma as is inseparable from religious acts; the pleasant feelings (produced by it) last but two moments: in the first moment it is acquired, in the second it is experienced, and in the third it is destroyed; this Karma is produced, comes into contact (with the soul), takes rise, is experienced, and is destroyed; for all time to come he is exempt from Karma.

72. Then when his life is spent up to less than half a muhûrta, he discontinues to act, and enters upon the third degree of pure meditation, from which there is no relapse to lower degrees and which requires most subtile functions only of his organs; he first stops the functions of his mind, then the functions of speech, then those of the body, at last he ceases to breathe. During the time required for pronouncing five short syllables, he is engaged in the final pure meditation, in which all functions of his organs have ceased, and he simultaneously annihilates the four remnants of Karma.

73. Then having, by all methods, got rid of his kârma bodies, the soul takes the form of a straight line, goes in one moment, without touching anything and taking up no space, (upwards to the highest Âkâsa), and there develops into its natural form, obtains perfection, enlightenment, deliverance, and final beatitude, and puts an end to all misery.

This indeed is the subject of the lecture called exertion in righteousness, which the Venerable Ascetic Mahâvîra has told, declared, explained, demonstrated.

## B. Akaranga Sutra

### Lesson 8

The wise ones who attain in due order to one of the unerring states (in which suicide is prescribed), those who are rich in control and endowed with knowledge, knowing the incomparable religious death, should continue their contemplation.

Knowing the twofold obstacles, i.e. bodily and mental, the wise ones, having thoroughly learned the law, perceiving in due order that the time for their death has come, get rid of karma.

Subduing the passions and living on little food, he should endure hardships. If a mendicant falls sick, let him again take food.

He should not long for life, nor wish for death; he should yearn after neither, life or death.

He who is indifferent and wishes for the destruction of karma, should continue his contemplation. Becoming unattached internally and externally, he should strive after absolute purity.

Whatever means one knows for calming one's own life, that a wise man should learn (i.e. practise) in order to gain time for continuing penance.

In a village or in a forest, examining the ground and recognising it as free from living beings, the sage should spread the straw.

---

Akaranga Sutra selections reprinted from Herman Jacobi, tr., *Jaina Sutras* (Part I), in *The Sacred Books of the East,* Vol. XXII (1884), pages 74–78. Modified.

Without food he should lie down and bear the pains which attack him. He should not for too long time give way to worldly feelings which overcome him.

When crawling animals or such as live on high or below, feed on his flesh and blood, he should neither kill them nor rub the wound.

Though these animals destroy the body, he should not stir from his position.

After the âsravas have ceased, he should bear pains as if he rejoiced in them.

When the bonds fall off, then he has accomplished his life.

We shall now describe a more exalted method for a well-controlled and instructed monk.

This other law has been proclaimed by *Gñ*â*tri*putra:

He should give up all motions except his own in the thrice-threefold way.

He should not lie on sprouts of grass, but inspecting the bare ground he should lie on it.

Without any comfort and food, he should there bear pain.

When the sage becomes weak in his limbs, he should strive after calmness.

For he is blameless, who is well fixed and immovable in his intention to die.

He should move to and fro on his ground, contract and stretch his limbs for the benefit of the whole body; or he should remain quiet as if he were lifeless.

He should walk about, when tired of lying, or stand with passive limbs; when tired of standing, he should sit down.

Intent on such an uncommon death, he should regulate the motions of his organs.

Having attained a place swarming with insects, he should search for a clean spot.

He should not remain there whence sin would rise.

He should raise himself above sinfulness, and bear all pains.

And this is a still more difficult method, when one lives according to it: not to stir from one's place, while checking all motions of the body.

This is the highest law, exalted above the preceding method:

Having examined a spot of bare ground he should remain there; stay O Brâhma*n*a!

Having attained a place free from living beings, he should there fix himself.

He should thoroughly mortify his flesh, thinking: There are no obstacles in my body.

Knowing as long as he lives the dangers and troubles, the wise and restrained ascetic should bear them as being instrumental to the dissolution of the body.

He should not be attached to the transitory pleasures, nor to the greater ones; he should not nourish desire and greed, looking only for eternal praise.

He should be enlightened with eternal objects, and not trust in the delusive power of the gods; a Brâhma*n*a should know of this and cast off all inferiority.

Not devoted to any of the external objects he reaches the end of his life; thinking that patience is the highest good, he should choose one of the described three good methods of entering Nirvâ*n*a.

# *Glossary of Hindu Terms*

| | |
|---|---|
| adharma | Demerit, vice, unrighteousness. Principle of rest. |
| Aditi | Earliest name given to Infinite Reality. |
| advaita | "Without a second." |
| Advaita Vedanta | Idealistic monism taught by Samkara. |
| Agni | Hindu fire god pervasive in ceremonies. Fire. |
| ahamkara | Sense of selfhood, feeling of individuality, egoism. |
| ahimsa | Principle of noninjury, nonviolence. |
| ajiva | The nonconscious, matter. |
| akasa | Space, ether. |
| ananda | Bliss, pleasures. |
| artha | Wealth, possessions. |
| Aryans | Nomadic migrants into India ca. 1500 B.C. Founders of Hindu civilization. |
| asat | Nonbeing. |

| | |
|---|---|
| asramas | Stages of life in Hinduism. |
| Atman | Ultimate Reality disclosed introspectively. Also, self, soul, breath, principle of life-sustenance. |
| avidya | Ignorance, imperfect knowledge, mistaking appearance for reality. |
| bhagavad | Blessed. |
| bhakti | Devotion, self-surrender in worship and action. |
| bhakti-yoga (bhakti-marga) | Way of devotion. Devotional practice of religion. |
| bodhi | Enlightenment, illumination. |
| Brahman | Final, transcendental Unconditioned Reality (viewed objectively). Also, sacred magic formula, stanza, priest. |
| Brahmin | Member of priestly caste. Sage, teacher. |
| buddhi | Faculty of awareness, presence of mind, attentiveness. |
| cit | Spiritual consciousness. |
| citta | Functions of thinking, desiring, observing, etc. |
| darsana | Critical expositions, systems of philosophy. |
| Dasyus | Non-Hindu, barbarian, one outside the caste system and Hindu humanity. |
| devas | Gods. |
| dharana | Yogic steadfastness of mind. |
| dharma | Moral law, virtue, righteousness, divine moral order. Also, principle of activity. |
| dhyana | Meditation, yogic concentration. |
| dhyana-yoga | Way of meditation. |

| | |
|---|---|
| Digambara | Sect of Jainist movement. "Sky-clad" (naked) monks. |
| Dyaus | Vedic god of the sky. |
| gunas | Qualities, attributes, modes of nature. |
| guru | Teacher, preceptor. |
| Indra | Vedic god of firmament. Warrior god. |
| Isvara | Personal god frequently mentioned in Hindu literature. |
| Jaina | Conqueror. Jainist hero who has achieved release. |
| jiva | Soul. In Jainism, the aggregate of life-monads. |
| jivan-mukti | Released, completely emancipated being, but one still partaking of earthly existence. |
| jnana | Knowledge. |
| jnana-yoga (jnana-marga) | Way of wisdom. |
| kaivalya | Isolation, complete independence of soul, absolute release. |
| kala | Time. |
| kalpa | World cycle. |
| kama | Pleasure, love, affection, carnal gratification. |
| karma | Work, deed, action bearing necessary consequences, law of causality. Ethically, the moral consequence of conduct. |
| karma-yoga | Renunciation in action. Way of action. |
| karuna | Compassion. |
| kevala | "Cut off." Transcended beings. |

| | |
|---|---|
| Krishna (Krsna) | Incarnation of Vishnu. A major character in the *Bhagavad-Gita.* |
| kshatriya | Member of warrior, aristocratic caste. |
| mahat | "Great principle" or primary substance of awareness. |
| manas | Thinking faculty, intellect. |
| mantras | Sacred formulas and prayers. |
| Mara | Evil One. The Tempter. Active cosmic principle of evil. |
| Maruts | Vedic wind gods. |
| maya | Cosmic illusion, magical appearance of worldly things. |
| moksa | Final emancipation |
| neti neti | Not this, not that. |
| nivrtti | Abstinence from activity or work. Resignation, renunciation. |
| niyama | Moral code constituted principally of sanctions against specific behavior. |
| Om | Sacred syllable of Hinduism. Symbolic of unity of all being, including speech, silence, self. |
| phala | "Result." Fruits of action. |
| Prajapati | Ancient god-creator of Vedic literature. |
| prajna | Discernment, knowledge. |
| prakrti | Nature, the realm of matter. |
| prana | Breath, life energies. |

| | |
|---|---|
| purusa | Self, spirit. The subject functioning in thought, desire, emotion, etc. |
| samadhi | Union, completion, absorption. |
| samsara | Round of transmigration. Birth, suffering, death, rebirth. Confusions of worldly experience. |
| samskara | "Latent impression," as in memory. Dispositional or habitual patterns in personality. |
| sastra | Holy scripture. |
| sat | Being. |
| Satya | Truthfulness, honesty, sincerity. |
| soma | A plant and its juice, an intoxicating drink used in Vedic rituals; also personified as a god. |
| sruti | Revealed truth. |
| sudra | Member of worker caste. |
| sutra | Teaching. Essay on doctrine. |
| Svetambara | Sect of Jainism. |
| tapas | "Heat." Ascetic austerities. |
| tat tvam asi | "That Thou Art." Asserts the unity of the self with the unconditional ground of all existence, Brahman-Atman. |
| Tirthankara | "Maker of the crossing." A Jainist conqueror who has achieved complete liberation. |
| turiya | Transcendental stage of consciousness. |
| vac | Speech, word. Also personified as a god in Vedic hymns. |
| vaisya | Member of merchant or agricultural caste. |

| | |
|---|---|
| varna | Caste. Color. |
| Varuna | Vedic god of the sky. Guardian of order and moral law. |
| Vedanta | "End of the Vedas." Hindu school of philosophy. |
| vidya | Knowledge. |
| Vishnu | Hindu god prominent in later Hinduism. |
| Visvarkarman | Creator of universe. |
| yama | Moral discipline designed to inculcate kindness, selflessness. |
| yoga | "Harnessing one's self to." Discipline. |

# *Selected Bibliography for Further Reading*


Campbell, Joseph, *The Masks of God: Oriental Mythology.* The Viking Press, 1962.

Eliot, Charles, *Hinduism and Buddhism: An Historical Sketch.* London: Routledge & Kegan Paul, Ltd., 1921. 3 vol.

Hiriyanna, M., *Outlines of Indian Philosophy.* George Allen & Unwin, Ltd., 1932.

Northrop, F. S. C., *The Meeting of East and West.* The Macmillan Company, 1946.

Prabhavananda, Swami, *The Spiritual Heritage of India.* Doubleday & Company, Inc., 1963.

Radhakrishnan, *The Hindu View of Life.* The Macmillan Company, 1962.

——— *Indian Philosophy,* Vol. I. The Macmillan Company, 1923.

Smith, Vincent A., *The Oxford History of India.* Oxford: At the Clarendon Press, 1968.

Zimmer, Heinrich, *Philosophies of India,* ed. by Joseph Campbell. Meridian Books, Inc., 1956.

*(Continued from front flap)*

"In the East the key concepts of religious thought are recognition, realization, release, and reunion," as seen in the scriptures translated here: Rg-Veda, Atharva-Veda, *Bhagavad-Gita,* Upanishads, Samkhya-Yoga, Vedanta, and Jaina Sutras.

The commentaries and translations are done by such famous experts on Eastern religions as Heinrich Zimmer, Mircea Eliade, and Paul Deussen. Also included are a Glossary of Hindu Terms and a Bibliography for further reading.

The Editor

ALLIE M. FRAZIER is Associate Professor of Philosophy and Religion at Hollins College. He is a graduate of Millsaps College, Boston University School of Theology, and Boston University (Ph.D.). He has held the Borden Parker Bowne Fellowship in Philosophy and was a Fulbright Scholar at Glasgow University. He has taught at the University of the Pacific, and was Chairman of the Department of Philosophy and Director of the Honors Program at Bethany College.